British Humour and
the Second World War

New Directions in Social and Cultural History

Series Editors: Sasha Handley (University of Manchester, UK),
Rohan McWilliam (Anglia Ruskin University, UK) and
Lucy Noakes (University of Brighton, UK)

Editorial Board:
Robert Aldrich, University of Sydney, Australia
James W. Cook, University of Michigan, USA
John H. Arnold, University of Cambridge, UK
Alison Rowlands, University of Essex, UK
Penny Summerfield, University of Manchester, UK
Mrinalini Sinha, University of Michigan, USA

The New Directions in Social and Cultural History series brings together the leading research in social and cultural history, one of the most exciting and current areas for history teaching and research, contributing innovative new perspectives to a range of historical events and issues. Books in the series engage with developments in the field since the post-cultural turn, showing how new theoretical approaches have impacted on research within both history and other related disciplines. Each volume will cover both theoretical and methodological developments on the particular topic, as well as combine this with an analysis of primary source materials.

Published:
New Directions in Social and Cultural History, ed. Sasha Handley,
Rohan McWilliam and Lucy Noakes (2018)
Art, Propaganda and Aerial Warfare in Britain during the Second World War,
Rebecca Searle (2020)
Welfare State Generation: Women, Agency and Class in Britain since 1945,
Eve Worth (2022)
Family History, Historical Consciousness and Citizenship: A New Social History,
Tanya Evans (2022)
Captive Fathers, Captive Children: Legacies of the War in the Far East,
Terry Smyth (2023)

Forthcoming:
Capital Labour in Victorian England: Manufacturing Consensus,
Donna Loftus

British Humour and the Second World War

'Keep Smiling Through'

Edited by Juliette Pattinson and Linsey Robb

BLOOMSBURY ACADEMIC
LONDON • NEW YORK • OXFORD • NEW DELHI • SYDNEY

BLOOMSBURY ACADEMIC
Bloomsbury Publishing Plc
50 Bedford Square, London, WC1B 3DP, UK
1385 Broadway, New York, NY 10018, USA
29 Earlsfort Terrace, Dublin 2, Ireland

BLOOMSBURY, BLOOMSBURY ACADEMIC and the Diana logo
are trademarks of Bloomsbury Publishing Plc

First published in Great Britain 2023
This paperback edition published in 2025

Copyright © Juliette Pattinson and Linsey Robb, 2023

Juliette Pattinson and Linsey Robb have asserted their right under the Copyright, Designs and Patents Act, 1988, to be identified as Editors of this work.

For legal purposes the Acknowledgements on p. viii constitute
an extension of this copyright page.

Series design by Liron Gilenberg | www.ironicitalics.com
Cover image © Imperial War Museum (B 8259)

All rights reserved. No part of this publication may be reproduced or transmitted in any form or by any means, electronic or mechanical, including photocopying, recording, or any information storage or retrieval system, without prior permission in writing from the publishers.

Bloomsbury Publishing Plc does not have any control over, or responsibility for, any third-party websites referred to or in this book. All internet addresses given in this book were correct at the time of going to press. The author and publisher regret any inconvenience caused if addresses have changed or sites have ceased to exist, but can accept no responsibility for any such changes.

A catalogue record for this book is available from the British Library.

A catalog record for this book is available from the Library of Congress.

ISBN:	HB:	978-1-3502-0166-8
	PB:	978-1-3502-0167-5
	ePDF:	978-1-3501-9947-7
	eBook:	978-1-3501-9948-4

Series: New Directions in Social and Cultural History

Typeset by Integra Software Services Pvt. Ltd.

To find out more about our authors and books visit www.bloomsbury.com
and sign up for our newsletters.

Contents

List of figures — vi
List of tables — vii
Acknowledgements — viii
Author biographies — ix

1. 'Few things in life are less funny than war': Reclaiming the humour in the horror *Juliette Pattinson and Linsey Robb* — 1
2. Observational comedy: Mass-Observation and the wartime joke, 1939–45 *Chris Smith* — 17
3. 'Good-natured as any folk in the world': The Ministry of Information Film and British Humour during the Second World War *Linsey Robb* — 41
4. Making people laugh on the wartime BBC *Siân Nicholas* — 63
5. 'I couldn't get a parrot, dear, so I brought a wren!': The British Cartoon Archive and wartime visual culture *Juliette Pattinson* — 85
6. ''E's a funny doctor': Dickie Orpen and the visual humour of the Second World War reconstructive surgery ward *Christine Slobogin* — 111
7. Taking 'the jagged edges off': British naval humour during the Second World War *Frances Houghton* — 137
8. 'Divided between *ITMA* and a sense of terror': Humour and remembering the war for the BBC People's War Archive *Corinna Peniston-Bird* — 161
9. Exploring *The Real Dad's Army* in the Imperial War Museum, London *Kasia Tomasiewicz* — 181
10. Listening very carefully to *'Allo 'Allo*: British comedy and the path to Brexit *Gavin Schaffer* — 199

Index — 216

List of figures

1.1	'Fighting Spirit' by Fox Photos. © Getty Images	6
5.1	Hitler and Mussolini pincushion. Courtesy of Richard and Alexander Marengo, British Cartoon Archive, KEM 18/2 Box 43	90
5.2	Storyboard for *Adolf and His Donkey Benito*. Courtesy of Richard and Alexander Marengo, British Cartoon Archive, KEM 7	92
5.3	British Cartoon Archive, CG/1/4/2/1/73/17, *Laughs on the Home Front*. Compiled by S. Evelyn Thomas (1943), 3	100
5.4	'Pore lil' feller – I told Emily when she went into munitions he'd never make a shopper', *Punch*, 3 September 1941, 201: no. 5243, 218. Courtesy of TopFoto	104
6.1	'The Spirit of the Sty'. Courtesy of the Guinea Pig Club	117
6.2	'Portrait of Corporal Buckett' and 'Bucket is Busy' from Dickie Orpen's personal papers. Courtesy of Bill Olivier	120
6.3	'Bucket Gets Still Busier' from Dickie Orpen's personal papers. Courtesy of Bill Olivier	122
6.4	'Sartorial Softening' from Dickie Orpen's personal papers. Courtesy of Bill Olivier	124
6.5	'Homo (Mowlemiensis) Sapiens (species Chirugo – Plasticus)' from Dickie Orpen's personal papers. Courtesy of Bill Olivier	125
6.6	'Maison Minestrone: Conforts Modernes + Chauffage Toutafait Centrale' from Dickie Orpen's personal papers. Courtesy of Bill Olivier	126
6.7	BAPRAS/DSB 6.5. Courtesy of The Collection of Plastic, Reconstructive and Aesthetic Surgeons	129

List of tables

2.1 List of Joke References in Each Channel, 1940. Source: MO, FR 229, Jokes, 7 August 1940, p. 44   24

2.2 Joke Categories by Age and Gender, 1942. Source: MO, FR 1400, February Directive: Jokes, 13 August 1942   35

Acknowledgements

This collection stems from a symposium held at the University of Kent in September 2019. The stimulating discussion from all the participants provided not only an enjoyable couple of days but also insightful comments which have helped shaped this collection. We would in particular like to acknowledge the encouragement of the late Clare Makepeace who was very supportive in the conference's planning stages. We are also grateful to the Social History Society for a conference grant which allowed us to support the attendance of PhD students and early career scholars. It perhaps goes without saying that only months after the symposium everyone's world became very different with the arrival of the Covid-19 pandemic. It is under that particular cloud that this collection was predominantly written and collated. We would therefore like to thank all the contributors for their ongoing patience and for still providing their valuable contributions while dealing with all the particular battles and challenges that the pandemic threw in their way. We would also like to thank the publishers for their patience with our original deadline as well as thank Abigail Lane in particular for her efficient support as we completed the various tasks big and small required for a project such as this.

Author biographies

Frances Houghton is Simon Research Fellow in History at the University of Manchester, with research specialisms in histories of emotion; memory and commemoration; gender and sexuality; race and ethnicity; and health and medicine in the Second World War. Key publications include her award-winning book *The Veterans' Tale: British Military Memoirs of the Second World War* (2019), and chapters in *Men, Masculinities and Male Culture in the Second World War* (2018) and *British Cultural Memory and the Second World War* (2014).

Siân Nicholas is Professor of Modern British History at the University of Aberystwyth, and co-founder and Co-Director of the Aberystwyth Centre for Media History. Her research interests include the history and memory of the First and Second World Wars and the role of the mass media in British society. She is the author of *The Echo of War: Home Front Propaganda and the Wartime BBC 1939–45* (1996), and co-editor of *Reconstructing the Past: History in the Mass Media 1890–2005* (2008), *Moral Panics, Social Fears and the Media: Historical Perspectives* (2013) and *Broadcasting in the UK and US in the 1950s: Historical Perspectives* (2016).

Juliette Pattinson is Professor of Modern History at the University of Kent, with a particular specialism in gender and war, clandestine warfare, personal testimonies and Home Front culture. Key publications include: *Women of War* (2020), *Men in Reserve* (2017) and *Behind Enemy Lines* (2007), two special issues on incarcerated masculinities (2014) and partisan and anti-partisan warfare (2008) and four co-edited collections: *Men, Masculinities and Male Culture in the Second World War* (2018), *Fighting for Britain?* (2015), *British Cultural Memory and the Second World War* (2014) and *War in a Twilight World* (2010).

Corinna Peniston-Bird is Professor of Gender and Cultural History at the University of Lancaster. Her research centres on gender dynamics in Britain in the World Wars, with an emphasis on the relationship between memories and cultural representations, and on gendered commemoration. She has published widely on the British military and civilian experience in the Second World War, as well as on innovative methodologies for working with diverse primary sources.

Linsey Robb is Associate Professor in Modern British History at the University of Northumbria. Her work focuses on cultural, social and gendered histories of the Second World War. Key publications include: *Men At Work* (2015), *Men in Reserve* (2017), *Men, Masculinities and Male Culture in the Second World War* (2018) and *Women and War: British Women and War, 1850–1950* (2020). She is currently writing a cultural and social history of conscientious objection in Britain during the Second World War. This work is currently funded by an AHRC Research, Development and Engagement Fellowship.

Gavin Schaffer is Professor of Modern British History at the University of Birmingham, specializing in immigration and racism in Britain. He has written books about multiculturalism and the broadcast media, and the history of eugenics. He is presently working on a Leverhulme Major Research Fellowship, writing a postwar history of British Jews.

Christine Slobogin is an art historian of medicine, currently a Postdoctoral Fellow in the History of Medicine and the Center for Medical Humanities & Social Medicine at John Hopkins University. She has published in *Medical Humanities* and *Visual Culture in Britain*, and she is working on her first monograph on Dickie Orpen and the visual culture of Second World War plastic surgery in Britain.

Chris Smith is Lecturer in History at Coventry University and works on the social and cultural history of Modern Britain. He has published on the history of intelligence and espionage in Britain, including *The Hidden History of Bletchley Park* (2015) and *The Last Cambridge Spy* (2019). He is currently co-writing, with Thomas Knowles, a history of Bletchley Park in British cultural memory and mythology.

Kasia Tomasiewicz is Visiting Researcher at the Centre for Memory, Narrative and Histories. She is a public and cultural historian of museum and memory studies, having completed a Collaborative Doctoral Partnership PhD with the University of Brighton and Imperial War Museums in 2020. She co-runs the Cursed Objects podcast.

1

'Few things in life are less funny than war'[†]: Reclaiming the humour in the horror

Juliette Pattinson and Linsey Robb

Speaking in a 1943 radio broadcast to women across the empire about female workers who downplayed the significance of their work to the wider war effort, Elizabeth Bowes-Lyon, the then Queen, noted that humour was a powerful component of the British war effort:

> The courage of our people is reinforced, too, by one of the strongest weapons in our national armoury: a sense of humour that nothing can daunt. With this weapon of amazing temper, that turns every way, our people keep guard over their sanity and their souls. I have seen that weapon in action many, many times in the last few years, and I well know how much it can help in the really bad times.[1]

Humour was a key defence in the nation's arsenal, facilitating high morale and giving a crucial edge over the enemy. The Queen was not alone in such a belief. Indeed, there is a widespread perception that there is something peculiarly British about humour: George Mikes, in *English Humour for Beginners*, for example, notes that 'the English possess a sense of humour which is specifically English, unintelligible to, and inimitable by, other people and – needless to add – superior to the humour of any other nation.'[2] The English sense of humour is categorized by Harold Nicolson, in his investigation into whether they have a monopoly over humour, as grim, kindly, wry, petty, sardonic, macabre and gay.[3] Such diverse forms of humour have been passed down

---

[†] Nicholas Barber, 'Is It Wrong to Find Humour in War?', BBC website https://www.bbc.com/culture/article/20160204-is-it-wrong-to-find-humour-in-war (2016) Accessed 23 November 2021.

[1] The Queen's radio broadcast to the Women of the Empire, 11 April 1943, *London Calling* (1943). British Cartoon Archive, CG/1/4/2/1/73/17, *Laughs on the Home Front*, Compiled by S. Evelyn Thomas (1943), 1.

[2] George Mikes, *English Humour for Beginners* (London: Andre Deutsch, 1980), 10.

[3] Harold Nicolson, *The English Sense of Humour* (London: Constable, 1956), 5.

through the generations. They have been nurtured by the characters, whose physical attributes and personality traits are each grossly exaggerated to comic effect, that populate the work of Shakespeare (the high-spirited prankster Toby Belch or the buffoonish John Falstaff spring to mind), Austen (especially her use of irony in the pen portraits of the absurd Mr Collins and the shallow Mrs Bennett), Dickens (pompous Bumble, dissolute Mrs Gamp and perky Micawber for example) and P. G. Wodehouse (including simple-minded Bertie Wooster and Gussy Finknottle). During the Second World War, humour was regarded as a key element of 'Britishness', serving to define British national character, much of which was constructed in opposition to the humourless Nazi automaton, as historian Sonya Rose asserts.[4] Humour was regarded as a national character trait, along with a love of animals, games, a cup of tea and queuing, a dislike for extremism, boastfulness and anything foreign, and a propensity towards reserve, insularity and superiority. In reflecting on who 'we are', a Ministry of Information file recorded that as well as being 'free', 'united', 'ready for sacrifice', 'ready for effort', 'truthful' and 'going to win', that the British are 'cheerful': 'We are happy, full of joy; we look on the bright side; we retain our sense of humour; we shall be happier in the end.'[5] Of course, as seen in other popular historical phenomenon and even academic writings, there is an elision of 'Britishness' and 'Englishness'. Yet as this collection will emphasize, the four nations did not share a uniform sense of humour and in reality nation and nation state were key influences on wartime comedy. '[T]he spirit of Clydesiders, typifying the Scottish sense of humour' was remarked upon in a report from the Scottish Women's Voluntary Service regarding the reception of 300 people who, having been bombed out of their homes and lost all their possessions, arrived in the early hours of the morning at a rest centre. When the person in charge apologized for having no food to offer them, one woman remarked dryly: 'Dinna worry. We had no time to send you a telegram to let you know we were comin'.[6] Close scrutiny of contemporaneous reports also reveals that regional specificities were often drawn: a member of the Women's Land Army observed 'the silent reticence, the understatement and the slow, quiet humour of Dorset', a Mass-Observation report considered Blitzed Liverpudlians as having 'good humour and laughter

---

[4] Sonya O. Rose, *Which People's War? National Identity and Citizenship in Wartime Britain, 1939–1945* (Oxford: Oxford University Press, 2003), 287.
[5] TNA, Ministry of Home Security, HO 199/434, 'Propaganda and Publicity Used to Measure and Boost Civilian Morale'.
[6] TNA, Ministry of Home Security, HO 207/388, 'Shelter Welfare Work: Assistance by Women's Voluntary Service, 1941–42', 5–6.

in [the] streets', while 'Nothing has affected the unconquerable optimism of the cockney, nor has anything restricted his ready, if graveyard humour, of which specific instances could be quoted indefinitely.'[7] There are also glimpses of the ways that different social groups were perceived: a member of the Women's Voluntary Service was recorded praising the Jewish and Irish communities of Stepney: 'I have never had much to do before with poor people, but I am full of admiration now for their grand humour, cheerfulness and courage.'[8]

The Second World War was in many ways an Age of Humour, a necessary reaction against the horrors unfolding during this time of total war. Indeed, humour served an important therapeutic function in wartime, having the potential to reduce anxiety and fear and enabling ordinary people to rebel against authority. Those living under foreign occupation or totalitarian regimes told jokes as a coping strategy, as a form of resistance or as a way to retain a sense of humanity.[9] Political jokes flourished under repressive conditions, fulfilling a function previously served by newspapers and parliamentary debate. Writing during the Nazi occupation of Czechoslovakia, Antonin Obrdlik notes that those living in occupied countries 'find a refuge in inventing, repeating and spreading through the channels of whispering counterpropaganda, anecdotes and jokes about their oppressors'.[10] The 'gallows humour' of those living in 'absolute uncertainty' offered 'an intellectual and emotional escape from the disturbing realities' of occupation. It had an 'importance as a compensation for fear', keeping alight 'the spirit of resistance' and 'bolster[ing] the morale of the Czech people'.[11] These small acts of bravado and defiance, which could have disproportionate ramifications if they were reported to the occupying authorities, were endorsed from the top: President Beneš reassured his people in a radio speech broadcast from London, where he was leading the government-in-exile, that the fact that other nations were now ridiculing Nazism ought to be taken as a good indicator that the end was in sight.[12]

---

[7] TNA, Ministry of Agriculture and Fisheries, MAF 59/22, 'Words, Words, Words!', *The Land Girl*, October 1943, 2; TNA, Ministry of Home Security, HO 199/442, 'Conditions in Selected Blitzed Towns: Findings by Mass Observation Group'; TNA, Ministry of Home Security, HO 199/444, 'Weekly reports dated July to November 1940'.

[8] TNA, Ministry of Home Security, HO 199/438, 'Ministry of Information Reports on Region No. 5 for the period 1 January 1941 to 19 April 1941'.

[9] Steve Lipman, *Laughter in Hell: The Use of Humour during the Holocaust* (Northvale: Aronson, 1997).

[10] Antonin J. Obrdlik, '"Gallows Humor": A Sociological Phenomenon', *American Journal of Sociology* 47, no. 5 (1942), 709–16. Here p. 712.

[11] Obrdlik, 'Gallows Humor', 710–12.

[12] Ibid., 711.

Of course, British war experience was very different to that of occupied Europe. While Britons faced privations, Britain was not a battleground nor did the public suffer the ignominies and dangers of living under occupation. British humour therefore was abundant and flourished in the daylight rather than in the shadows. Indeed, in wartime Britain, humour was held in particularly high esteem, and lack thereof, viewed with considerable scepticism. The ability to laugh at oneself, to smile at one's misfortune and to see the humour in the mundane was especially needed in wartime, as circumstances became increasingly bleak with mounting military losses and civilian deaths, increased shortages and curtailments of movement. As noted by Chair Mrs McNeill in a talk to the Wigtownshire branch of the Women's Land Army, 'Their work called not only for physical endurance, but for common-sense, initiative, patience, and, above all, a sense of humour.'[13] There was an evident demand for an opportunity to laugh: a release from the increased working hours, the separation from loved ones, the dual burdens of work and maintaining a household, the fear of sustaining battle wounds and death. Laughter made the unbearable bearable. It was a coping mechanism and a form of escapism. As ARP Officer Mr W. Mason observed, 'The grim side of air raids is often tinged with humour … It is felt that the sense of humour existing among the personnel has done much to maintain their morale, and it is often said that the day the Britisher does lose his sense of humour is the day when the war effort will decline.'[14] Indeed, war and comedy are intimately connected as laughter was invoked as a weapon with which to prosecute the war, as the Queen identified. And it provided a means to demonstrate allegiance to the British war effort. There was a strong communal aspect to humour: shared jocularity served to establish bonds between individuals, creating and maintaining group identity, defining the 'in' group as well as outsiders. People more readily laughed when they were with others. Thus, as Noel Carroll asserts, humour had a significant role to play in constructing communities.[15]

Humour was everywhere: funny occurrences happened continually and were incorporated into anecdotes that were frequently repeated, it was read on the pages of novels, magazines and newspapers, sung about, incorporated into everyday parlance, heard on the radio and seen on the cinema screen. Novelists were keen to inject some comic relief: E.M. Delafield's eponymous diarist in *The Provincial Lady in War-Time* paints a satirical picture of the Phoney War:

---

[13] The National Archives (henceforth TNA) MAF 59/21 Ministry of Agriculture and Fisheries, 'Scottish Notes', *The Land Girl*, March 1942, 10.

[14] TNA, HO 192/1238, Civil Defence Services, 'Impressions of the Growth and Working of the Civil Defence Services', 6.

[15] Noel Carroll, *Humour: A Very Short Introduction* (Oxford: Oxford University Press, 2014).

Meet several people in the village, and exchange comments on such topics as food-rationing, possible shortage of sugar, and inability ever to go anywhere on proposed petrol allowance. Extraordinary and characteristically English tendency on the part of everybody to go into fits of laughter and say Well, we're all in the same boat, aren't we, and we've got to show 'itler he can't go on like that, haven't we? Agree that we have, and that we will.[16]

Newspapers and magazines often featured cartoon strips portraying in pictorial form current events or lampooning Nazi leaders. Comedic songs recorded by Flanagan and Allen, George Formby and Tommy Trinder were wildly popular. 'Hitler has only got one ball', sung to the tune of the 'Colonel Bogey March' that was popular during the First World War, tapped into a childish mentality by ridiculing Hitler, Goebbels, Göring and Himmler for having undersized or missing testicles. So pervasive was this mocking, both during the war and after, that it is featured in three of our chapters (Robb on wartime cinema, Pattinson on cartoons and Schaffer on 'Allo 'Allo!). Moreover, the Local Defence Volunteers were affectionately referred to as the Look, Duck and Vanish brigade, while ENSA became Every Night Something Awful. Humorous captions were also evident on the high street with the owners of blitzed shops, their goods exposed to the elements, displaying signs joking 'More Open than Usual'. Such examples of wry humour, which were captured for posterity in photographic form such as Figure 1.1 and articulated by the deadpan delivery of Quentin Reynolds in the filmic short *London Can Take It!*, speak to a determination to see the lighter side of dark occurrences.[17] A highly popular radio programme was *ITMA (It's That Man Again)* starring Tommy Handley. This fast-paced sketch show, which broadcast twelve series of over 300 episodes between 1939 and 1949, had a variety of characters, many with accents, including Funf, the dull-witted German, and the Colonel who read every remark as an invitation to have a drink, and repetition of catch phrases such as Mrs Mopp's 'Can I do yer now, sir?' was a key part of its success in building a loyal fan base. Films that were not billed as comedies routinely wove in comedic characters for light relief, often with marked regional accents: the postmistress in *Went the Day Well?* (1942), the railway porter and waitress in *Brief Encounter* (1945) and the Canadian soldier who goes awol in *Waterloo*

---

[16] E.M. Delafield, *The Provincial Lady in War-Time* (New York: Harper & Brothers, 1940), 39.
[17] 'In the centre of the city the shops are open as usual. In fact, many of them are *more* open than usual.' A shopkeeper is shown brushing away broken glass and a woman enters the shop through the window. *London Can Take It!* Dir. Humphrey Jennings and Harry Watt, GPO Film Unit (1940).

Figure 1.1 'Fighting Spirit' by Fox Photos. © Getty Images.

Road (1944), for example.[18] Humorous lines were often inserted into films for similar effect: for example, the audience is reminded that an orange is 'a spherical pulpish fruit of reddish-yellow colour' in *Millions Like Us* (1943). This unequivocal approach of injecting humour at every opportunity was thought to have a positive impact on morale as one 1940 Home Intelligence

---

[18] *Went the Day Well?* Dir. Alberto Cavalcanti (1942); *Brief Encounter* Dir. David Lean (1945); *Waterloo Road* Dir. Sidney Gilliat (1944).

Report suggested: 'Reports have shown that direct talk with broad humour, or spirited comment goes down very much better than the intellectual approach demanded at the beginning of the war. Propaganda should not be subtle: for ordinary people are not subtle.'[19]

Home Front popular culture, in the form of radio programmes, feature films, documentary films, newsreels, cartoons and songs, parodied the conflict and were crucial morale-boosters as the war evolved into a protracted struggle. Whereas radio programmes and pictorial cartoons were reliant on just one sense, cinematic films interwove the spoken word with visual humour. Comedy was also often performative, acted out on the stage. RAF Gang Shows included comedy sketches, humorous songs and frequently men in drag in the tradition of the music hall, which was later satirized by the BBC television series *It Ain't Half Hot, Mum!*[20] They were performed from summer 1940 for servicemen in various theatres of war and provided an essential means of respite from both the boredom and the horror of battle. Post-war household names such as Tony Hancock, Dick Emery and Peter Sellers were regulars.

Furthermore, few events have resonated so comprehensively in modern British culture as the Second World War.[21] Indeed, since 1945, the Second World War has sparked the imagination of scriptwriters. Jimmy Perry and David Croft drew on their experiences in the Home Guard to write *Dad's Army*, much as they had done with their participation in Royal Artillery concert parties in India when scripting *It Ain't Half Hot, Mum!*, and Croft paired up with Jeremy Lloyd to write *'Allo 'Allo!*[22] Unlike the First World War, the cultural memory of the later war is replete with stories about the conflict that use humour as a device.

Despite the pervasiveness of humour throughout British wartime life, the popularity of post-war comic representations of the British experience of war and the recognition that humour has long been acknowledged as a key component of the British attitude and response to the Second World War, scholars have never systemically approached the topic. Indeed, humour has been on the margins of

---

[19] TNA, HO 199/446, Ministry of Home Security, 'Summary of Morale June – July 1940', 4.
[20] By 1945, there were fifteen home-based units of Gang Shows, two of which comprised members of the Women's Auxiliary Air Force, which had first performed in Normandy in June 1944, and ten overseas units. Richard Fawkes, *Fighting for a Laugh: Entertaining the British and American Armed Forces, 1939–1946* (London: Macdonald & Jane's, 1978), 58.
[21] Lucy Noakes and Juliette Pattinson, 'Keep Calm and Carry On: The Cultural Memory of the Second World War in Britain', in Lucy Noakes and Juliette Pattinson (eds.), *The Cultural Memory of the Second World War in Britain* (London: Bloomsbury, 2013), 1–24.
[22] The BBC broadcast eighty episodes of *Dad's Army* between July 1968 and November 1977, 56 episodes of *It Ain't Half Hot, Mum!* between January 1974 and September 1981 and 85 episodes of *'Allo 'Allo!* between December 1982 and December 1992.

historical research more broadly, rarely the subject of scholarly study.[23] Humour is generally only reflected in the scholarship in a piecemeal and fragmented way. For example, Jeffrey Richards and Sonya Rose both clearly articulated that humour was a key part of British national identity in wartime. Richards argues as part of his wide-ranging volume on British film, that they were imbued during the war with 'a self-deprecating good humour'.[24] Similarly, Rose asserted that 'The British prided themselves on being a virile nation, but its virility was temperate. They were fighting a war with their sense of humour intact; they were "good tempered" and modest'.[25] While Rose's concept of 'temperate masculinity' has proven to be extremely influential, such analysis on the importance of humour was a small aside in a much wider study. Such fleeting glances are typical of the historiography. For example, Penny Summerfield's seminal *Reconstructing Women's Wartime Lives* has a section analysing the teasing faced by women in industrial workplaces.[26] Similarly, Claire Langhamer, Lucy Noakes and Claudia Siebrecht's edited collection *Total War: An Emotional History* has some examples of the ways in which humour features in wartime emotional lives.[27] Indeed, it was the scattered but persistent nature of references to humour in our previous edited collection *Men, Masculinities and Male Culture in the Second World War* that was the inspiration behind the symposium held at the University of Kent in 2019 and this volume.[28] Perhaps the most notable exception to these piecemeal allusions is the work of Penny Summerfield and Corinna Peniston-Bird on the Home Guard and their explorations of the multi-faceted ways in which humour was used during the war and after. They make special reference to the enduring

---

[23] In Valerie Holman and Debra Kelly's special edition of *Journal of European Studies* 31:123 (2001) on war and humour in Europe during the two world wars, there are two articles that refer to Britain during the Second World War. See also David Slucki, Gabriel N. Finder and Avinoam Patt, *Laughter after: Humor and the Holocaust* (Detroit: Wayne State University Press, 2020); Shepherd Mpofu (ed.), *The Politics of Laughter in the Social Media Age: Perspectives from the Global South* (Houndmills: Palgrave, 2021); Pierre Serna, *A Politique du Rire: Satires, Caricatures et Blasphèmes XVIe-XXIe Siècles* [The Politics of Laughter: Satires, Caricatures and Blasphemies 16–21st Centuries] (Ceyzerieu: Champ Vallon: 2015); Martina Kessel and Patrick Merziger (eds.), *The Politics of Humour: Laughter, Inclusion and Exclusion in the Twentieth Century* (Buffalo: University of Toronto Press, 2012); George E.C. Paton, Chris Powell and Stephen Wagg (eds.), *The Social Faces of Humour: Practices and Issues* (London: Routledge, 1996).

[24] Jeffrey Richards, *Films and British National Identity: From Dickens to Dad's Army* (Manchester: Manchester University Press, 1997), 106.

[25] Rose, *Which People's War?*, 287.

[26] Penny Summerfield, *Reconstructing Women's Wartime Lives* (Manchester: Manchester University Press, 1998), 139–40.

[27] Clare Langhamer, Lucy Noakes and Claudia Siebrecht (eds.), *Total War: An Emotional History* (Oxford: Oxford University Press, 2020).

[28] Linsey Robb and Juliette Pattinson (eds.), *Men, Masculinities and Male Culture in the Second World War* (Basingstoke: Palgrave Macmillan, 2018).

legacy of the television sitcom *Dad's Army* in the public consciousness and those who served in Civil Defence.[29] Moreover, given the vast array of work on the culture, and cultural legacy, of the war in Britain it is somewhat surprising that humour has never been the serious focus of scholars and instead is incidental in wider themes. For example, wartime commercial cinema has been thoroughly analysed by scholars but work on humour is rare; a notable exception is a chapter on humour in Robert Murphy's *British Cinema and the Second World War*.[30] While these works are invaluable additions to the scholarship on the Second World War, they are but few of the myriad ways in which humour featured and functioned in wartime life and in the war's legacy. As such, this collection makes a vital contribution as the first attempt to take a prolonged look at wartime humour by looking at a broader range of cultural media and lived experiences.

This collection also fits within a broader turn to the emotions within historical enquiry over the last two decades: fear, shame, jealousy, hatred, grief and love have each been the subject of rigorous examination.[31] Such emotions have also been recently subjected to critical scrutiny during wartime: as Lucy Noakes, Claire Langhamer and Claudia Siebrecht note, war is often experienced at the time and remembered subsequently as a period of heightened emotional intensity.[32] But another emotion, that of amusement, is yet to be exposed to the same rigour. This edited collection seeks to restore the serious topic of humour to the historical record, illuminating often overlooked aspects of Britain's war in popular culture and cultural memory by analysing what generated laughter. Understanding the humour of a given culture provides important insights into that society. An analysis of humour during and about the Second World War

---

[29] Penny Summerfield and Corinna Peniston-Bird, *Contesting Home Defence: Men, Women and the Home Guard in the Second World War* (Manchester: Manchester University Press, 2007); Corinna Peniston-Bird and Penny Summerfield, '"Hey, You're Dead!": The Multiple Uses of Humour in Representations of British National Defence in the Second World War', *Journal of European Studies* 31 no. 123 (2001), 413–35.

[30] Robert Murphy, *British Cinema and the Second World War* (London: Continuum, 2005).

[31] Jan Plamper, *The History of Emotions: An Introduction* (Oxford: Oxford University Press, 2017); Michael Laffan, Max Weiss (eds.), *Facing Fear: The History of an Emotion in Global Perspective* (Princeton: Princeton University Press 2012); Joanna Bourke, 'Fear and Anxiety: Writing about Emotion in Modern History', *History Workshop Journal*, 55, no. 1 (2003), 111–33; Peter N. Stearns, *Shame: A Brief History* (Champaign: University of Illinois, 2017); David Konstan and N. Keith Rutter (eds.), *Envy, Spite and Jealousy: The Rivalrous Emotions in Ancient Greece* (Edinburgh: Edinburgh University Press, 2003); Berit Brogaard, *Hatred: Understanding Our Most Dangerous Emotion* (New York: Oxford University Press, 2020); Lucy Noakes, *Dying for the Nation: Death, Grief and Bereavement in Second World War Britain* (Manchester: Manchester University Press, 2020); Claire Langhamer, *The English in Love: The Intimate Story of an Emotional Revolution* (Oxford: Oxford University Press, 2013).

[32] Lucy Noakes, Claire Langhamer and Claudia Siebrecht (eds.), *Total War: An Emotional History* (Oxford: Oxford University Press, 2020).

provides the key to the cultural codes and sensibilities of the past, revealing what people laughed at, how and when they laughed.

Yet it is a truth universally acknowledged that a collection about humour is, sadly, unlikely to be overly funny. This is because the nature of humour is historically variable, changing over time and from one culture to another. What appeared funny to wartime audiences may be read as lame and outdated or even highly offensive to modern-day eyes with very different cultural attitudes. Some cartoons, for example, had explicitly racist overtones. A cartoon by Jones that featured in a pamphlet entitled *Good Humour Annual* depicts a white man tied by his hands and feet to a cane carried by smiling men with simian features, black skin, large eyes, oversized white lips and button noses, who are barefoot, wearing fringed skirts and have hoops around their biceps and ankles and dangling from their ears. Another white man is sitting naked in a giant cooking vessel, overseen by men in chefs' hats holding a large carving knife and a giant spoon. 'Ha! There you are Ponsonby: I was getting quite worried about you.'[33] The cultural context in which humour is produced is therefore key, as humour is local, both context- and temporally specific, and difficult to translate. Some aspects simply do not travel well across the borders of time, culture and language, dependent as they are on contemporary attitudes and habits. An understanding of the political, cultural and social context(s) of its creation is thus vital in understanding humour's construction and reception, what Victor Raskin terms 'situational context'.[34] Humour is also highly subjective: what amuses one person can be regarded as distasteful or simply unfunny by another. Some found humour inappropriate in a time of war. In a survey about Ministry of Information pamphlets, 67 per cent of the nearly 6,000 people interviewed replied 'no' when asked 'Do you think more humour should be introduced into these books?' One respondent noted that 'war must be remembered as grim.'[35] This unease about undermining the seriousness of war was also made apparent on the pages of *London's New Statesman and Nation*. This weekly magazine ran literary competitions, announcing the theme one week and publishing the winning entries another. On 25 October 1941, the printed 'ruthless rhymes' focused primarily on death: bodies used to manure vegetable gardens, cannibalism and murder all featured.

---

[33] Kent Cartoon Archive, CG/1/4/2/1/73/4, *Good Humour Annual*, Compiled by S. Evelyn Thomas (1943), 60.
[34] Victor Raskin, *Semantic Mechanisms of Humor* (Dordrecht: D. Reidel Publishing Company, 1985).
[35] TNA, Ministry of Information, HO 262/16, 'Special Surveys on War and Postwar Matters', 11. The six MoI publications under consideration were *Man Power, Front Line, Eighth Army, Combined Operations, Coastal Command* and *East of Malta, West of Suez*.

A reader wrote in to complain: 'Do not woes of total war this weekly competition bar? Who put in his own last breath should be pardoned jokes on death.'[36] This elicited a strong editorial response:

> Ruthless rhymes are essentially satires upon Man's indifference to the fate of others except in so far as this affects his personal convenience. Evidently jokes about death can all be thought in bad taste, but the fact that most of us have, during the last year, been in danger does not, as far as I can see, aggravate the offence; it merely increases the desire to make such jokes. I note that a rhyme about an undisposed bomb exploding comes from a member of a bomb-disposal unit, and one about a propeller killing somebody comes from an aerodrome.[37]

As this editor noted, humour had an important role to play in helping the (majority of the) public navigate the tragic experiences of total war. It is this that the volume, in part, seeks to scrutinize in more depth. However, this is not simply a collection on humour on the British Home Front. The collection extends past 1945 to examine representations of wartime humour in post-war British culture. It brings together cutting-edge historical research by leading and emerging researchers in the field on the utilization of humour during Britain's Second World War experience and, through the adoption of a critical approach which sees humour as a product of the present rather than a simple reproduction of the past, its legacy in British popular culture. These focused case studies provide fresh perspectives on a wide variety of aspects enabling readers to place humour within a historical context, analysing not only cultural representations but also how humour featured in everyday wartime life and after. It explores humour in a diverse range of wartime locations, including the surgical ward and the naval ship, across a variety of media, such as cartoons, radio, filmic shorts and longform films, in post-war repositories, such as the BBC People's War Archive, Mass-Observation, the Imperial War Museum Sound Archive and the British Cartoon Archive, and in retrospective accounts, including the popular television comedy *'Allo 'Allo!* and the IWM's *Dad's Army* exhibition. And in revealing the prevalence of references to the exceptionalism of Britain and the superiority of the British to the German enemy, case studies provide fresh insights into British national identity and the British psyche.

---

[36] Cited in Charles R. Gruner, *The Games of Humor: A Comprehensive Theory of Why We Laugh* (New Brunswick: Transaction Publishers, 1977), 50.
[37] Cited in Gruner, *The Games of Humor*, 51.

'Playing hookey, little Tom
Teased an unexploded bomb.
At the Pig and Whistle bar
They'd always said he would go far.'

'Straying near the prop, a WAAF
Managed to get cut in half
'See, the wood's not even frayed',
Jim said, as he wiped the blade.'

The collection examines the ways humour functioned, and was deployed, both during the war and after. Across the chapters we see recurrent humorous themes and motifs which persist across varied media, wartime services and even time periods as these ideas continued to provoke mirth long after peace had come. For example, chapters by Linsey Robb and Juliette Pattinson examine the ways Nazis were ridiculed in wartime media (specifically propaganda films and cartoons). These ideas are later re-examined in Gavin Schaffer's chapter on the 1980s and 1990s British sitcom *'Allo 'Allo!* which heavily ridiculed Nazi officers. We see the same topics repeatedly being mined for their comedic value. The privations of war were, somewhat surprisingly, rich fodder for humour. Nicholas, Pattinson and Peniston-Bird each note the ways in which wartime rationing was played for laughs both during the war and after. Pattinson and Houghton both examine the ways in which humour functioned as a bonding strategy and mark of friendship in the face of danger and difficulties. Slobogin, writing about wartime medical drawings, and Peniston-Bird, on postwar recollections in the BBC's People's War Archive, both examine the ways trauma and humour were often irretrievably intermingled in both experience and memory. Similarly, Peniston-Bird, Tomasiewicz and Schaffer look at the ways these challenges, hardships and wartime peculiarities filtered into the memories and cultural legacy of the war in Britain. Indeed, while the war may have ended in 1945, its comedic lifespan, as this collections shows, was far greater.

The collection opens with various chapters on the way humour as a construct explicitly functioned in wartime society. Chris Smith sets the scene by noting the attention given to humour while total war was being waged. He adopts an almost forensic approach in his examination of the reports on humour in Mass-Observation. In addition to enhancing our understanding of this fascinating organization, he chronologically plots significant wartime events and fortunes of the nation against fluctuations in the British mood through an analysis of jokes that were circulating widely. He argues that the war joke was not as prominent in wartime as one might think with many patrons and professionals preferring classic jokes which relied on slapstick or sexual humour. The collection then turns its focus on to various types of media, specifically film, radio and cartoons. Linsey Robb explores humour in official wartime filmic propaganda. She analyses a wide range of shorts and feature-length films and, in doing so, develops themes that are often overlooked in studies of propaganda. The portrayal of common bonds between apparently disparate groups is one such angle. She argues that humour was used to make information memorable and, more importantly, was deployed as a key indicator of essential British humanity and morality. Like Smith, Siân Nicholas adopts a chronological approach to plot the ways BBC radio broadcasts incorporated humour into wartime programming as well as the waxing and waning of official and popular responses to this humour. While lampooning Hitler was largely acceptable, and even appreciated, at the start of the war, this quickly faded as wartime life became more entrenched. While scholars of British popular culture have generally argued that the British people sought to escape the war, Nicholas demonstrates that it was the very topicality of the material which was so well received by listeners of *ITMA*. Juliette Pattinson's chapter reveals the richness of cartoons as a historical source by examining what they can tell us about attitudes towards the enemy, Home Front privations and shifting gender roles. This chapter speaks to how humour expressed in cartoon form could provide an outlet to wartime vexations, enabling the public to pass critical comment on certain situations without undermining the war effort.

The collection then moves away from examining Home Front humour circulating in the public domain to exploring private forms of humour that were never intended to be disseminated. The first of two case studies exploring very distinct forms of humour situated within closed communities is from a militaristic setting: Frances Houghton examines the humour of officers of the Royal Navy by examining novel sources such as naval signals and cartoons. Houghton shows that humour was used to both enliven dull routines as well as to 'take the jagged edge off' dangerous situations. The second case study is sited in a facial surgery ward: Christine Slobogin analyses the marginalia and cartoons of medical illustrator Dickie Orpen. In examining this unique source Slobogin argues that, as with other such documented wards, humour was integral to the surgical unit and was a fundamental tool not just for the patients but also for the staff tasked with the literal reconstruction of men damaged in some of the worst ways possible in warfare.

The collection then moves away from the contemporaneity of wartime humour and onto the various ways humour has filtered into post-war depictions and understandings of the war. Corinna Peniston-Bird's chapter examines the deployment of humour in the entries to the BBC's People's War online archive. Peniston-Bird provides a masterclass on how to work meaningfully with a very large online data set while rescuing from obscurity the mundane and the everyday which are so often overlooked. She shows that humour was used for a dual purpose: both to engage the audience and connect them to a past they had not experienced but also, conversely, to highlight the absurdity of wartime experience and ultimately highlight to readers their estrangement from the experiences of war. The collection ends with discussions of two of the most popular post-war sitcoms. Kasia Tomasiewicz discusses *Dad's Army* through the lens of an exhibition about the programme held at the Imperial War

Museum. Due to the crisis of the 1970s, the show and the exhibition provided a much-needed cultural outlet for humour and nostalgia. While less explicitly focused on a comedic product, the exhibition enhances our understanding of how the war might be more easily remembered from a comedic perspective that circumvents unpleasant aspects of the conflict. Moving away from an explicit focus on the Second World War and taking us up to the present day, the collection ends with Gavin Schaffer's analysis of *'Allo 'Allo!*'s enduring legacy. He argues that the persistent assertion that this show represents something unique about Britain and its humour points to a wider and long-term cultural discomfort with Britain's relationship with Europe which found its nadir in Brexit.

The collection, therefore, covers the use of humour in a broad range of situations and media. Humour, comedy and laughter, in their various guises, were clearly integral to the war and its memory in Britain, performing to negate the horrors of war, brighten its tedium and strengthen bonds among those who found themselves serving in new and unfamiliar environments.

Bibliography

Nicholas Barber, 'Is It Wrong to Find Humour in War?', BBC website https://www.bbc.com/culture/article/20160204-is-it-wrong-to-find-humour-in-war (2016) Accessed 23 November 2021.

Joanna Bourke, 'Fear and Anxiety: Writing about Emotion in Modern History', *History Workshop Journal*, 55, no. 1 (2003), 111–33.

Berit Brogaard, *Hatred: Understanding Our Most Dangerous Emotion* (New York: Oxford University Press, 2020).

Noel Carroll, *Humour: A Very Short Introduction* (Oxford: Oxford University Press, 2014).

E.M. Delafield, *The Provincial Lady in War-Time* (New York: Harper & Brothers, 1940).

Richard Fawkes, *Fighting for a Laugh: Entertaining the British and American Armed Forces, 1939–1946* (London: Macdonald & Jane's, 1978).

Charles R. Gruner, *The Games of Humor: A Comprehensive Theory of Why We Laugh* (New Brunswick: Transaction Publishers, 1977).

Martina Kessel and Patrick Merziger (eds.), *The Politics of Humour: Laughter, Inclusion and Exclusion in the Twentieth Century* (Buffalo: University of Toronto Press, 2012).

David Konstan and N. Keith Rutter (eds.), *Envy, Spite and Jealousy: The Rivalrous Emotions in Ancient Greece* (Edinburgh: Edinburgh University Press, 2003).

Michael Laffan and Max Weiss (eds.), *Facing Fear: The History of an Emotion in Global Perspective* (Princeton: Princeton University Press, 2012).

Claire Langhamer, *The English in Love: The Intimate Story of an Emotional Revolution* (Oxford: Oxford University Press, 2013).

Clare Langhamer, Lucy Noakes and Claudia Siebrecht (eds.), *Total War: An Emotional History* (Oxford: Oxford University Press, 2020).

George Mikes, *English Humour for Beginners* (London: Andre Deutsch, 1980).

Robert Murphy, *British Cinema and the Second World War* (London: Continuum, 2005).

Harold Nicolson, *The English Sense of Humour* (London: Constable, 1956).

Lucy Noakes, *Dying for the Nation: Death, Grief and Bereavement in Second World War Britain* (Manchester: Manchester University Press, 2020).

Lucy Noakes and Juliette Pattinson, 'Keep Calm and Carry On: The Cultural Memory of the Second World War in Britain' in Lucy Noakes and Juliette Pattinson (eds.), *The Cultural Memory of the Second World War in Britain* (London: Bloomsbury, 2013), 1–24.

Antonin J. Obrdlik, '"Gallows Humor": A Sociological Phenomenon', *American Journal of Sociology*, 47, no. 5 (1942), 709–16.

George E.C. Paton, Chris Powell and Stephen Wagg (eds.), *The Social Faces of Humour: Practices and Issues* (London: Routledge, 1996).

Avinoam Patt, *Laughter after: Humor and the Holocaust* (Detroit: Wayne State University Press, 2020).

Corinna Peniston-Bird and Penny Summerfield, '"Hey, You're Dead!": The Multiple Uses of Humour in Representations of British National Defence in the Second World War', *Journal of European Studies*, 31 no. 123 (2001), 413–35.

Jan Plamper, *The History of Emotions: An Introduction* (Oxford: Oxford University Press, 2017).

Victor Raskin, *Semantic Mechanisms of Humor* (Dordrecht: D. Reidel Publishing Company, 1985).

Jeffrey Richards, *Films and British National Identity: From Dickens to Dad's Army* (Manchester: Manchester University Press, 1997).

Linsey Robb and Juliette Pattinson (eds.), *Men, Masculinities and Male Culture in the Second World War* (Basingstoke: Palgrave Macmillan, 2018).

Sonya O. Rose, *Which People's War? National Identity and Citizenship in Wartime Britain, 1939–1945* (Oxford: Oxford University Press, 2003).

Pierre Serna, *A Politique du Rire: Satires, Caricatures et Blasphèmes XVIe-XXIe Siècles* [*The Politics of Laughter: Satires, Caricatures and Blasphemies 16–21st Centuries*] (Ceyzerieu: Champ Vallon, 2015).

David Slucki, Gabriel N. Finder and Shepherd Mpofu (eds.), *The Politics of Laughter in the Social Media Age: Perspectives from the Global South* (Houndmills: Palgrave, 2021).

Peter N. Stearns, *Shame: A Brief History* (Champaign: University of Illinois, 2017).

Penny Summerfield, *Reconstructing Women's Wartime Lives* (Manchester: Manchester University Press, 1998).

Penny Summerfield and Corinna Peniston-Bird, *Contesting Home Defence: Men, Women and the Home Guard in the Second World War* (Manchester: Manchester University Press, 2007).

2

Observational comedy: Mass-Observation and the wartime joke, 1939–45

Chris Smith

The Second World War generated, largely through the machinery of wartime propaganda and then amplified in post-war mythology, a notion that the British were a unified people during wartime.[1] Many of course were not. While some did come together, others remained divided along class, gender, national and ethnic grounds, as noted by various historians.[2] Even if some people were not really in 'it' together, propagandists worked hard to inculcate an image of good-humoured unity. They drew upon comedic writers to present messages with the veneer of cheer to sweeten an otherwise bitter reality. As such, humourists, including the *Punch* editor and cartoonist, Fougasse (Cyril Kenneth Bird) were drafted to produce propaganda for the state.[3]

In the minds of the propagandists, these efforts were successful. In October 1940, R. H. Parker, head of the Home Publicity Division of the MOI, recorded that 'Nothing has affected the unconquerable optimism of the cockney, nothing has restricted his ready, if graveyard, humour.'[4] The telling of jokes was, then, in the midst of death and crisis, evidence to the propagandists that they were

---

[1] Paul Addison and Jeremy A. Crang (eds.), *Listening to Britain: Home Intelligence Reports on Britain's Finest Hour – May to September 1940* (London: Jonathan Cape, 2011), 5.
[2] Angus Calder, *The People's War* (London: Pimlico: 1969); Clive Ponting, *1940: Myth and Reality* (London: Hamish Hamilton, 1990); Stuart Hylton, *Careless Talk: The Hidden History of the Home Front, 1939-1945* (Stroud: The History Press, 2001, 2010); David Edgerton, *Britain's War Machine: Weapons, Resources and Experts in the Second World War* (London: Penguin, 2012). The legacies of these mythologies and their construction have also been the subject of study: Angus Calder, *The Myth of the Blitz* (London: Pimlico, 1991); Mark Connelly, *We Can Take It!: Britain and the Memory of the Second World War* (Harlow: Pearson Education, 2007).
[3] Bird published a short 'broadcast talk' entitled, 'Strictly between these four walls', which outlined his philosophy in producing humorous visual propaganda. See, Fougasse, *... And the Gatepost* (London: Chattos & Windus, 1940).
[4] Lola Serraf, 'Writing the "People's War": Evaluating the Myth of the Blitz in British Women's Fiction of the Second World War' (Universitat Autònoma de Barcelona: Unpublished PhD thesis, 2018), 13-14.

succeeding. But did wartime jokes actually demonstrate the sentiments that Parker believed they did? Were they a reflection of a united people, thumbing their noses at German efforts to destroy their morale? This chapter argues that they were not. Jokes often showed defeatism, but by and large they served as a form of escapism. This was a fact not lost on many professional comedians in music halls who, finding that topical war jokes did not go down well, turned to other topics to entertain.

So, what, instead, did people joke about and what do those jokes tell us about British wartime society? To answer this question, it is worth turning to Mass-Observation, an ethnographic project started by the anthropologist Tom Harrisson, the poet Charles Madge and the documentary filmmaker Humphrey Jennings, which sought to record everyday life in Britain. The project began life in 1937 as, according to Harrisson, a reaction to the 'disturbed condition of Western Europe under the threat of fascism'. The project 'sought [to] supply accurate observation of everyday life and *real* (not just published) public mood … a vast sector of normal life … which did not seem adequately covered by the media, the arts, the social scientists, even by the political leaders'.[5] To this end, hundreds of volunteer Observers kept diaries, recorded conversations (and not only their own) and filled out questionnaires – grandly titled 'directives'.[6] Despite one Mass-Observation analysis noting that 'There are probably few subjects about which so many dull books have been written as humour',[7] from its inception, Mass-Observers were very interested in what made people laugh and the mechanics of humour. Observers recorded jokes they had heard told to them and to others, as well as jokes made in music halls, theatres, books and cartoons. In all, during this period from 1937 to 1948 (when joke collection ceased), over 10,000 examples were sent in to Mass-Observation, who compiled reports and categorized them by type and by frequency with which they were told.[8] They found that for the most part, the war was a popular source of topical jokes. Yet these were collectively dwarfed in number by subjects which the British public had always laughed at: the humdrum of everyday life, sex and lavatories, work and home.

Such a rich and varied archive offers a unique insight into the British wartime sense of humour. It is possible to gain an idea of what people were laughing at,

---

[5] Tom Harrisson, *Living through the Blitz* (London: Penguin, 1990), 13.
[6] Nick Hubble, *Mass Observation and Everyday Life: Culture, History, Theory*, 2nd ed. (Basingstoke: Palgrave Macmillan, 2010).
[7] Mass Observation [MO], File Report [FR] 3026, The British Sense of Humour, August 1948, 5.
[8] MO, FR 3026, The British Sense of Humour, August 1948, 8.

the types of jokes they told one another, the jokes that drew patrons into the music halls to listen to professional comedians and performers, and the humour that sold newspapers and magazines. The methods, successes, imperfections and legacies of Mass-Observation – for example, Observers tended to be educated and (often lower) middle class, thus skewing the sample and rendering the picture provided unrepresentative of wider British society – have been discussed at length by other historians.[9] The jokes Mass-Observation collected and the analysis of these jokes, by contrast, have not. This chapter is the first exploration of this rich vein of material.

Surprisingly, historians have offered little attention to British wartime humour. That is not to say that historians have not considered humour at all – they have.[10] Initially, historians treated wartime humour as a form of escapism or a coping mechanism when dealing with the extreme stresses of war. For instance, Norman Longmate noted that the blackout was 'the first great source of wartime jokes, one of those disagreeable but universal experiences which might as well be laughed at as it could not be remedied'.[11] Jokes, then, were a manifestation of stoicism and the mythical British stiff-upper-lip.[12] This logical conclusion, that humour served as a crutch to deal with the onerous yet ubiquitous problems of war, appears to be borne out by examination of wartime collections of humour. Certainly D. B. Wyndham Lewis, editor of a joke book which saw three editions produced during the war, included significant volumes of material on the blackout, rationing (eggs being particularly funny: 'The job of the experts is to keep the eggs moving'[13]), evacuation, and so on.

This was the humour of high (or at least middle)-brow professional humourists. This was an 'English sense of humour', characterized by Harold Nicolson as possessing 'a very large admixture of kindliness, sentiment, reasonableness, and fancy'.[14] Wyndham Lewis was a professional literary humourist who often

---

[9] Penny Summerfield, 'Mass-Observation: Social Research or Social Movement?', *Journal of Contemporary History*, 20, no. 3 (1985), 441–3; Joe Moran, 'Mass-Observation, Market Research, and the Birth of Focus Groups, 1937–1997', *Journal of British Studies*, 47, no. 4 (2008), 827–51; Hubble, *Mass Observation and Everyday Life*; J. Michael Hogan, 'The Road Not Taken in Opinion Research: Mass-Observation in Great Britain, 1937–1940', *Rhetoric and Public Affairs*, 18, no. 3 (2015), 409–40.
[10] For a recent example see: Alan Weeks, *Cheer Up. Mate: Second World Humour* (Stroud: The History Press, 2011).
[11] Norman Longmate, *How We Lived Then: A History of Everyday Life during the Second World War* (London: Pimlico, 2002), 40.
[12] Calder, *The People's War*, 174.
[13] D. B. Wynhham Lewis, *I Couldn't Help Laughing: An Anthology of War-Time Humour* (London: Lindsay Drummond Ltd., 1943), 108.
[14] Harold Nicolson, *The English Sense of Humour and Other Essays* (London: Constable and Company Limited, 1956), 37.

penned columns in the newspapers under the pseudonym Beachcomber and, later, as Timothy Shy, co-wrote with the cartoonist Ronald Searle, *The Terror of St Trinian's* (1952).[15] From Wyndham Lewis's perspective, British humour had 'grown up' since the First World War, which was characterized by 'its anxious refinement, and its unerring social sense'. In the years since, the importation of American humour, from Hollywood and New York had changed British humour. These were places with:

> rich racial mixtures, a crisper air and tempo, a swifter and more deafening daily racket of existence, a rather adolescent, or pimply (si j'ose m'exprimer ainsi [if I dare to express myself so]) cult of destructiveness for destructiveness sake, bigger and better hangovers, dizzier blondes, ruder policemen, and a quicker uptake, not to say uppercut. [...] It does, I think, explain why the British public now stands, with scarcely a yelp, drawings, prose, and verse with a tang of mordancy from which it would have recoiled a quarter of a century ago with cries inspired by spiritual experiences at Lord's and the Oval.[16]

Conversely, the historian and wartime military veteran, Paul Fussell, found that the Second World War largely proved, at least in official quarters, a low point for humour. The official humour – that is the material of cinema, wireless and publications – was, he argued, dull fluff in which writers churned out drab, uniform patriotic pronouncements, all of which pleased the wartime powers that be. To prove his point, Fussell contended that even the corniest of patriotism could pass as 'profound and ennobling'. The troops, however, were 'impatient of dullness high purpose and official euphemisms' and instead 'delighted in automatic obscene abuse'. Theirs was 'a different wartime tradition, [a] precise, skeptical, demotic mode'.[17] Such jokes among the troops railed against the injustices and ludicrous nature of service life, the ignorance of civilians and so on. But this is the humour of the hyper-masculine and militaristic environment of the troops and Wyndham Lewis's of the refined middle classes. What of the jokes told in the music halls and in everyday life between people?

A key consideration regarding humour and the Home Front was how they were produced and circulated. As Mass-Observation identified, there were six main means through which jokes entered public consciousness. These were the

---

[15] Timothy Shy and Robert Searle, *The Terror of St Trinian's* (London: Parish, 1952).
[16] Wynhham Lewis, *I Couldn't Help Laughing*, 7–8.
[17] Paul Fussell, *Wartime: Understanding and Behaviour in the Second World War* (Oxford: Oxford University Press, 1989), 152. For a delightfully vulgar collection of RAF ballads, see Harold Bennett (ed.), *Bawdy Ballads & Dirty Ditties of the Wartime RAF* (Bognor Regis: Woodfield Publishing Ltd., 2000). For the mindset of the British soldiers, often amusing, see Alan Allport, *Browned Off and Bloody Minded: The British Soldier Goes to War, 1939–1945* (New Haven, CT: Yale University Press, 2015).

cinema, printed literature, broadcasts by the BBC on the wireless, in the music halls and theatres, visual jokes in the form of cartoons and images, and jokes told between private individuals.[18] But where did these jokes actually come from?

The first thing to note is that many jokes were old gags, recycled for consumption. Once initially told, they would fade from memory, except for a few individuals, to later be resurrected for a new generation. Even the great comedians of the day were not above flogging derivative material. Indeed, George Formby, who dominated British comedy before and during the war, began his stage career imitating the act of his late father, who had also been a music hall comedian.[19] In the context of wartime, the old jokes from the First World War would be repackaged for the new conflict. However, there were limits to this; once a joke had entered the conscience of the new generations of audience, it could rarely be repeated by professional comedians. Indeed, Cecil Hunt, author of the joke book *Laughing Gas* (1940), noted that every 'story' in his collection was 'a "chestnut" to someone' and that they included 'many stories I have cherished for years.' Of course, he was not alone in reproducing jokes he had collected over the years and he, himself, fell victim to the same process. He observed that his previous series, the *Howler* books, had 'been milked by so many comedians and ventriloquists', that the jokes had gone stale for him because, 'I know all the answers.'[20] That was certainly true; some of the jokes which appeared in Hunt's collection were later replicated in newspapers:

> 'Sergeant, to untidy recruit: "Pull yourself together, man; remember you're wearing the King's uniform." Recruit: "Oh, it is, is it? I knew by the fit it couldn't be mine."'

This joke was repeated not only in various British newspapers but was also found in an Australian paper in 1943.[21] Another joke appeared in a Wisconsin newspaper in 1942 and reappeared decades later, in 1965, in a New York-based paper:

> '"Anyone here know shorthand?" asked the sergeant of the recruits. Two men stepped forward. "Good," he said, "go and help with the potato peeling. They're shorthanded there."'[22]

---

[18] MO, FR 229, Joke Report, 25 June 1940, 4a.
[19] Richard Anthony Baker, *Old Time Variety: An Illustrated History* (Barnsley: Remember When, 2011), 90.
[20] Cecil Hunt, *Laughing Gas: The Best Jokes* (London: Methuen & Co. Ltd., 1940), v.
[21] Hunt, *Laughing Gas*, p. 21; *The Mirror* [Perth, Western Australia], 'King's Uniform', 18 December 1943.
[22] *Manitowok Sun-Messenger*, 20 February 1942, 1; *The Kingston Daily Freeman*, 8 December 1965, p. 22; Hunt, *Laughing Gas*, 11.

Such jokes were simple wordplays and were, in essence, timeless. They were not context-specific and the joke derived from the generic situation and language of the joke. They were related to military affairs and thus were prescient in a wartime joke book. Whether Hunt had authored or potentially resurrected such jokes, they had their place in 1940 and beyond. Unsurprisingly, therefore, the professional comedians that the Mass-Observers spoke to emphasize the utility of drawing upon old jokes for a new time.[23] Will Wise, a writer for music hall comedians, told them that, 'we used a lot of old gags from the last war – I don't file them, I have a good memory – which were all new to this generation. What's wrong with some comedians is that they bring them up again too soon; you should wait for them to be old enough to be new as the saying goes.' He further added,

> The same things are happening to-day as yesterday, you have got to make them essential, and it's up to you to twist them and make them sound new. There must have been someone who made the first aviation joke and the first wireless joke; but apart from that there is love, beer, sausages, black puddings, soldiers, sailors, policemen, all the same things which only need a new overcoat. You have got to give the old gags a modern finish.[24]

It is worth reflecting again on D. B. Wyndham Lewis's view that the British sense of humour had, under the influence of American comedy, become more cynical, more satirical and would have been unrecognizable to readers of a First World War audience. That might have been true for authors like himself, writing for *Punch* with its higher brow and middle-class readership.[25] Certainly, it was echoed by Fougasse, who told the Mass-Observers that old jokes could still have merit for their 'technical pleasure' but that a comedian would never run out of new material 'until humanity is perfect'. Fougasse's point, however, was a practical one: 'Every now and again none of us remember the joke and then the original author says that it was first printed in 1905 and what are we going to do about it?'[26] This legal and commercial concern stood in contrast to Wyndham Lewis's assertion that the British sense of humour had culturally moved on. However, in the music halls, for performers like Wise, as well as writers of joke compendiums like Cecil Lewis, old material was clearly no bar, provided sufficient time had passed or it could be spruced up for the present age. Indeed, in a caveat to his earlier objection to old material, Fougasse made much the same observation as

---

[23] MO, FR 229, Joke Report, 25 June 1940, 7–8.
[24] Ibid., 8.
[25] Wyndham Lewis, *I Couldn't Help Laughing*, 7–8.
[26] MO, FR 229, Joke Report, 25 June 1940, 8.

Wise regarding placing a new spin on old gags: 'basically I suppose there is no such thing as a new joke any more than there is a new man. But that man can do a thousand different things. All those people dishing up pictures of our troops in trenches seem to forget there are no trenches in this war.'[27]

The lifecycle of the joke was much speculated by the Observers and served as the primary point of discussion of a June 1940 'Joke Report', which sought to statistically and qualitatively analyse the jokes collected by the Observers thus far. The general thesis was that the public told jokes, or at least iterations of jokes they had heard from other venues, which the public then repeated to one another. According to the Report, comparatively few of the music hall comics wrote their own jokes. Instead, they relied on professional joke writers to author much of their material. Meanwhile, the performers who made their living on the BBC similarly drew upon the services of professional comedians. Interestingly, there was little overlap between the music hall joke and the radio joke, because once a joke had appeared on the radio, it had been released to a mass audience, and thus could not be repeated to a different audience – its originality was spent. Second, because of the vast spectrum of audience, jokes necessarily were required to be inoffensive lest they antagonize a portion of the audience. Thus, jokes with regional appeal, poking fun at another part of the country, were out. So too were regionally abstruse jokes with only limited appeal to specific locales.[28] Printed jokes, appearing in magazines like *Punch*, were also the products of the professional writer – individuals like the humourist and journalist Hubert Phillips.[29] The cartoonist David Low, quoted in Mass-Observation's 1947 analysis of British humour, argued that, 'I am convinced that the music halls and such like never made up a joke, they get all their material second hand. An event happened; it is the wits in the street sitting over their cups of tea or glasses of beer that think of the funny remark about it.'[30]

The various file reports in which Mass-Observation laboured over and statistically analysed jokes showed a clear trajectory. In the opening twelve months of the war, the war joke, that is, a joke about the war, the military or some facet of explicitly wartime life, was popular but became increasingly less so rapidly towards the end of the year and into 1941, likely because there was little funny about the Blitz and a desire to escape, rather than reflect on, reality. The music hall comedians, therefore, were most likely to be attuned to the

---

[27] MO, FR 229, Joke Report, 25 June 1940, 8.
[28] MO, FR 229, Joke Report, 25 June 1940, 5.
[29] MO, FR 229, Joke Report, 25 June 1940, 6.
[30] MO, FR 229, Joke Report, 25 June 1940, 6.

public's appetite for humour. After all, they directly interacted with audiences and did not wish to 'die' on stage. If a type or theme of joke ceased to be funny, and the comedian did not adapt with the public mood, that comic could suffer the embarrassment of a silent audience and see ticket sales collapse. For such performers, the volume and length of a laugh was a direct gauge of the appetites of their audience.[31]

The Anglo-American film industries were also attuned to the same shifts in public mood. As Table 2.1 (a limited reconstruction of a table produced in August 1940 by Mass-Observation) shows, war-related references made in jokes, across a variety of different types of media, were relatively popular in 1940. War jokes were most popular in illustrations, with 61 per cent of jokes referencing the war, and magazines, where just under half did. As Table 2.1 also shows, in 1940 30 per cent of jokes told in music halls concerned the war. This would drop to 10 per cent within a year.[32]

Although no comparative statistical analysis was conducted, the author of a subsequent 1941 File Report felt that 'clearly the number here [war jokes in films] has dropped considerably'. Print media, by contrast, continued to produce war-related material at front and centre.[33] In 1940, 47 per cent of the jokes examined

Table 2.1 List of Joke References in Each Channel, 1940.[34]

	Music Hall	Panto	BBC	Film	Magazine	Newspaper	Illustration
War	30%	25%	22%	2%	47%	8%	61%
Sex	19%	11%	11%	15%	20%	18%	24%
Health	8%	8%	20%	22%	4%	2%	2%
Clothes	7%	13%	4%	6%	5%	20%	<1%
Domestic affairs	7%	8%	7%	10%	5%	10%	3%
Other	29%	35%	36%	48%	19%	42%	10%

Source: MO, FR 229, Jokes, 7 August 1940, p. 44. Note that the original table contains 11 'channels' (media) and 22 categories of joke reference. For simplicity only key types of media and major joke categories have been reproduced here.

[31] MO, FR 177, Report from Mass-Observation on WAR JOKES in Music Halls, 7 June 1940.
[32] MO, FR 943 0–3, War Jokes 1941, 1 November 1941.
[33] MO, FR 943 0–3, War Jokes 1941, 1 November 1941.
[34] MO, FR 229, Jokes, 7 August 1940, 44. Note that the original table contains eleven 'channels' (media) and twenty-two categories of joke reference. For simplicity only key types of media and major joke categories have been reproduced here.

in magazines, such as *Punch*, were war-related; by 1941 that tally had remained largely the same (48 per cent). As the File Report noted, unlike the music hall comedian who could directly gauge an audience's reaction, magazine editors had no such immediate method to see how the jokes were going down.[35] In addition, *Punch*, a satirical magazine, unsurprisingly retained its focus on current war-related events.

Film as a medium is interesting to consider. Prior to the bombing of Pearl Harbor on 7 December 1941, the Hollywood film industry had remained largely reticent on the conflict, not wishing to challenge the Roosevelt administration's position of neutrality.[36] As such, English-language films commenting on the conflict prior to 1942 were largely British productions. A Mass-Observation analysis conducted in August 1940 showed that the public was still largely watching pre-war films. The jokes listed in the report, included in comedies such as Charlie Chaplin's *Modern Times* (1936) and George Formby's *It's in the Air* (1939), were generated in response to a competition, run by the *Sunday Dispatch*, to find the funniest incidents in film. Given the competition was run in February 1940, few of the films had been produced and released during the war itself.[37] Nevertheless, it appears that filmmakers followed general trend as regards war jokes – they included fewer as the war progressed.[38] This, however, took longer because, like magazine humourists, film makers (though able to test screen audiences) were unable to measure the impact of their jokes until after production had completed – in the case of films, this was several months.

Clearly, despite the reduction in popularity of the war-themed joke in the music hall and cinema, it should not be assumed that the war joke was necessarily unpopular in every format. Nor should it be concluded that magazine writers and editors were poor judges of the public mood. There was, and remained, an audience for the war joke in printed form. As noted, *I Couldn't Help Laughing*, a collection of explicitly war-related humour, saw three editions between December 1941 and October 1943 and was reprinted again in November 1944. Clearly, there was a market for such material and publishers, like Lindsay Drummond Ltd., and writers, like Wyndham Lewis, were keen to capitalize on that element of the public appetite.

---

[35] Ibid., 1941.
[36] Mark. H. Glancy, *When Hollywood Loved Britain: The Hollywood 'British' Film, 1939–1945* (Manchester: Manchester University Press, 1999), 38.
[37] MO, FR 198, Film Joke Competition Report, 13 June 1940.
[38] MO, FR 943 0–3, War Jokes 1941, 1 November 1941.

Publishers saw an opportunity to cash in on the situation and produced almanacs, some of which explicitly and implicitly drew upon the war to sell copy. For instance, *The Black-Out Book: One-hundred-and-one black-out nights' Entertainment* by Evelyn August, included jokes, quizzes, puzzles, riddles and aphorisms, designed to be consumed by children during the blackout periods.[39] Given the audience were young children, the jokes contained tended to be fairly simple puns and rhymes: 'The weeping Whale just cries and cries. He'll be nothing but blubber till he dies.'[40] Others, however, were situational, often related to the realities of war. For instance, in an imagined conversation between a shopkeeper and female client,

> Dye it black, please.
> Black, madam?
>
> Yes, my boy's an A.R.P. Warden, and he says he can't take me out because I contravene the black-out regulations.[41]

Or to take another example, between an ARP warden and young woman,

> What is the meaning of that A.R.P. on your car?
> Why didn't you know officer?
> My boy friend put it there – it means A Real Peach.[42]

The book was designed to be both entertaining, keeping children out of the way of adults while in the shelter, but also instructive. Clearly, jokes like the ones above played on the unusual realities of wartime restrictions, yet also reminded children of those regulations.

It also should not, however, be assumed that joke books were necessarily littered with war-related themes. For instance, Cecil Hunt's *Laughing Gas*, which contained a rich variety of jokes, included only a few war jokes or even military jokes. No more than thirty individual jokes, of a packed 135-page book, referenced military matters, the political situation of 1940 or even the politics of recent years dating back to the First World War. As noted above, these were, in many cases, simple wordplays, which could be applied to many scenarios, including the war, as the reader chose. Of those that did obliquely reference

---

[39] Evelyn August, *The Black-Out Book: One-hundred-and-one Black-out Nights' Entertainment* (Oxford: Osprey, 1940, 2009).
[40] August, *The Black-Out Book*, 43.
[41] Ibid., 17.
[42] Ibid., 39.

current events, these were only situational to the war through the addition of contemporary details. For instance:

> A U.S. journalist suspected that much of his mail had been tampered with by Japanese military authorities. So in the next letter to a friend, he said: 'I don't know when or if this letter will arrive, because the Japanese censor will probably open it.'
>
> Some days afterwards he received a polite note from the Japanese Censor's department. It said: 'The statement in your letter of the 12th was not correct. We do not open letters.'[43]

This could have been applied to any censorship office. That Hunt referenced Japan and the United States, during a period of growing international tension between the two, is incidental to the mechanics of the joke.

The initial popularity of war-related jokes plainly was a result of the emergent situation, with the novelties and changes to life that it brought. As one Mass-Observer noted in 1940, 'I liked a joke on the wireless. "I'd give you my four most precious possessions in the world – a fountain pen and three torch batteries." We see the point, it seems impossible to buy batteries.'[44] However, the public rapidly grew bored of tiresome restrictions such as the blackout and rationing, stress and, of course, danger. These issues, mundane and unpleasant, saw comedians rapidly discover that their audiences soon preferred jokes that recalled less fraught times. They had little desire to be reminded that there was a war on, which of course they knew full well. Moreover, in 1940 and 1941, Britain appeared to be losing. It is understandable, therefore, that when they spent their hard-earned money at the music hall, they wanted to escape the conflict. This was also reflected in private jokes. For instance, the most popular joke of 1943 had nothing to do with the war, but was a shaggy dog story which gained its humour from its absurdity:

> A man went into a restaurant and ordered cabbage. When it came up, he picked up the dish and plastered the contents over his head. When he was asked 'What do you think you are doing with that cabbage?' he replied, 'Is that cabbage? I thought it was spinach.'[45]

When jokes were about the war, how did they reflect on the conflict? Unsurprisingly, some were patriotic, lauding the heroism particularly of the

---

[43] Hunt, *Laughing Gas*, 50.
[44] MO, TC 77, Jokes 1939–1947, 13 March 1940, 74.
[45] MO, FR 3026, The British Sense of Humour, August 1948, 6.

British forces and their allies. After the Battle of Britain, the airmen of the RAF, including Polish pilots, became national heroes. As Mark Connelly has observed, 'The British like to see themselves as the few and so Fighter Command became the fewest of the few.'[46] A rare victory in a period of military calamity, the Battle of Britain became a source of national pride and this was very much reflected in the jokes of the period. One such joke, repeated throughout the conflict and well into the post-war era, went:

> The Queen was talking to one of the Polish airmen who had just been decorated, and she asked him about his experiences. 'I was flying over France,' he said haltingly, 'and I met four great big Fokkers, and I shot them all down. And when I come back, over the Channel there was one great big Fokker, and I shot that down too.' 'That was splendid,' said the Queen. 'What were the machines? Were they Messerschmidts?'[47]

Others also mocked the competence of the German bombers during the Blitz. One joke, recorded in April 1941, during the dying days of the London Blitz picked just such a theme: 'A German pilot took his plane back to Germany still fully loaded with bombs. When his officer asked him why, he said: "I spent five hours searching for my target, and when I found it I was just about to drop my bombs when the "all-clear" sounded."'[48]

Jokes then were dependent on the situation. The Battle of Britain offered a period of relief and victory. But more generally in 1940, such respite was rare. Following the fall of France, jokes in the music halls about the state of the war largely evaporated, 'not merely references to Hitler and Germany disappeared, but also rationing, black-out, warden and so on'. The basis for this, according to one Mass-Observation analyst, was that 'since the beginning of total warfare people no longer think the Germans a subject to laugh at'.[49]

It was only following rare military successes that war jokes were to re-emerge in any significant number. Often these were fairly innocuous with absurdist elements. For example, 'It is reputed that the Germans have a decoy aerodrome, all the aeroplanes being made of wood. But we aren't taken in.

---

[46] Connelly, *We Can Take it!*, 96.
[47] MO, TC 77, Jokes, 1939–1947, 18 February 1944, p. 75. The joke was repeated by the comedian Stan Boardman on *Des O'Connor Tonight* in the mid-1980s. See, 'Stan Boardman and Des O'Connor the Fokker Joke', https://www.youtube.com/watch?v=-8Yf5B6GbYk [Accessed 5 December 2021]. See also, Colin Bycroft, *End 2 End 4 Parkinson's: Cycling from Land's End to John O' Groats – a Second Midlife Crisis* (Great Britain: Vita Fugit), 119.
[48] MO, TC 77, Jokes 1939–1947, 3 May 1941, 83.
[49] MO, FR 177, War Jokes in Music Halls, 7 June 1940.

We've been over there and dropped a wooden bomb!'[50] Others, however, revelled in military successes. This was specifically in relation to the military conflict against Mussolini's Italy. On 28 October 1940, Italy invaded Greece, which proved to be disastrous. Within days, on 14 November, Greek forces had launched a counter-offensive and by 23 November had restored the pre-war border and soon advanced into Albania. In the meantime, on 11 November, the Royal Navy attacked the Italian fleet at Taranto, securing British supply lines in the Mediterranean. The result was a flurry of jokes in music halls made at the expense of Mussolini and Italian forces, which went down very well. For instance, 'Every navy has its own drink. The Americans like rye whiskey, the British has its rum, but the Italians stick to port.' On a similar note, 'Mussolini is having a bad Christmas. He can't even cook a turkey because he can't get hold of Greece.' Some also deployed xenophobic terminology: 'If you want to get rid of hornet's nests, apply to the R.A.F. who are very good at burning out Wops (Wasps) nests.' These jokes, as the Mass-Observer who collected them noted, were relatively unusual, in that they were specific and topical, referencing recent wartime news. These differed, for example, from jokes about Hitler, which tended to be generically abusive and could be 'applied to anybody'.[51] A good example of this being the rhyme 'Hitler has only got one ball', which first circulated in 1939.[52]

Yet even laughing at enemy leaders, a rich vein of humour prior to the Battle of France, had begun to run thin by June 1940.[53] Clearly, few were in the mood to laugh at the existential threat posed to the nation. They were, however, quite willing to laugh at the state of the war effort, which plainly required improvement. Indeed, some poked fun at unwarranted patriotism taken to ludicrous extremes:

> '…. had an awful time getting it. You see,' I went in and asked for Apfl Kuchen. The man sort of looked at me, evidently thought I was a Fifth Columnist, talking German, and said 'I beg yourr [sic] pardon?' So I said '[o]ne of those things - those German apple tarts'. And he said 'Excuse me Sir, they are not German now, they are Continental.' (General laugh)[54]

---

[50] MO, TC 77, Jokes 1939-1947, 3 May 1941, 83.
[51] MO, TC 77, Jokes 1939-1947, Note on War Jokes, 27 December 1940, 136.
[52] This rhyme, sung to the tune of Colonel Bogey March, was dutifully recorded by Mass-Observation: MO, TC 77, Jokes 1939-1947, 18 October 1942, 60.
[53] MO, FR 177, War Jokes in Music Halls, 7 June 1940.
[54] MO, Topic Collection, Jokes 1939-1947, Jokes, 30 June 1940, 96.

Others, by contrast, played on the idea that some men were attempting to dodge conscription through various nefarious means:

> Man in the Army went about everywhere picking up pieces of paper, throwing them away and saying 'they're not 'em.'
>
> He was medically examined and discharged as unfit. When he was given his discharge papers, he pounced on them and said:
> 'Ah, that's 'em.'[55]

Another, from the height of the Blitz in October 1940, several months after the British Army had retreated from Dunkirk to relative security across the Channel, joked of 'The girl who gave her boy-friend a white feather because he was leaving London to join the army.'[56] By joining the army the boyfriend had fled the bombs raining down in London to the safety of military training and deployment. This type of joke was contingent on the military situation. Later defeatist jokes, such as one from 1942 when the British army was fighting all over the world, suggested that the patriotic desire to join the Armed Forces was insanity, thus providing medical grounds for being excused conscription:

> The young man was having his medical exam for the army. The doctor reported him to be perfectly fit. The young man smiled with apparent pleasure. 'Good. Good, Doctor', he said, rubbing his hands. 'Now I want you to send me straight away to the front line. I want to be in all the biggest battles and worst retreats. I want to risk my life in the air, on the land and on the sea. I want to be in the midst of it all.'
>
> 'Well, I must say, you're a very patriotic young man' said the doctor somewhat taken aback by this enthusiasm.
>
> 'Are you sure, doctor', asked the young man softly, 'are you QUITE sure, I'm not just a little MAD?'[57]

Other forms of defeatist jokes played upon and punctured ideas of general British military and technical efficiency. For instance, a popular joke in 1940 was:

> Two men see a group of soldiers on motor cycles are going past.

---

[55] MO, TC 77, Jokes 1939–1947, 3 May 1941, 83.
[56] MO, TC 77, Jokes, 1939–1947, 18 October 1940, p. 145. A 'white feather', ironically used here, is a reference to the practice of shaming men not in military service during the First World War.
[57] MO, TC 77, Jokes, 1939–1947, War Jokes, PJ 31 March 1942, 69.

They must be Nazis ... ... All on motor bicycles that actually work
(At that moment one of the motor bicycles refuses to start again after stopping for the red light. Both men laugh loudly).

'It's all right – they <u>are</u> British all right.'[58]

Corinna Peniston-Bird and Penny Summerfield have made a similar observation of humorous cartoons in 1940. The Home Guard came in for a ribbing based on 'the improvisation and play-acting that such involvement required, and by the uncertain relation of this part-time army to the regular armed forces'.[59] The Home Guard were not the only ones to have caustic pot-shots delivered in their direction. Other wartime services had recruited men deemed inferior in some fashion or other and who proved ripe for mockery. For instance, in 1940, a policeman received similar mockery, dutifully recorded by the Mass-Observers:

> On the night of the first raid warning a policeman in Westhoughton rushed out and it wasn't till he had gone 1 1/2 miles and spoke to someone he realized he'd not got his false teeth. He stopped an AFS lorry and made them turn back to get it.[60]

Even after the military situation appeared to have improved in 1941, when Britain gained additional allies in the form of the Soviet Union and the United States, a new set of jokes appeared now criticizing the British for an alleged lacklustre attitude towards the conflict. Indeed, the period prior to the failed operation by British forces in Norway in April 1940 was acerbically known as the 'Bore War'. Even after the invasion of France, the apparent inactivity of British forces, despite heavy fighting by British troops, sailors and airmen on numerous fronts and theatres, led to politicians being ridiculed for a lack of mettle. As one joke from November 1942 went:

> The Pope thought the war should stop. He approached Hitler, 'What!' said Hitler, 'After England declaring war on me first? Oh no, <u>I'm</u> not going to stop it.'
>
> The Pope went to Stalin, 'Stop the war?' said Stalin, 'With the Germans occupying half my country? Oh no!'
>
> The Pope asked Roosevelt. He said, 'We fight for the right – for honour, for freedom. We can't stop.'

---

[58] MO, Topic Collection, Jokes 1939–1947, Jokes, 3 July 1940, 98.
[59] Corinna Peniston-Bird and Penny Summerfield, '"Hey, you're dead!": The Multiple Uses of Humour in Representations of British National Defence in the Second World War', *Journal of European Studies*, 31 no. 123, (2001), 433.
[60] MO, Topic Collection, Jokes 1939–1947, bolton Airraid Jokes, 29 June 1940, 95.

At last the Pope came to Churchill. 'I say,' he begged, 'Do stop this fighting.' 'Fighting? Fighting?' said Churchill, 'Who's fighting?'[61]

Another joke, from a few months earlier in June, similarly implied Britain was contributing little to the defeat of the Axis powers:

> A group I knew were discussing the ways of obtaining victory in this war. They decided that 3 things were necessary, Industrial power, Man power & Time – Americans supply the Industrial power.
> Russia the Man power. Gt. Britain the Time.[62]

Clearly, war jokes could be cynical, unkind or display a surprising degree of defeatism. Meanwhile, many of the usual, old, unkind stereotypes and prejudices were apparent in jokes. For instance, one joke regarding alleged Scottish frugality read, 'Did you hear the one about the Scotsman who had seven children? He went out into the garden & fired a revolver, then he went in & told the kids Father Christmas shot himself.'[63] Others revealed morbid gallows humour. As one woman complained of black humour, 'I find desperately unfunny a recent B.B.C. joke about a pilot who bailed out into the Channel and an old bus conductor in a rescue launch which was full up calling out: "Full up, No standing" and leaving him to drown.'[64] Others wearied by the war found their humour evaporate. As one Observer wrote in 1943, 'when people are overcome by apathy they don't make jokes.'[65]

Yet the important point remains that such jokes, though common enough, were hardly the main source of humour during the war and should not be taken as representative of the mood in Britain or of humour on the Home Front. Although by February 1943 the war joke remained the most popular, it was only marginally more so than sex jokes.[66] Although the war was the most popular single category of joke, they still made up no more than a third of the material collected for that particular February 1943 bulletin. Like the jokes of professional comedians in the music halls and, increasingly as the war went on, the cinema and BBC, jokes told in person tended to reflect themes of everyday life. Perhaps unsurprisingly, sex jokes remained popular throughout the period, particularly in the music halls and in private. As the 1947 Report noted, 'throughout all

---

[61] MO, TC 77, Jokes 1939–1947, 23 November 1942, 74.
[62] MO, TC 77, Jokes 1939–1947, 4 May 1942, 78.
[63] MO, TC 77, Jokes, 1939–1947, War Jokes, DH 29 December 1944, 72.
[64] MO, FR 3026, The British Sense of Humour, August 1948, 16.
[65] MO, TC 77, Jokes, 1939–1947, 15 December 1943, 159.
[66] MO, TC 77, Jokes 1939–1947, Draft Bulletin for Feb 1943, Jokes, 16 February 1943, 224.

media the most popular subjects of humour are invariably ill-health, sex and domestic affairs.'[67] It is difficult to know which of these jokes actually were, as many were often described as unprintable by those who submitted jokes to Mass-Observation.[68]

George Formby, the comedian, singer and actor, fell foul of the BBC's Director General, John Reith, for his popular song, 'The Window Cleaner', which had featured in the film *Keep Your Seats, Please* (1936) and which went on to be one of Formby's signature tunes. It placed the voyeuristic protagonist as a window cleaner, observing the various bedroom activities of those behind the windowpanes being cleaned:

> Honeymoonin' couples too
> You should see them bill 'n coo
> You'd be surprised at things they do
> ...
> The blushin' bride, she looks divine
> The bridegroom he is doin' fine
> I'd rather have his job than mine
> ...
> Ladies' nighties I have spied
> I've often seen what goes inside.[69]

This level of brazen sexual innuendo proved too much for Reith, who promptly banned the song from being played on the BBC, stating that 'if the public wants to listen to Formby singing his disgusting little ditty, they'll have to be content to hear it in the cinemas, not over the nation's airwaves'.[70]

During the Second World War, Formby answered his country's call and weaponized his talents with the ukulele and innuendo in the service of the war effort. His films and recordings retained the 'everyman', regional and low-brow – or at least anti-high-brow – themes. Charlie Chaplin's excoriating anti-Nazi political picture, *The Great Dictator* (1940), in which he played an 'everyman' Jewish barber living under a fascist, anti-Semitic dictatorship, showed his character stand up to authoritarian power. Like Chaplin, Formby was to pit his own variant of the ordinary British man on the street comedic persona against

---

[67] MO, FR 3026, The British Sense of Humour, August 1948, 8.
[68] MO, FR 1400, February Directive: Jokes, 13 August 1942, 5.
[69] George Formby, Harry Gifford and Fred E. Cliffe, *The Window Cleaner*, Regal Zonophone (1936).
[70] Steven Gerrard, 'The Great British Music Hall: Its Importance to British Culture and "The Trivial", *Culture Unbound*, 5 (2013), 506.

the brutality and militarism of the Third Reich, Fascist Italy and Imperial Japan. For his part, Formby threw himself into the entertainment of the troops and was a leading figure within the Entertainments National Service Association (ENSA) – an organization which arranged entertainment for service personnel.[71] His working-class image, Lancashire accent and cheeky stage persona ensured that he was a hit with the troops. His popularity was such that he was forced to decline performances at home as he filled his calendar with engagements for the troops abroad.[72] During the war he often played soldiers and sailors, but his jokes retained their sexual innuendo and double entendre. For example, 'Mr Wu's An Air Raid Warden Now', blended racial comedy ('So if you've a chink in your window/You'll have another one at your door') with voyeurism ('He'll flash his torch into the dark/And the girls all cover their laundry mark').[73]

His brand of sex-themed humour was standard fair for the period. An albeit methodologically flawed joke report, which significantly over-represented male respondents, compiled in August 1942, is instructive on this point. The analysis showed that sex jokes, which numbered fifty-eight, comprised 16 per cent of the total submitted.[74] The only category higher were war-related jokes, of which there were fifty-nine. Table 2.2 partially recreates a table drawn by the Mass-Observer, which was categorized by the type of joke submitted and the age and gender of the respondents. Like Table 2.1 with data from 1940, Table 2.2's 1942 numbers showed sex jokes remained popular, particularly with younger men.

War jokes actually comprised a whole host of material, much of which included other categories – including sex, of which six were included as 'war jokes'. Meanwhile, the 'sex joke' was also underrepresented in the sample because respondents (of which there were 106), despite 32 per cent stating that they 'liked "dirty" jokes', found that:

> the funniest were quite unrepeatable. All told, there were only some 9 jokes told that would probably not have passed the Lord Chamberlain; the worst of these was the story of the bride who went up to her room, undressed, took chloroform and left the Vaseline on the mantelpiece.[75]

Although precise figures were not provided, of twenty themes recorded by frequency on a scale of 1 to 20, sex jokes were the most frequent. A year later,

---

[71] Andy Merriman, *Greasepaint & Cordite: How ENSA Entertained the Troops during World War II* (London: Aurum, 2013), 35.
[72] *The Times*, 'Mr. George Formby's Company', 12 February 1940, 4.
[73] Eddie Latta and George Formby, 'Mr Wu's An Air Raid Warden Now', Regal Zonophone (1942).
[74] MO, FR 1400, February Directive: Jokes, 13 August 1942.
[75] MO, FR 1400, February Directive: Jokes, 13 August 1942.

Table 2.2 Joke Categories by Age and Gender, 1942.

	Men under forty	Men over forty	Women under forty	Women over forty
War	43	6	8	2
Sex	30	8	16	4
Health	33	5	9	5
Religion	14	10	7	3
Domestic Affairs	21	4	6	1
Food	13	4	3	0
Law	10	2	3	0
Jobs	12	2	0	0
Lavatory	7	4	1	0
Money	9	3	0	0
Alcohol	9	2	0	0
Other	33	2	14	0
Total	243	52	67	15

Source: MO, FR 1400, February Directive: Jokes, 13 August 1942. Note that the table has been condensed for simplicity.

in another report, a Mass-Observer noted that 'Among private jokes there were slightly more about sex, but not nearly so large a predominance as in wartime music-hall.'[76]

Unsurprisingly, some of these jokes were merely smutty, while others were deliberately outrageous and played upon the victimization or objectification of women. To take a dark example from one respondent, which made light of sexual assault: 'rape impossible, lady with drawers up run faster than man with trousers down.'[77] Some jokes also criticized the alleged loosening of morality of the public, particularly women – a well-observed phenomenon of general moral panic related to young women's sexuality during the war.[78] These could easily be made topical when refashioned into a war joke. Women of the three military services, the Women's Auxiliary Air Force (WAAF), the Auxiliary Territorial Service (ATS) and the Women's Royal Naval Service (WRNS) were all subjects

---

[76] MO, Topic Collection, Jokes 1939-1947, Draft Bulletin for Feb 1943, Jokes, 16 February 1943, 224.
[77] MO, TC 77, Jokes 1939-1945, 17 May 1940, 198. Confucius (551-479 BCE) was a Chinese philosopher.
[78] Gerard J. DeGroot, 'Lipstick on Her Nipples, Cordite in Her Hair: Sex and Romance among British Servicewomen during the Second World War', in Gerard J. DeGroot and Corinna Peniston-Bird (eds.), A Soldier and a Woman: Sexual Integration and the Military (London: Routledge, 2000), 100-18.

of crude sexually themed jokes, alleging promiscuity. Women of the WAAF were referred to as 'pilot's cockpits' and ATS women as 'officers' ground sheets'.[79] One joke from 1941 went, 'What's better than a cap full of WAAFs? A hand on a Wrens' Nest'.[80]

Later, when American troops arrived in Britain in large numbers, they and Britain's young women more generally, became the subjects of such jokes. One, for instance, from December 1944: 'Have you seen the new sort of knickers that girls are wearing lately? No. Yes, one "Yank" and they're down.'[81] Another from the same individual, 'Do you know what the fashionnable [sic] girl does nowadays? No. She menstruates with a drawl and excretes chewing gum.'[82] As a last example, a lost child when asked about his missing mother, 'We'll find her soon. What's she like? Double gins and American soldiers'.[83] This was in response to a moral panic which suggested that British women were likely to fall prey to the charms of American servicemen, while Britain's own young men were posted elsewhere. Such fears even translated into works of history. Norman Longmate reminisced that 'Although the Americans' reputation for pursuing any female who looked remotely available was richly deserved, there was often at least an equal determination to "get off" on the part of British women.'[84] As the unfair wartime adage went, the American troops were 'oversexed, overpaid, overfed, and over here'.[85]

What, then, can we draw from this examination of wartime jokes? Although the exploration of wartime humour remains in its infancy, the findings presented in this chapter offer some pointers regarding the nature of British wartime jokes and wider British society during the Second World War. First, the Mass-Observers, keen to statistically analyse jokes, demonstrate to us that while professional comedians always retained war-related material in their repertoires, this rapidly reduced in volume after 1940, as did the war joke in

---

[79] Dan Ellin, 'The Many Behind the Few: The Lives and Emotions of Erks and WAAFs of RAF Bomber Command 1939–1945' (University of Warwick, Unpublished PhD thesis, 2015), 87, note 256; BBC, BBC People's War, John Cocker, A7769532, 'With the ATS on a Search-Light Squad (Chapter One)', 14 December 2005, https://www.bbc.co.uk/history/ww2peopleswar/stories/32/a7769532.shtml.
[80] MO, TC 77, Jokes 1939–1947, 23 December 1941.
[81] A version of this joke 'a new brand of knickers, "One Yank and they're off"', was repeated in the *Daily Express* in 1979. David Reynolds, *Rich Relations: The American Occupation of Britain, 1942–1945* (London: Random House, 1995), xxiii.
[82] MO, TC 77, Jokes 1939–1947, 6 December 1944 172–3.
[83] MO, TC 77, Jokes 1939–1947, 28 January 1944, 163.
[84] Norman Longmate, *The G.I.'s: The Americans in Britain 1942–1945* (London: Hutchinson & Co, 1975), 247.
[85] Reynolds, *Rich Relations*, xxiii.

the cinema. Clearly, the view was that when audiences went to be entertained, they wanted escapism not continual reminders of the war itself. While they were happy to enjoy some topical war-related material, they plainly did not wish to be inundated with it. A similar trend can be observed in Hollywood's output. Meanwhile, in published material, the war joke enjoyed a considerably greater longevity, the subject of satirists and humourists typically writing for a middle-class audience. Clearly, from the early midpoint of 1940 on, which unsurprisingly coincided with the series of calamitous defeats for British forces, the war ceased to be funny – or at least comedians found significantly less reception to it than they had.

Unsurprisingly, war jokes were often repackaged or at least thematically similar to pre-existing jokes which dealt with funny themes. This much is clear from examination of those jokes collected by the Mass-Observers. As they noted, common subjects of jokes – sex, bodily functions, slapstick and so on being the most popular – remained popular and could easily be reconfigured to comment on topical war-related subjects: thus, the bobby losing his dentures, the incompetence of the Italian military or the alleged promiscuity of young British women when faced with the sexual magnetism of the American serviceman. These jokes also railed against the official propaganda which would forge the mythology of The People's War. Rather than stoic and good-natured humour in the face of adversity, jokes often belittled, othered and revelled in defeatism. As the 1948 Mass-Observation Report on the 'British Sense of Humour' observed, 'It cannot be said from a study of these jokes that the traditional British sense of tolerance is carried over into the field of jokes.'[86]

This all suggests a gendered approach to the question of wartime humour, as well as class, race and sexuality, are future avenues of important research. This exploration of wartime humour represents only a first look at what Mass-Observation has to offer and only a casual glance at the wider array of joke books, BBC programmes, films, periodicals and cinema which utilized jokes. Humour is a vital resource through which to understand a culture and society. It is no surprise that historians of Nazi Germany have already done so, while scholars of Britain's Second World War history remain largely left behind. It is clear that historians of Britain's propaganda effort, as well as social historians of the war more generally, would greatly benefit from examining Mass-Observation's joke files.

---

[86] MO, FR 3026, The British Sense of Humour, August 1948, 16.

Bibliography

Paul Addison and Crang, Jeremy. A, (eds.), *Listening to Britain: Home Intelligence Reports on Britain's Finest Hour – May to September 1940* (London: Jonathan Cape, 2011).

Alan Allport, *Browned Off and Bloody Minded: The British Soldier Goes to War, 1939–1945* (New Haven, CT: Yale University Press, 2015).

Evelyn August, *The Black-Out Book: One-hundred-and-one black-out nights' Entertainment* (Oxford: Osprey, 1940, 2009).

Richard Anthony Baker, *Old Time Variety: An Illustrated History* (Barnsley: Remember When, 2011).

Harold Bennett, (ed.), *Bawdy Ballads & Dirty Ditties of the Wartime RAF* (Bognor Regis: Woodfield Publishing Ltd., 2000).

Colin Bycroft, *End 2 End 4 Parkinson's: Cycling from Land's End to John O' Groats – a Second Midlife Crisis* (Great Britain: Vita Fugit, 2008).

Angus Calder, *The People's War* (London: Pimlico, 1969).

Angus Calder, *The Myth of the Blitz* (London: Pimlico, 1991).

Mark Connelly, *We Can Take It!: Britain and the Memory of the Second World War* (Harlow: Pearson Education, 2007).

Gerard J. DeGroot, 'Lipstick on Her Nipples, Cordite in Her Hair: Sex and Romance among British Servicewomen during the Second World War', in Gerard J. DeGroot and Corinna Peniston-Bird (eds.), *A Soldier and a Woman: Sexual Integration and the Military* (London: Routledge, 2000), 100–18.

David Edgerton, *Britain's War Machine: Weapons, Resources and Experts in the Second World War* (London: Penguin, 2012).

Dan Ellin, 'The Many Behind the Few: The Lives and Emotions of Erks and WAAFs of RAF Bomber Command 1939–1945' (University of Warwick, Unpublished PhD thesis, 2015).

Fougasse, *… And the Gatepost* (London: Chattos & Windus, 1940).

Paul Fussell, *Wartime: Understanding and Behaviour in the Second World War* (Oxford: Oxford University Press).

Steven Gerrard, 'The Great British Music Hall: Its Importance to British Culture and "The Trivial"', *Culture Unbound*, 5 (2013), 487–514.

Mark. H. Glancy, *When Hollywood Loved Britain: The Hollywood 'British' Film, 1939–1945* (Manchester: Manchester University Press, 1999).

Tom Harrisson, *Living through the Blitz* (London: Penguin, 1990).

Micheal J. Hogan, 'The Road Not Taken in Opinion Research: Mass-Observation in Great Britain, 1937–1940', *Rhetoric and Public Affairs*, 18, no. 3 (2015), 409–40.

Nick Hubble, *Mass Observation and Everyday Life: Culture, History, Theory*, 2nd ed. (Basingstoke: Palgrave Macmillan, 2010).

Cecil Hunt, *Laughing Gas: The Best Jokes* (London: Methuen & Co. Ltd., 1940).

Stuart Hylton, *Careless Talk: The Hidden History of the Home Front, 1939–1945* (Stroud: The History Press, 2001, 2010).

Norman Longmate, *The G.I.'s: The Americans in Britain 1942–1945* (London: Hutchinson & Co, 1975).

Norman Longmate, *How We Lived Then: A History of Everyday Life during the Second World War* (London: Pimlico, 2002).

Andy Merriman, *Greasepaint & Cordite: How ENSA Entertained the Troops during World War II* (London: Aurum, 2013).

Joe Moran, 'Mass-Observation, Market Research, and the Birth of Focus Groups, 1937–1997', *Journal of British Studies*, 47, no. 4 (2008), 827–51.

Harold Nicolson, *The English Sense of Humour and Other Essays* (London: Constable and Company Limited, 1956).

Corinna Peniston-Bird and Summerfield, Penny, '"Hey, you're dead!": The Multiple Uses of Humour in Representations of British National Defence in the Second World War', *Journal of European Studies*, 31, no. 123 (2001), 413–35.

Clive Ponting, *1940: Myth and Reality* (London: Hamish Hamilton, 1990).

David Reynolds, *Rich Relations: The American Occupation of Britain, 1942–1945* (London: Random House, 1995).

Lola Serraf, 'Writing the "People's War": Evaluating the Myth of the Blitz in British Women's Fiction of the Second World War' (Universitat Autònoma de Barcelona: Unpublished PhD thesis, 2018).

Timothy Shy, and Ronald Searle, *The Terror of St Trinian's* (London: Parish, 1952).

Penny Summerfield, 'Mass-Observation: Social Research or Social Movement?', *Journal of Contemporary History*, 20, no. 3 (1985), 439–52.

Alan Weeks, *Cheer Up. Mate: Second World Humour* (Stroud: The History Press, 2011).

D. B. Wyndham Lewis, *I Couldn't Help Laughing: An Anthology of War-Time Humour* (London: Lindsay Drummond Ltd., 1943).

3

'Good-natured as any folk in the world': The Ministry of Information Film and British Humour during the Second World War

Linsey Robb

In July 1940 the GPO (General Post Office) Film Unit of the Ministry of Information released the film *Britain at Bay*.[1] It documents that specific tense and fractious moment in the war as Britain stood alone in Europe having watched much of the continent fall to the Nazi war machine, with real fear that the invasion of British shores was not only likely but imminent. The film looks to the past, for example Britain's defiance of Napoleon, and the present, for instance the swift formation of the Local Defence Volunteers, to highlight Britain's fortitude in the face of the enemy. The film was written and narrated by noted author and broadcaster J. B. Priestley whose infamous weekly *Postscripts* talks had commenced the previous month. As part of his narration he declared: 'These people of ours are as easy-going and good-natured as any folk in the world, who've asked for nothing belonging to others but only fair dealing among nations'. Leaving aside the glaring tension between such a statement and Britain's role as an imperial power, Priestley makes clear a central tenet of British self-identity in this period: good humour. Historian Sonya Rose describes a 'lauded British sense of humour and camaraderie as a national and masculine characteristic, one which was popularized in the wartime song lyrics that advised those having a difficult time to "keep smiling through".[2] Yet, despite the ubiquity of this sentiment the way humour manifested itself in wartime culture has never

---

I would like to thank the members of Northumbria University's Conflict and Society Research Group for their invaluable suggestions on this chapter. Any errors which remain are, of course, my own.

[1] *Britain at Bay* Dir. Harry Watt (1940).
[2] Sonya O. Rose, *Which People's War?: National Identity and Citizenship in Wartime Britain 1939–1945* (Oxford: Oxford University Press, 2004), 154.

been directly addressed by historians, a lacuna this chapter will begin to fill by examining wartime propaganda films.

Cinema-going was phenomenally popular in Britain during the Second World War. Despite all cinemas being briefly closed early in the war, film-viewing continued to be an enormously popular leisure pursuit throughout the conflict. Cinema attendance grew from 19 million a week in 1940 to 30 million a week by the end of the war.[3] A Wartime Social Survey showed that 32 per cent of adults went to the cinema at least once a week and the average adult saw around two feature films a month.[4] As AJP Taylor famously asserted, cinema was the 'essential social habit of the age'.[5] As well as being a widespread leisure activity, film also had fantastic possibilities for propaganda, as historian Michael Spicer notes:

> Film interpreted great events, made sense of the world and the past. And because film operates on the emotions it was also an effective medium of mass persuasion. In the darkened auditorium, the audience become part of the unfolding narrative on the screen, identifying with those portrayed on film, sharing their struggles, their fears, and aspirations; and when the audience left the theatre, some small residue of that experience remains, helping to shape their response to similar situations and moulding attitudes to the issues and problems shown on the screen.[6]

Because of this, film was a central pillar in the British Ministry of Information's (MOI) propaganda strategy. Yet, for many, a trip to the cinema was a chance to escape from the war and 'war pictures' were not necessarily a box office draw. Indeed, one of the most popular films of the war was *Gone With the Wind* (1939) which played in London's West End for four years straight during the war.[7] While a 'war film' in some respects, it is likely that British wartime audiences were attracted more by the melodrama, romance and sumptuous costumes than an investment in the outcome of the American Civil War. Therefore, while film may be ideal for propaganda purposes, the British public were far from an unthinkingly receptive audience. Propaganda needed to engage and entertain.

---

[3] Antonia Lant, *Blackout: Reinventing Women for Wartime British Cinema* (Princeton: Princeton University Press, 1991), 24.
[4] J.P. Mayer, *British Cinemas and Their Audiences: Sociological Studies* (London: Dennis Dobson, 1978), 253–69.
[5] A.J.P. Taylor, *English History 1914–1945* (Harmondsworth: Penguin, 1970), 392.
[6] Michael Paris, 'Introduction: Film, Television, and the Second World War – The First Fifty Years', in Michael Paris (ed.), *Repicturing the Second World War: Representations in Film and Television* (Basingstoke: Palgrave Macmillan, 2007), 2.
[7] Mark Glancy, 'Going to the Pictures: British Cinema and the Second World War', *Past and Future*, 8 (2010), 8–9.

James Chapman notes there were three key themes present in official MOI propaganda. Firstly, what Britain is fighting for, secondly, how Britain fights and finally, the need for sacrifices if the fight is to be won.[8] As already noted, film was a key method in putting across these messages to wartime audiences. However, in the many texts which have been written about wartime cinema little has been said, in a concerted way at least, about the use of humour. However, wartime humour was a serious undertaking; the British state used it for far more than simple entertainment. This chapter, therefore, examines the extant filmic material produced by the Ministry of Information (and its associated production companies) during the Second World War. Over 250 films held by the Imperial War Museum and the British Film Institute as well as those released commercially on DVD were analysed for the comedic content and effects.[9] Throughout the war, the MOI produced both longform films and filmic shorts to inform the British public, generally adult Home Front audiences, and to ensure their behaviour was conducive to eventual victory. As this chapter will show, many of these films were imbued with, as a minimum, comedic elements. In examining this phenomenon, this chapter will show that humour was a key aspect of the British government's propaganda strategy and comedy was used to allay fears, brighten up dull wartime instructions as well as forming a cornerstone of the way Britain, and its allies, were portrayed.

Making films in wartime

Propaganda and communications were an important and vast undertaking during the Second World War. Planning for what would become the Ministry of Information (MOI) during the Second World War started in the mid-1930s but was only announced to the British public in June 1939. However, as is well documented elsewhere, its early months were turbulent with several high-profile personnel changes in just a very short period.[10] Similarly, early wartime propaganda poster campaigns (most famously 'Your Courage, Your

---

[8] James Chapman, 'Cinema, Propaganda and National Identity: British Film and the Second World War', in Justine Ashby and Andrew Higson (eds.), *British Cinema, Past and Present* (London: Taylor and Francis, 2000), 198.

[9] Please note this chapter was produced under the strictures of Covid-19 lockdowns. These archives may hold physical copies of films which have not been digitized but were inaccessible during the research and writing of this volume. The films discussed here are a large cross section of the material produced but are, therefore, not exhaustive.

[10] David Welch, *Propaganda, Power and Persuasion: From World War I to Wikileaks* (London: IB Tauris, 2013), 80–1.

Cheerfulness, Your Resolution, Will Bring Us Victory') met with public disdain. The MOI was therefore tagged with derogatory nicknames such as the 'Ministry of Dis-information' and the 'Ministry of Muddle'.[11] However, as Robert Mackay notes, the initially didactic attempts 'were gradually replaced by a more sophisticated understanding of the nature of the relationship between what people were told and how they felt and behaved'.[12] The MOI was, however, an amorphous and fluid government department, and this was especially true when it came to films. For example, it helped to create propaganda for other government ministries but also outsourced its own production. Indeed, the line between commercial cinema and government productions, for example, was not always clearly delineated. The MOI worked with companies like Ealing and Gainsborough as they produced wartime feature films. Similarly, many of the MOI's filmic shorts were not shot 'in-house' but rather outsourced to production companies. Indeed, Verity Films was set up by film producer Sydney Box for that very specific purpose.[13]

The MOI itself made, or commissioned, two key types of film. The first of these was the longform documentary. It has long been said there was a 'wartime wedding' between the previously distinct documentary and commercial filmmaking traditions. As James Chapman notes: 'The war also marked a high watermark for the British documentary movement, whose skills and experience were now much in demand for the provision of "propaganda for democracy".'[14] In 1940 the MOI absorbed the GPO Film Unit which had had a prominent role in the interwar documentary film movement. Renamed the Crown Film Unit they produced some classics of the genre which were remembered and watched long after the war had ended, such as *Target for Tonight* (1941), *Fires Were Started* (1943) and *The Silent Village* (1943).[15] These films enjoyed cinematic releases but were also shown by the non-theatrical film unit of the MOI which took films directly to wartime communities to be shown in, for example, Scout huts, Miners' Institutes and community centres.[16]

---

[11] James Chapman, '"War" versus "Cultural" Propaganda: Institutional and Ideological Tensions over the Projection of Britain during the Second World War', in *Propaganda, Power and Persuasion: From World War I to Wikileaks*, ed. David Welch (London: I.B. Tauris, 2013), 80–1.

[12] Robert Mackay, *Half the Battle: Civilian Morale in Britain during the Second World War* (Manchester: Manchester University Press, 2003), 141.

[13] Andrew Spicer, 'Extending People's Minds for a Brief Time Every Day: The Wartime Propaganda Short', *Journal of Media Practice*, 4 no. 2 (2003), 107.

[14] James Chapman, *A New History of British Documentary* (Basingstoke: Palgrave Macmillan, 2015), 90.

[15] *Target for Tonight* Dir. Watt (1941); *Fires Were Started* and *The Silent Village* Dir. Humphrey Jennings (1943).

[16] Robert Murphy, *British Cinema and the Second World War* (London: Continuum, 2000), 59.

The other central type of film produced by the MOI was the short film. Over 1,800 of these 'inspirational' and 'instructional' films were produced during the course of the war.[17] Initially, a five-minute short was produced weekly but in 1942 the running time was increased to 15 minutes and the production rate decreased to monthly.[18] They were distributed free to cinemas to form part of the cinematic programme (feature film, cartoon, newsreels, etc.) and, as Murphy argues, 'were a relatively painless way of absorbing government propaganda'.[19] Mass-Observation records note, however, that these shorts were not infrequently missed from the cinematic programme altogether or placed in ignominious places in the running order such as directly after the main feature.[20] These films have faded into obscurity far more than their longform counterparts. Equally, as Spicer notes, they have generally been overlooked by historians.[21] They were often designed to be responsive to a particular wartime moment and as such left little cultural trace. As Robert Mackay notes no one went to the cinema primarily to see the short films.[22] Box office receipts reflected the demand for the main picture and tell us nothing of the general popularity of the shorts that happened to be in the programme. Similarly, they left little and sporadic trace, compared to their longer form counterparts, in newspaper archives and other usual repositories such as Mass-Observation. Indeed, as with any cultural source, gauging audience reaction to any film is the most difficult part of the analysis. Comedy, as with other media, is highly subjective depending not just on different time periods but viewing experience, class, gender as well as personal experiences. However, where possible, this chapter incorporates the cultural traces of these films. For example, Mass-Observation made some efforts, especially early in the war, to trace and track the popularity of MOI short films. Similarly, longer form documentaries and some shorts received reviews and discussions in the newspapers. While these sources are far from representative – MO for example had, unintentionally, a very specific type of respondent and critics very rarely tally with popular opinion – these sources give a small window into understanding how contemporary audiences viewed and understood these filmic sources.[23] Moreover, given that the films were generally instructional in

[17] Andrew Spicer, 'Extending People's Minds for a Brief Time Every Day', 105.
[18] Ibid., 106.
[19] Murphy, *British Cinema and the Second World War*, 59.
[20] MOA: TC Films 1937–48 17-8-B.
[21] Spicer, 'Extending People's Minds for a Brief Time Every Day', 105.
[22] Mackay, *Half the Battle*, 180.
[23] Mike Savage, 'Mass Observation and Social Class.' Mass Observation Online. 2013. Accessed 1 July 2021. http://www.massobservation.amdigital.co.uk/FurtherResources/Essays/MassObservationAnd SocialClass.

some capacity we can analyse the ways the state attempted to influence and change public behaviours, even if it is difficult to know how successful they were.

Uses of humour

What is initially striking about the Ministry of Information films is the clear lines drawn between what is and isn't humorous (or at least what is and isn't permissible to laugh at in a government-sanctioned production). As Pierre Purseigle notes:

> The very mention of humour as a strategy in war, and especially in the age of total war, may seem to entail an inherent paradox. War in the twentieth century led to mass slaughter, large-scale destruction, economic disturbance, and above all was the greatest source of loss, grief and mourning.[24]

Despite the seemingly unfunny source material, commercially produced feature films about the armed services during the war – for example *The Way Ahead* (1944) and *In Which We Serve* (1942)[25] – often featured comical moments and light-hearted exchanges even in moments of battle and high danger. This was a logical strategy as humour invited the audience to, without heavy-handedness, question their morals and certainties. As Kamm et al. note:

> Comedy temporarily suspends the rigid regimes of normality with performances, behaviour patterns, practices, dialogues and images of surreal absurdity, grotesque exaggeration and drastic vehemence, inviting viewers to interrogate the moral ground of cherished norms and established values.[26]

Despite the prevalence of this theme, official MOI productions focusing on the military, with perhaps the exception of depictions of training, were generally straightforwardly serious records of various parts of the war effort. For example, 1940's *Kill or Be Killed* detailed the work of Army snipers. Similarly, 1944's *By Sea and Land* depicted the work of British commandos in the reinvasion of Europe.[27] Indeed, most of the filmic productions by the MOI very much live up to its name: they are informational and little else. Many are light in tone but are far from humorous. Indeed, this was something noted by prolific Mass-Observation

---

[24] *The Way Ahead* Dir. Carol Reed (1944) and *In Which We Serve* Dir. Noël Coward and David Lean (1942).
[25] Pierre Purseigle, 'Mirroring Societies at War: Pictorial Humour in the British and French Popular Press during the First World War', *Journal of European Studies* 31, no. 123 (2001), 289.
[26] Juergen Kamm, Birgit Neumann, Ken McGregor and Frank Klepner, *British TV Comedies: Cultural Concepts, Contexts and Controversies* (Basingstoke: Palgrave Macmillan, 2015), 3.
[27] *Kill or Be Killed* Dir. Len Lye (1940); *Sea and Land* Dir. Jack Lee (1944).

contributor Len England, who went on to co-direct MO in the 1950s and 1960s, when summarizing his thoughts on the early months of the MOI short:

> In very few of the films is there any real attempt at making jokes: those that have contained them have been almost invariably successful. There is no need for elaborate farce, but simply for homely, everyday humour [...] It is not suggested that a message can be put over by means of jokes, but rather humour puts the audience into the right frame.[28]

What humour there is in MOI films is nearly all found on the Home Front. Nearly every conceivable Home Front topic from rationing to air-raid shelters and schooling to evacuation received filmic treatment during the war, often with lightly comic touches. For example, in the 1940 film *Shipbuilders* each man interviewed, with comedic regularity, states that his is 'the most important job in shipbuilding'. Similarly, in the 1940 film *Bringing It Home*, about evacuation, one boy remarks in astonishment when approaching their new village home 'Look Bill. Apples. On trees'. A man from the evacuees' new village quickly adds wryly 'And that evening our village was just one big bellyache', implying that the evacuees had all eaten too many apples. In the 1943 short *Manpower*, centred on a shop whose staff are being called up one by one, each member of staff replies with an overblown and incredulous 'who, me?' every time the voiceover announces they are to be deployed to a different wartime role. The Nazis too, consistent with other wartime media, are often figures of fun but only when discussed in relation to Home Front topics. This is seen, for example, in the National Savings short *Get Cracking* (1944) which begins with Goebbels reading the newspaper, presumably over breakfast, before cracking his egg with his spoon, causing it to explode.[29] In response, he throws the egg cup at a portrait of Hitler, smashing the glass and the portrait to flip to a frown. The audience is then encouraged to 'get cracking' to defeat these 'bad eggs' by investing in national savings.

Moreover, format also often dictated the amount of explicitly humorous content. Longform MOI films tended towards the serious, but the shorts were often comical. This is logical. Each of these films only had a brief amount of time to get across an important, often timely message, and a humorous approach was perhaps more likely to grab the audience's attention. Although their remit was generally Home Front issues, a vast array of big and small topics were presented to wartime audiences in this way. In winter 1942 audiences were presented with

[28] MOA: TC Films 1937–48 17-8-B.
[29] *Shipbuilders* Dir. Leon Schauder (1940); *Bringing It Home* Dir. John E. Lewis (1940); *Manpower* No director listed (1943); *Get Cracking* No director listed (1944).

a postal worker having nightmares about catching and sorting an increasing number of letters falling from the sky as a reminder to post in good time for Christmas. The same message was shown in 1944 by cartoonists Halas and Batchelor, most famous for their 1954 version of *Animal Farm*, who depicted a vision of Santa Claus too weighed down with last minute post to be able to fly at all.[30] Indeed, these films could not only be humorous but actively surreal. To promote a message of 'make do and mend', British audiences in 1944 were treated to a 13-minute film about the life of a suit, narrated by 'the suit' itself. The suit describes its fourteen-year life from best wear to its eventual fate in being cut up for children's clothes, a final act which prompts the suit to ask of its assassin – its owner's wife – 'will it hurt, Mary?' Collectively, these examples find the humour in the mundanity of wartime life in an attempt to have their messages remembered by the audience long after they have left the darkness of the cinema.

The MOI,[31] and of course its commercial contributors, were also adept at using well-known comedians and actors for their films for similar reasons. Indeed, such 'star turns' often relied on the public's knowledge of the performer for most of the comedy. For example, the 1942 film *Go to Blazes* features comic actor Will Hay, then a highly profitable film actor best known for satirizing authority figures' comic failings.[32] In the film Hay plays a character very much in line with his wider known oeuvre, the father of the house, whose home is struck by an incendiary bomb. His ineffectual flapping about with a previously half-read pamphlet causes the incendiary to burn through the floor to the basement where it, luckily and coincidentally, falls into a bucket of water. When a second bomb hits the house, his wife and daughter, played by Muriel George and Thora Hird, respectively, show both Hay and the cinema audience how to correctly deal with such devices. Similarly, 1942 short film *Save Your Shillings and Smile*, a call to invest in war savings, relies on comedian Tommy Trinder's celebrity much more than the very thin story about him deciding which of his chorus girls he will take out after his variety show, eventually choosing the sensible girl who knows all about war savings and investments. Trinder's status as an unlikely ladies' man was also played upon in the 1941 short *Eating Out with Tommy Trinder* in which he avoided yet another unedifying dinner with his fiancée's parents by taking them to a British Restaurant to extol both the quality of the food and the efficiency of cooking on scale.[33] Collectively, therefore, it is clear that the MOI consciously used humour as a vehicle for driving home important propaganda.

---

[30] *Animal Farm* Dir. Halas and Batchelor (1954).

[31] *In Which We Live: Being the Life Story of a Suit Told by Itself* Dir. Richard Massingham (1944).

[32] *Go to Blazes* Dir. Walter Forde (1942).

[33] *Save Your Shillings and Smile* No director listed (1942); *Eating Out with Tommy Trinder* Dir. Desmond Dickinson (1941).

The meanings of humour

Humour had a role beyond the simple transmission of necessary information. As seen elsewhere in this collection, humour played an important part in bonding in various wartime relationships. Indeed, psychologists note that humour can help form group cohesion and a group identity in a variety of interpersonal relationships from workplace to romantic.[34] These relationship cues were often translated into filmic depictions. It was even used in serious and dramatic pieces to underline and underscore tragedy and melancholy. For example, in 1940 the Crown Film Unit produced the film *Men of the Lightship*.[35] The film recreated, using real lightship men rather than actors, the events of 29 January 1940 in which the British East Dudgeon lightship was attacked by the Luftwaffe, violating the long-held neutrality of such vessels in wartime, resulting in the death of all seven men on board. The attack took place when the war had still, for Britain at least, not really begun in earnest and the attack was widely seen as proof of Nazi barbarity and cruelty. The tragic nature of the lightship men's death is underscored on film by their friendship and bond – a point emphasized to the audience through humour. The men joke around and tease each other affectionately. For example, in one scene the character of Lofty is playing the accordion and there is clamour for him to play a different tune to which he retorts 'I don't know any others'. They also hide Lofty's tortoise as a practical joke and fix it so Lofty has to be the one to empty the 'slops', both of which are taken in good grace by Lofty.[36] When Lofty does take out the bucket, the contents blow back in his face as he empties them overboard, an action which, according to Mass-Observation observers, received a big laugh throughout the country.[37] Despite this mild slapstick, a review in *The Times* noted: 'The effect of the film depends on the skill with which the crew are made to seem real people in a real situation.'[38] Indeed, far from being mean-spirited these humorous actions highlight to the audience the realistic bond these men have formed working in close quarters together and neatly juxtaposes their lives together with their collective deaths.

In many ways *Men of the Lightship* bears, sometimes in protean format, the hallmarks of the Crown Film Unit's wartime productions. This is most notably

---

[34] Rod A. Martin, *The Psychology of Humor: An Integrative Approach* (London: Elsevier Science & Technology, 2006), 122.
[35] *Men of the Lightship* Dir. David MacDonald (1940).
[36] Lofty's tortoise is, unfortunately, left behind when they abandon ship.
[37] MOA: TC Films 1937–48 17-8-A.
[38] 'Gaumont Cinema,' *Times*, 25 July 1940, 6.

seen in the non-professional cast but also can be seen in the way humour is deployed to emphasize later pathos and tragedy. The best example of this is in Humphrey Jennings's *The Silent Village* (1943).[39] In this film Jennings transposes the events of the Lidice Massacre, where the entire Czech village of Lidice was destroyed with 340 killed as a reprisal for the assassination of Reich's Protector Reinhard Heydrich, to the Welsh mining village of Cwmgiedd. For the most part, the citizens of Cwmgiedd speak only in Welsh or are presented silently under an English language voiceover narration. *The Manchester Guardian* noted of this filmic device: 'The very restraint of the brilliant camera work and economy of dialogue intensify the sense of brooding tragedy [...] This is a stark, immensely moving, and at times, strangely beautiful record of a crime that shocked civilisation.'[40] However, despite this their essential bonds are still made clear through humour. In one scene, two men laugh together as they wash in the pithead showers. In another, a daughter laughs as she pours water over her father's head as he bathes. Collectively they laugh in the pub or while watching a Daffy Duck cartoon in the cinema. Despite the lack of verbal cues it is made evident that these people love each other, and their deeply human bond is cemented to the audience through laughter. This serves to make the end of the film all the more distressing when the women and children are loaded on to trucks bound for concentration camps and the men, all defiantly singing Welsh national anthem 'Old land of our fathers', are lined up against the churchyard wall and shot one by one. As such, the depiction of humour is an integral part of the intent of the film which aimed to humanize and personalize a tragedy which happened far from British shores, in a town of which few British people had heard and even fewer could pronounce, while simultaneously serving as a stark reminder of what they were fighting for and against.

By contrast, humour could also serve to dilute and make palatable some of the more uncomfortable parts of the British war experience. Some of these can now look rather shocking and, sometimes, downright callous. For example, the 1940 film *War and Order* documented, in a light-hearted way, how policing changed in wartime.[41] It includes many wry asides and lighter comical moments. During a scene showing a police uniform fitting, the voiceover actor puts on a comical voice to declare 'bit tight round the bust sir'. Moreover, during a weapons donation a woman brings in very outdated weapons, including a mace and armour, much to the amusement of the officers who declare, in a now clearly racist aside, that it is a 'good thing Abyssinia's with us'. According to Mass-Observation contributors

---

[39] *The Silent Village* Dir. Humphrey Jennings (1943).
[40] N, J. N. D. 'Picture Theatre', *The Manchester Guardian*, 20 July 1943, 3.
[41] *War and Order* Dir. Charles Hasses (1940).

this scene was received with laughter in the cinemas, although it is of course impossible to know which exact part of this scenario sparked mirth.[42] Perhaps more shockingly, over footage of Italians being rounded up for internment and the closure of their café, the voiceover remarks 'just the weather for ice cream too'. While to modern eyes these seem culturally insensitive, it is clear that it was intended to reassure the presumed audience of ethnically white and ethnically British citizens that these wartime developments were unremarkable.[43]

Such a trope is also seen in portraying the social changes which war necessitated. This is clearly seen in the 1942 film *Night Shift* which documented a 10-hour night-time shift in an armaments factory.[44] The majority of the 2000-strong workforce depicted in the film are women, just a tiny fraction of those who were recruited into previously male-dominated industrial spaces.[45] The film approaches this disturbance of the social order with humour. While a girl is working one of her male co-workers approaches her and jokes 'are you trying to win the war on your own? You need a man about the place.' She replies tartly 'no we don't'. In a later scene another male worker remarks cheekily to a girl banging a hammer on her loaded lathe 'mind it doesn't go off.' She rather incongruously replies 'I'd rather be firing them than making them any day'. The female voiceover restores gender norms by noting 'We're putting all we've got in to making them for the men who can.' Two things are noticeable from these exchanges. Firstly, the men are not given the upper hand in these comic exchanges, neatly reflecting the partially changed gender dynamics in the wartime workplace. Secondly, the film mainly approaches the entrance of women into new types of industrial work with humour, therefore signalling to the viewing audience that these changes are non-threatening and tolerable.

Humour and national identity

Fundamentally, as noted in the opening of this chapter, humour, and especially good humour in the face of adversity, was presented as a foundational British trait. This is seen very clearly in the 1941 Crown Film Unit production *Ordinary People*.[46] The film opens with the sound of the all-clear from the

---

[42] MOA: TC Films 1937–48 17-8-A.
[43] For more on the experience of Italians in Britain in this period see Wendy Ugolini, *Experiencing War as the 'Enemy Other': Italian Scottish Experience in World War II* (Manchester: Manchester University Press, 2011).
[44] *Night Shift* Dir. JD Chambers (1942).
[45] For more on this see Penny Summerfield, *Reconstructing Women's Wartime Lives: Discourse and Subjectivity in Oral Histories of the Second World War* (Manchester: Manchester University Press, 1998).
[46] *Ordinary People* Dir. Jack Lee and JB Holmes (1941).

air raid sirens as the audience watches some of London's citizens, played by non-actors, emerge from the shelters ready to go about their lives. They are in good spirits, unbowed from their night underground. Indeed, the very first words uttered in the film are an exchange between two male friends. A simple question about getting tea is met with the joking response of 'if you're going, there won't be enough for us.' Later in the film a GPO worker, who then maintained the telephone network, enters the remains of a bombed-out house to check its telephone line. As he calls the exchange he declares with mock exasperation 'only another 473 to do'. The film ends back at the shelter as its occupants settle down for the evening with a sing-song. The good humour in this film features as a crucial indicator of the indomitable spirit of London and, as the film states, 'why Hitler cannot win.' As Claire Langhamer notes of the film and the broader period:

> In this wartime context, ordinariness was located within the everyday, but was not synonymous with it. The 'People's War' provided a space within which ordinariness – as a set of values, social characteristics and emotional styles, as well as specific behaviours in particular places – was asserted and celebrated. The extreme demands of wartime seemed to colourise the ordinary and draw attention to its texture.[47]

This sort of good-humoured attitude to the work and hardships of war is a persistent and recurrent motif throughout wartime cinema. For example, in the 1942 film *Builders* the men joke around with the narrator and tease each other playfully.[48] One man, Bob, jokingly complains that 'I shift more with my boots than I do with my machine.' Another, Old Charlie, jokes 'we'd have got a lot more done if we hadn't brought old George with us' before adding mock-incredulously 'Blimey, is he working?' In the 1941 Ministry of Food short *Mrs T and Her Cabbage Patch* about growing food in allotments we see the titular Mrs T and her husband and grown-up daughter, Mary, eating breakfast and preparing packed lunches for their various days of war work.[49] Mrs T encourages Mary to eat some watercress 'for her skin' when Dad asks if he should have some too before adding 'Well my skin has always been my key claim to beauty.' British wartime films are replete with these small moments of humour which indicate both positivity in the face of adversity and strong bonds between family, friends and fellow citizens. As Sonya Rose notes humour is an integral part of British identity in

---

[47] Claire Langhamer, 'Who the Hell Are Ordinary People? Ordinariness as a Category of Historical Analysis', *Transactions of the Royal Historical Society*, 28 (2018), 3.
[48] *Builders* Dir. Pat Jackson (1942).
[49] *Mrs T and Her Cabbage Patch* Dir. Mary Field (1941).

this period because it contrasted favourably with the stereotypical image of the Nazis and Germans as humourless and brutish.[50]

Of course, if finding levity in the midst of war was seen as a paragon of British virtue then to be the butt of the joke conveyed the precise opposite. As renowned French philosopher Henri Bergson argued, humour can be an effective measure of social control:

> Therefore, society holds suspended over each individual member, if not the threat of correction, at all events the prospect of a snubbing, which, although it is slight, is none the less dreaded. Such must be the function of laughter. Always rather humiliating for the one against whom it is directed, laughter is, really and truly, a kind of social 'ragging.'[51]

Throughout wartime cinema, and particularly in the informational films created by the MOI, there was persistent use of a comical bumbling fool character to demonstrate the incorrect way to approach a variety of wartime scenarios. This character was nearly always male and always middle-aged or elderly. He was also invariably rather dim-witted. For example, in the 1940 film *Goofer Trouble* two middle-aged men leave their air-raid shelters to watch dogfights, or 'goofers' in RAF parlance, thereby preventing the British pilots from using their machine guns in battle.[52] The two unnamed goofers are played by well-known comic actors Fred Emney and Edward Chapman and their dress, demeanour and action clearly mark them out as risible. Indeed, one Mass-Observation observer noted this film was well received 'because of the humour of Emney's fatness, and the right type of bomb joke'. The film ends with an RAF pilot, the paragon of British wartime masculinity, reminding the goofers, and therefore the viewing audience, 'Give us a break, back us up – take shelter and don't give us any more goofer trouble.'[53]

Similarly, the 1940 short film *The Backyard Front* (produced for the Ministry of Agriculture) featured actor and comedian Claude Dampier and gardening expert and broadcaster Cecil H. Middleton as 'neighbours' to encourage digging for victory.[54] Claude is comically inept; for example, he thinks 'proteins' is the name of a local couple. Yet his ineptitude creates the space for Middleton to impart his complex knowledge about proper garden management in a way which is memorable and entertaining. Similarly, the 1942 film *The Owner Goes*

---

[50] Rose, *Which People's War?*, 154.
[51] Henri Bergson (translated by Cloudesley Brereton and Fred Rothwell), *Laughter: An Essay on the Meaning of the Comic* (New York: Dover Publications, 2005), 65.
[52] *Goofer Trouble* Dir. Maurice Elvey (1940).
[53] For more on wartime masculinities see Linsey Robb and Juliette Pattinson (eds.), *Men, Masculinities and Male Culture in the Second World War* (Basingstoke: Palgrave Macmillan, 2018).
[54] *The Backyard Front* Dir. Andrew Buchanan (1940).

Aloft is the story of a bumbling middle-aged man who is arrested trying to enter an RAF fighter station and is presumed a spy. However, he declares he is not trespassing as he is the 'owner' of the site because his National Savings helped to pay for the site and planes. This rather ludicrous conceit leads to him getting a tour of the base and even a turn in a flight trainer. As such, his idiocy, yet again, provides a digestible way for the audience to be informed about, and encouraged to participate in, the National Savings scheme. Collectively, it is clear that this trope creates a straightforwardly enjoyable way to get across necessary information to an audience. However, it also tells us who it is permissible to laugh at in wartime society. Indeed, the middle-aged man, very clearly not of fighting age, is often the butt of the joke throughout wartime media. For example, a whole series of 'Careless Talk Costs Lives' posters centred on the gossiping of middle-aged men. Moreover, 'Dig For Victory' campaigns often centred on the middle-aged man. Even in static media like posters it was clear these men were figures of fun as they were often comically rotund or laughably puny.[55]

This phenomenon of the laughable middle-aged man has a class dimension too. The 'ordinary' man, the hero of wartime media, was generally portrayed as working class or lower middle-class. Those of obviously higher socio-economic strata became legitimate figures of fun in this 'people's war'. Indeed, laughing at 'betters' may have provided an element of the humour as inverted the generally accepted social order. This phenomenon is seen, for example, in the 1941 film *Mr Proudfoot Show a Light*.[56] Mr Proudfoot, played by comic actor Sydney Howard, speaks in an affected upper-class accent and his acts of buffoonery, namely showing a light by removing his blackout protections for some fresh air, cause the Luftwaffe to drop a bomb directly on his house. A large part of the humour of the short comes from the ridiculous overblown aristocratic nature of Mr Proudfoot's demeanour and actions. While, according to a Mass-Observation contributor, this film received a lukewarm reception, not least because of the implausibility of the Germans dropping a bomb with such accuracy, Howard's performance as the eponymous Mr Proudfoot was received more favourably, showing that this stereotype of the buffoon resonated with the audience.[57] Of course, class in general shaped both the viewing experience and the interpretation of filmic messages. For example, a Mass-Observation survey

---

[55] Juliette Pattinson, Arthur McIvor and Linsey Robb, *Men in Reserve: British Civilian Masculinities in the Second World War* (Manchester: Manchester University Press, 2017), 10.
[56] *Mr Proudfoot Show a Light* Dir. Herbert Mason (1941).
[57] MOA: TC Films 1937–48 17-8-A.

did find that more middle-class than working-class viewers liked MOI shorts (94 per cent to 78 per cent), a fact Len England blames on the 'middle class attitude of most of the films'.[58]

This discussion of 'Britishness' obscures the fact that Britain was not, and is not, a single nation but instead a collection of four separate nations with their own independent identities, although Northern Ireland (controversially partitioned from the rest of Ireland in 1921 and often subject to different wartime regulations) was only infrequently seen or discussed in wartime propaganda.[59] However, national and regional divisions were sometimes brought to the fore, most notably through accent. Before the war, regional accents had had limited exposure in cinema, with some high-profile exceptions such as character actors Gracie Fields and George Formby, and had little box office draw. This changed markedly during the war. The most popular BBC wartime broadcasters were Wilfred Pickles and J. B. Priestley who spoke with soft regional, namely Yorkshire, accents. Film, too, moved to include a wide range of accents to denote 'authenticity' in the story being told. Many wartime films, such as *Millions Like Us* (1943) and *The Way Ahead* (1944), included a range of regional and national accents to suggest essential wartime unity. However, any regional or non-English accent was often subject to, generally gentle, mocking. *Squadron 992* was released in mid-1940 and detailed the work of RAF Barrage Balloon crew working in Edinburgh and the surrounding areas (especially around the Forth Bridge).[60] One balloon is due to be located on a farm. The elderly Scots farmer points out that the building the RAF wants to use as storage is the 'wash hoose', a phrase which has to be translated for the superior officer: 'he means a laundry sir'. In this exchange it is unclear who the butt of the joke is and as such it can perhaps be read as an attempt at presenting a united front through mutual mockery.

This, therefore, raises questions not just of who it was appropriate to laugh at but also who was in on the joke. As we have seen, humour and laughter were used to convey fundamental humanity upon the subjects depicted and to suggest that they were 'like us' to the viewing audience. In the context of both a global war and Britain's imperial standing it is revealing to see who is granted the right to laugh. This is shown, for example, in Czech refugee Jiří Weiss's 1945 film Crown

---

[58] MOA: TC Films 1937–48 17-8-B.
[59] For more on Northern Ireland during the Second World War, see, for example, Guy Woodward, *Culture, Northern Ireland, and the Second World War* (Oxford: Oxford University Press, 2015). For discussion of Britishness, see Wendy Ugolini and Juliette Pattinson (ed.), *Fighting for Britain? Negotiating Identities in Britain during the Second World War* (New York: Peter Lang, 2015).
[60] *Millions Like Us* Dir. Sidney Gilliat and Frank Launder (1943) and *The Way Ahead* Dir. Carol Reed (1944); *Squadron 992* Dir. Harry Watt (1940).

Film Unit, *Night and Day*.[61] In the film, the Czechoslovak airmen are represented in a way which would have been familiar to British audiences. Despite being largely silent, for obvious language reasons, they are shown having strong bonds to each other, bonds which are affirmed by comedy and laughter. In one scene, while eating a meal the men laugh and play pranks on each other, for example placing a flower in one man's sandwich while his head is turned. The message to the audience is clear: while these effective pilots are not humourless Nazis they are very like the British men the audience knew and loved.

Humour was also often used to explain the relationships between nations and to smooth over cultural differences. This is most obviously seen in the 1943 film *Welcome to Britain*, produced by the MOI for training the American armed forces.[62] Starring American actor Burgess Meredith the whole film has a wryly comical air. The film begins with Meredith declaring 'I'm the best person to show you around, I've been here for 3 weeks' and ends with him rushing to get out final pieces of information before heading off to 'battle'. Meredith does poke gentle fun at the citizens of the United Kingdom, for example when he gently complains in the pub about having to drink warm beer. However, he too is often equally the butt of the joke, for example when he is caught out not knowing the difference between bitter and mild – 'well one's bitter and one's mild, you'll just have to find out for yourself'. As such, mutual teasing and mockery are cemented as the basis of a friendly relationship. A similar theme is seen in the 1942 film *Common Cause*.[63] This film centres on two fictionalized conversations between two different pairs of men, one between a British naval man and a Soviet pilot and the other between two Chinese and American soldiers. Through these conversations the film tries to convey the message of both a common cause, as per the title, and common ground between different races and nations. The Brit and Russian trade war stories over their respective national drinks laughing as they do so. The Chinese and American soldiers learn about each other's culture, often gently teasing each other in the process. In one scene the American soldier remarks 'you talk English quite well, learn it at school I suppose.' The Chinese soldier responds by asking the American 'you speak it also quite good [sic], did you learn it in school too?' In doing so, the film is able to gently mock and probe the soldier's, and presumably the audience's, preconceived notions about foreign nationals. Again, we see humour is at the heart of this implication of a common bond.

This is even more fascinating in the context of Britain's status as an imperial power. The empire was central to British survival and victory which necessitated

---

[61] *Night and Day* Dir. Jiří Weiss's (1945).
[62] *Welcome to Britain* Dir. Burgess Meredith and Anthony Asquith (1943).
[63] *Common Cause* Dir. Henry Cass (1942).

a concerted propaganda campaign to promote the empire at home and to encourage imperial subjects to see themselves as part of the British war effort. For example, in 1941 film *India Marches* British audiences were treated to a blended image of specific Indian activities – dance and wrestling for example – as well as activities which cemented their quasi-Britishness – bagpipes and army drill. Mass-Observation contributor 'KT' noted of the film:[64]

> The film seemed to go down well with the audience and as has been previously pointed out the shots of activity which were different from that of the army ordinarily aroused more interest than those which might be the army anywhere: the Indian Ballet and wrestling which are common only to India received much better response than those shots which showed the Indian Army drilling and firing machine guns. There was a certain amount of emphasis on the idea that India is proud to be part of the empire and is united to withstand aggression; the audience seemed to swallow this.[65]

Documentary News Letter, a wartime magazine about documentary film, noted of the film's integral irony that the portrayed Indians were apparently fighting for 'freedom and democracy'; the same government that would have us believe that these Indians 'would immediately start killing each other if they were given the said freedom and democracy'.[66] Similarly, efforts were made by the BBC to, as Thomas Hajkowski argues, present the empire as 'egalitarian, and committed to stewarding the dependent colonies towards self-rule'.[67] However, what is striking about most of these films is that colonial subjects, with the exception of white people from the dominions, are largely mute or relegated to small, often serious, speaking roles. They are never granted the opportunity of being humorous. Instead, the relationship is transactional and paternalistic. The lack of humour underscores their inability to capture a parity of esteem. Imperial subjects were never unequivocally presented as 'like us' to British audiences but rather were denied laughter as a key humanizing trait.

Conclusions

This analysis of one strand of the myriad types of wartime culture which abounded in this propaganda war merely scratches the surface in analysing the purposes and uses of comedy in wartime. While highlighting the need for

---

[64] *India Marches* No director listed (1941).
[65] MOA: TC Films 1937–48 17-8-A.
[66] *Documentary News Letter*, 2 August 1941, 149.
[67] Thomas Hajkowski, 'The BBC, the Empire, and the Second World War, 1939–1945', *Historical Journal of Film, Radio and Television*, 2, no. 2 (2002), 151.

further study in this area, what this chapter has shown is humour was a central part of the Ministry of Information's wartime filmic propaganda strategy. At a basic level it was used to bring interest to propaganda films and to make vital, but often not particularly interesting, information memorable to the viewing audience. It could even make palatable the difficult and necessary changes to life and society in wartime. Moreover, this humour had a policing function too. While it was fine to laugh in wartime no one wants to be laughed at and the MOI made continually plain that those who flouted or ignored necessary wartime regulations were legitimate figures of fun.

However, humour and comedy had uses and meanings far beyond the practical. 'Good humour' was a vital part of the British self-image, confirming to themselves that they were the 'good guys' in opposition to the humourless brutish Nazis. Humour underpinned not only the filmic British relationship to the war but also to each other. Humour, whether between individuals or the constituent nations of the United Kingdom, made plain bonds of affection and mutual understanding. This is also seen where humour is used to humanize to a British audience those from different allied nations to emphasize that they were 'like us' not only in common cause against the Axis powers but in temperament too, a technique which was stretched to breaking point when it came to depictions and discussions of the citizens of imperial territories.

Filmography

The Backyard Front (1940), Dir. Andrew Buchanan. United Kingdom: British Films Limited.
Bringing It Home (1940), Dir. John E. Lewis.
Britain at Bay (1940), Dir. Harry Watt. United Kingdom: GPO Film Unit.
Builders (1942), Dir. Pat Jackson. United Kingdom: Crown Film Unit.
By Sea and Land (1944), Dir. Jack Lee. United Kingdom: Crown Film Unit.
Common Cause (1942), Dir. Henry Cass. United Kingdom: Verity Films.
Christmas Wishes (1944), Dir. Halas and Batchelor. United Kingdom: Halas and Batchelor.
Eating Out with Tommy Trinder (1941), Dir. Desmond Dickinson. United Kingdom: Strand Film Company.
Fires Were Started (1943), Dir. Humphrey Jennings. United Kingdom: Crown Film Unit.
Get Cracking (1944), No director listed. United Kingdom: No Production Company Listed.
Gone with the Wind (1939), Dir. Victor Fleming. United States of America: Metro-Goldwyn-Mayer.

Go to Blazes (1942), Dir. Walter Forde. United Kingdom: Ministry of Information.
Goofer Trouble (1940), Dir. Maurice Elvey. United Kingdom: Ministry of Information.
In Which We Live: Being the Life Story of a Suit Told by Itself (1944) Dir. Richard Massingham. United Kingdom: Ministry of Information.
In Which We Serve (1942), Dir. Noël Coward. United Kingdom: British Lion Film.
Kill or Be Killed (1942), No director listed. United Kingdom: Realist Film Unit.
Manpower (1943), No director Listed. United Kingdom: Strand Film Production.
Millions Like Us (1943), Dir. Sidney Gilliat and Frank Launder. United Kingdom: Gainsborough Pictures.
Men of the Lightship (1940), Dir. David MacDonald. United Kingdom: Crown Film Unit.
Mr Proudfoot Show a Light (1941), Dir. Herbert Mason. United Kingdom: 20th Century Fox.
Mrs T and Her Cabbage Patch (1941), Dir. Mary Field. United Kingdom: The Electrical Association for Women.
Night and Day (1945), Dir. Jirí Weiss. United Kingdom: Czechoslovak Film Unit.
Night Shift (1942), Dir. J. D. Chambers. United Kingdom: Paul Rotha Productions.
Ordinary People (1941), Dir. Jack Lee and J. B. Holmes. United Kingdom: Crown Film Unit.
The Owner Goes Aloft (1942), Dir. Ivan Scott. United Kingdom: Spectator Short Films.
Post Early for Christmas (1942), No director listed. United Kingdom: Ministry of Information.
Save Your Shillings and Smile (1942), Dir. Harry Watt. United Kingdom: Ealing Studios.
Shipbuilders (1940), Dir. Leon Schanuder. United Kingdom: CB Instructional.
The Silent Village (1943), Dir. Humphrey Jennings. United Kingdom: Crown Film Unit.
Squadron 992 (1940), Dir. Harry Watt. United Kingdom: GPO Film Unit.
Target for Tonight (1941), Dir. Harry Watt. United Kingdom: Crown Film Unit.
War and Order (1940), Dir. Charles Hasse. United Kingdom: GPO Film Unit.
The Way Ahead (1944), Dir. Carol Reed. United Kingdom: Two Cities Films.
A Welcome to Britain (1943), Dir. Burgess Meredith and Anthony Asquith. United Kingdom: Strand Film Company.

Bibliography

Henri Bergson (translated by Cloudesley Brereton and Fred Rothwell), *Laughter: An Essay on the Meaning of the Comic* (New York: Dover Publications, 2005).
James Chapman, 'Cinema, Propaganda and National Identity: British Film and the Second World War', in Justine Ashby and Andrew Higson (eds.), *British Cinema, Past and Present* (London: Taylor and Francis, 2000), 193–206.
James Chapman, '"War" versus "Cultural" Propaganda: Institutional and Ideological Tensions over the Projection of Britain during the Second World War', in David

Welch (ed.), *Propaganda, Power and Persuasion: From World War I to Wikileaks* (London: I.B. Tauris, 2013).

James Chapman, *A New History of British Documentary* (Basingstoke: Palgrave Macmillan, 2015).

Mark Glancy, 'Going to the Pictures: British Cinema and the Second World War', *Past and Future*, 8 (2010), 7–9.

Thomas Hajkowski, 'The BBC, the Empire, and the Second World War, 1939–1945', *Historical Journal of Film, Radio and Television*, 22 no. 2 (2002), 135–55.

Jeremy Havardi, *Projecting Britain at War: The National Character in British World War II Films* (Jefferson: McFarland & Company, 2014).

Jeurgen Kamm, BirgitNeumann, Ken McGregor and Frank Klepner, *British TV Comedies: Cultural Concepts, Contexts and Controversies* (Basingstoke: Palgrave Macmillan, 2015).

Claire Langhamer, 'Who the Hell Are Ordinary People? Ordinariness as a Category of Historical Analysis', *Transactions of the Royal Historical Society*, 28 (2018), 175–95.

Antonia Lant, *Blackout: Reinventing Women for Wartime British Cinema* (Princeton: Princeton University Press, 1991).

Robert Mackay, *Half the Battle: Civilian Morale in Britain during the Second World War* (Manchester: Manchester University Press, 2003).

Rod A. Martin, *The Psychology of Humor: An Integrative Approach* (London: Elsevier Science & Technology, 2006).

J.P. Mayer, *British Cinemas and Their Audiences: Sociological Studies* (London: Dennis Dobson, 1978).

Robert Murphy, *British Cinema and the Second World War* (London: Continuum, 2000).

Michael Paris, *Repicturing the Second World War: Representations in Film and Television*. (Basingstoke: Palgrave Macmillan, 2007).

Juliette Pattinson, Arthur McIvor and Linsey Robb, *Men in Reserve: British Civilian Masculinities in the Second World War* (Manchester: Manchester University Press, 2017).

Pierre Purseigle, 'Mirroring Societies at War: Pictorial Humour in the British and French Popular Press during the First World War', *Journal of European Studies* 31 no. 123 (2001), 289–328.

Linsey Robb and Juliette Pattinson (eds.), *Men, Masculinities and Male Culture in the Second World War* (Basingstoke: Palgrave Macmillan, 2018).

Sonya O. Rose, *Which People's War?: National Identity and Citizenship in Wartime Britain 1939–1945* (Oxford: Oxford University Press, 2004).

Mike Savage, 'Mass Observation and Social Class', Mass Observation Online (2013). Accessed July 01, 2021. http://www.massobservation.amdigital.co.uk/FurtherResources/Essays/MassObservationAndSocialClass.

Andrew Spicer, 'Extending People's Minds for a Brief Time Every Day: The Wartime Propaganda Short', *Journal of Media Practice*, 4 no. 2 (2003), 105–12.

Penny Summerfield, *Reconstructing Women's Wartime Lives: Discourse and Subjectivity in Oral Histories of the Second World War* (Manchester: Manchester University Press, 1998).

A.J.P. Taylor, *English History 1914–1945* (Harmondsworth: Penguin, 1970).

Wendy Ugolini, *Experiencing War as the 'Enemy Other': Italian Scottish Experience in World War II* (Manchester: Manchester University Press, 2011).

Wendy Ugolini and Juliette Pattinson (ed.), *Fighting for Britain? Negotiating Identities in Britain during the Second World War* (New York: Peter Lang, 2015).

Guy Woodward, *Culture, Northern Ireland, and the Second World War* (Oxford: Oxford University Press, 2015).

4

Making people laugh on the wartime BBC

Siân Nicholas

When one thinks of humour and wartime radio one tends to think automatically of *ITMA (It's That Man Again)*, the iconic BBC Variety series that attracted over 14 million listeners weekly during the Second World War and gifted the British people a range of catchphrases as baffling nowadays as they were ubiquitous then. However, *ITMA* was only the most famous of an extraordinary effort by the wartime BBC Variety Department to bring entertainment and laughter to not just the Home Front but also service personnel listening at home and overseas. In the 1930s the BBC had consolidated an approach to radio comedy that was typically middlebrow, avuncular, and family-oriented. During the war, the BBC found itself needing to cater to a wider and more diverse set of audiences and audience tastes than ever before, and to audiences for whom diversion and escapism was an ever more important need. This challenge, which went to the very heart of the 'Reithian' philosophy of the BBC, saw the Corporation attempt a range of approaches, from anti-Nazi satire to nostalgic 'English' humour, from 'canteen' comedy to aural carnival. Sometimes the humour fell flat; sometimes it came from unexpected places. But over the course of the war the BBC Variety Department would create a common vocabulary and set of cultural reference points that would transcend class, age and gender, and that would become an essential part of British popular memory of the war.

BBC comedy before the war

Variety was the Cinderella department of the inter-war BBC. Sir John Reith, the BBC's first and most influential Director-General, had recognized that if the BBC was to provide the comprehensive national service he envisioned ('the best of everything into the greatest number of homes'[1]), this had to include light entertainment. The BBC offered Variety performers national fame and unprecedented audiences – but also poor remuneration and the potential overexposure of long-standing comedy routines. Meanwhile, while many music hall comedians based their acts around calculated vulgarity and innuendo, the BBC was the 'guest in the home', with a self-imposed responsibility not to offend its audience. The BBC's Handbook of Variety Routine, issued in 1936, notoriously proscribed, among other topics, religion or biblical quotations; any physical or fatal medical condition; drunkenness; any prominent person; marital infidelity, immorality, or effeminacy in men,[2] while writing in late 1939, the BBC's Director of Variety, John Watt, noted, 'It is said that there are only six jokes in the world, and I can assure you that we cannot broadcast three of them ....'[3] Music hall comedy was, alongside dance music, considered something better left to the continental-based English-language commercial stations Radios Luxembourg and Normandie. By the late 1930s these stations were attracting up to a third of the British domestic audience, with their blend of sponsored Variety and dance music, and risqué comedians such as Max Miller.

Some music hall routines did successfully make the transition to radio, particularly the character-based comedy of Jeanne de Casalis (as the querulous 'Mrs Feather'), Rob Wilton (as the bumbling 'Mr Muddlecombe, J.P., Principal Magistrate of Nether Backwash') and Mabel Constanduros (as the poisonous East End matriarch Grandma Buggins). The music hall tradition was also explicit in such programmes as *The Kentucky Minstrels* and the BBC's own Variety showcase, *Music Hall*. However, the BBC also developed its own more allusive form of humour, with echoes of *Punch* and 'Beachcomber', exemplified by the radio monologues of Ronald Knox and A. J. Alan. And although BBC radio producers returned from the United States with tales of Jack Benny and Burns and Allen, quick-fire comedy based around distinctive personalities and sharp repartee, BBC listeners preferred Gillie Potter ('England's egregious patrician philosopher') with his anecdotes from the rural backwater of 'Hogsnorton', invariably introducing himself, 'Good evening, England. This is Gillie Potter speaking to you in English.'[4]

---

[1] J.C.W. Reith, *Broadcast over Britain* (London: Hodder and Stoughton, 1924), 147.

[2] 'Artists Material' supplement to BBC Handbook of Variety Routine, 1936, quoted in Martin Dibbs, *Radio Fun and the BBC Variety Department 1922–67: Comedy and Popular Music on Air* (Basingstoke: Palgrave Macmillan, 2019), 62.

[3] John Watt (ed.), *Radio Variety* (London: J.M. Dent and Sons Ltd., 1939), xiii–ix. Though he added a postscript: 'Since writing the above, there is an addition to the list of permissible jokes in the person of Hitler.'

[4] Andy Foster and Steve Furst (eds.), *Radio Comedy 1938–68* (London: Virgin Publishing, 1996), 69–70; Siân Nicholas, 'Potter, Gillie', *Oxford Dictionary of National Biography*.

There was, however, one really innovative BBC comedy show in the late 1930s. *Band Waggon*, which premiered in January 1938, was conceived as a dance band show compered by a comedian, and was loosely based on an American radio show of the same name. But its signature ten-minute comic interlude, performed by up-and-coming cockney music hall star Arthur Askey and his public-school straight man Richard 'Stinker' Murdoch (itself an innovation), swiftly developed into a new kind of radio humour based on absurd situations and aural slapstick. Punning on Askey's status as the show's 'resident comedian', the weekly comedy sketch removed itself to his fictional flat on the roof of Broadcasting House, and in short time introduced his landlady Mrs Bagwash and her daughter Nausea, Basil and Lucy the pigeons, and Lewis the goat. The comedy was based on a daring combination of repartee and sound effects that encouraged the audience's imagination in making fun of some cherished BBC institutions, whether the six time-pips (nominally in Askey's care), the BBC Theatre Organ (in which Basil and Lucy got loose), or when, while vacuuming the flat, Askey accidentally sucked up to the ceiling the entire BBC Symphony Orchestra practicing in the room below. The most famous sound effect of all was the 'Band Waggon Crash': at some point in the proceedings, something would crash to the ground with an enormous noise – including the BBC Symphony Orchestra, when Askey turned his vacuum cleaner off.[5]

BBC comedy in the early months of the war: making fun of Hitler

With the early days and weeks of the war predicted to be a wholesale blitzkrieg of the country, the BBC had assumed that its initial wartime role would be little more than the provision of news, information and soothing music, before, hopefully, returning to something more like normal output. Comedy had not originally been considered as a priority, or even particularly appropriate: war was not funny and making jokes would likely be seen in poor taste. Under the BBC's War Plan ('Document C'), the Variety Department itself was reduced to a skeleton staff and evacuated to Bristol.[6]

The first live programme from the displaced Variety Department was *For Amusement Only*, on Wednesday evening, 6 September 1939, on the barely

---

[5] *Band Waggon* would have one short wartime series before Askey moved on and Murdoch was called up.
[6] See Asa Briggs, *The History of Broadcasting in the United Kingdom, Vol III: The War of Words* (London: Oxford University Press, 1970), 29; Dibbs, *Radio Fun*, 111–12.

week-old emergency BBC Home Service. The show was a conscious attempt to evoke the atmosphere of a First World War concert party – though with jokes about air raid wardens and the blackout – and caused something of a sensation by featuring the first comic song about Hitler ever broadcast on the BBC, *Who Is this Man Who Looks Like Charlie Chaplin?* (chorus: 'We think he's Charlie Chaplin all the time'), written in haste by Max Kester and John Watt, and performed by Tommy Handley. This song represented a sea change for the BBC, not least in its abandonment of the courtesies it had conventionally accorded all political figures. (Grace Wyndham Goldie, radio critic of *The Listener*, commented that 'though not in the best of taste, the song was a necessary correction of perspective'.[7]) This change of policy can also be seen in the robust new verse added to an Arthur Askey broadcast of Flanagan and Allen's *Run, Rabbit, Run*:

> Run, Adolf, run, Adolf, run, run, run.
> Look what you've been gone and done, done, done.
> We will knock the stuffing out of you,
> Old fat-guts Goering, and Goebbels too [etc][8]

An ostensibly more cerebral approach was taken by *Adolf in Blunderland*, broadcast on Friday evening 6 October 1939, 'a political parody' in the style of an undergraduate revue by Max Kester and James Dyrenforth, closely based on Lewis Carroll's *Alice in Wonderland* and featuring, as well as the titular 'Little Adolf', the White Von Ribbit (White Rabbit/Von Ribbentrop), Mad Flatterer (Mad Hatter/Himmler), March Into (March Hare/Goering), Deutch-Hess (Duchess/Rudolf Hess), Mock Gurbles (Mock Turtle/Goebbels) and Doormat (Dormouse/ 'just the average German. He's asleep half the time …. doped by propaganda. He's unconscious of what's going on around him'.[9]) The script relied on pastiche, puns and a close knowledge of its source material, viz. Adolf's recitation during the Mad Flatterer's Tea Party:

> 'Twas the voice of the Fuehrer! I heard him declare
> If you want a good massacre, bomb from the air.
> When his silly moustache isn't bristling with wrath
> It's kept in mein camphor to save it from moth.[10]

---

[7] Grace Wyndham Goldie, *The Listener*, 14 September 1939, 544.
[8] Recording of Jack Hylton and his Band, featuring Arthur Askey, BBC Sound Library, Broadcasting House London.
[9] James Dyrenforth and Max Kester, *Adolf in Blunderland* (London: Frederick Muller, 1939), 31.
[10] Quoted in 'Little Adolf in Blunderland – New Satire by BBC', *Daily Telegraph*, 6 October 1939.

Dyrenforth later proudly recalled that the script was considered so controversial that it had to be scrutinized by *three* censors and was being altered even during the broadcast.[11] It appears to have been well received by audiences and critics alike, was published in book form in December 1939 (going through four editions in three months) and was repeated 'by popular demand' in February 1940.

However, popular approval of Hitler jokes on the radio had already peaked. Barely a fortnight after *Adolf in Blunderland*, John Watt announced to the press that there were too many anti-Nazi jokes and songs on the BBC.[12] A trenchant letter to *The Times* queried the entire approach of ridiculing one's enemies ('surely it is wrong psychologically to encourage us to think of our present enemies as being contemptible and ridiculous').[13] Producers of pantomimes and Forces shows also offered their opinions, warning that 'today's soldiers are intelligent, sophisticated. They like clever wit. They don't like hearing the old old Army jokes ... do like clever burlesque of some side of Army life ... don't like Hitler jokes ....'[14] In January 1940, Goldie offered her own take on patriotic propaganda: 'If a comedian sings "Run, rabbit, run" or "There'll always be an England" one single time more, I'll buy a twopenny bomb and blow up my radio'.[15]

The Variety Department's formal ban on jokes about Nazi leaders appears to have been honoured more in the breach than the observance. Twice in the spring of 1940, the BBC's Northern Ireland Director Melvin Dinwiddie complained to Controller of Programmes Basil Nicolls after hearing jokes that made reference to Goering's weight: the first, that owing to the shortage of fats in Germany, Herman Goering had presented his stomach to the nation; second, that the Air Force had made a flight over Goering's paunch but had not had time to make the round trip. Nicolls apparently conceded defeat after the second instance, commenting, 'It looks as if we should give up struggling against Goering's paunch'.[16] In August 1941 two highly charged satirical talks broadcast by the American commentator Quentin Reynolds, 'Dear Dr Goebbels' and 'Dear Mr Schickelgruber' (a reference to Hitler's supposed original surname), received high public approval. Tellingly, however, when the British journalist, William Connor ('Cassandra' of the *Daily Mirror*) took a similar approach in a

---

[11] Dyrenforth and Kester, *Adolf in Blunderland*, foreword.
[12] 'Too Many Anti-Nazi Jokes', *Daily Telegraph*, 16 October 1939.
[13] 'Propaganda', R.S. Forman to The Editor, *The Times*, 25 October 1939.
[14] 'Wrong Stuff to Give the Troops', *Daily Express*, 16 December 1939.
[15] Grace Wyndham Goldie, *The Listener*, 4 January 1940, 43.
[16] NID to CP 19 February 1940 and 17 March 1940, and replies, 26 February 1940 and 2 April 1940. BBC Written Archives Centre, Caversham (hereafter BBC WAC) file R34/275/1.

broadcast attacking the comic author P. G. Wodehouse, who had been accused of broadcasting for the Germans while interned in the South of France, the public response was very different. What was considered humorous in an American accent was considered bad taste in an English one, and Connor's broadcast was roundly condemned as 'un-British'.[17] Also controversial was a broadcast – permitted after much internal BBC soul-searching – by Noël Coward in July 1943 of his satirical song *Don't Let's Be Beastly to the Germans*. BBC's fears that parts of the radio audience might take Coward's sarcastic lyrics literally were ultimately outweighed by the information that Winston Churchill had already been treated to a performance of the song and had 'appreciatively joined in the chorus'.[18] Nazi leaders remained the regular butt of jokes throughout the war, on the BBC as well as in films and cartoons, as both Linsey Robb and Juliette Pattinson explore in their chapters.

'Canteen' comedy and 'the stuff to give the troops'

As the anticipated blitz failed to materialize, and the novelty of emergency conditions (and the emergency broadcasting schedule) began to pall, the most entertaining thing on the radio for a time appeared to be William Joyce, Lord Haw Haw's, broadcasts in English from Germany.[19] The BBC sought to combat this by, among other initiatives, creating a sense of quasi-military unity by 'going all canteen'.[20] The popular Saturday evening Variety show *In Town Tonight* returned in October as *In the Canteen Tonight*, and from November a new show, *Garrison Theatre*, sought to revive for a new war the style and humour of the First World War's Northern Command Garrison Theatre. *Garrison Theatre* gave wartime Britain its first new Variety star in Jack Warner, a music hall entertainer and occasional broadcaster overshadowed at the time by his far more famous sisters Elsie and Doris Waters (aka the comedy housewives 'Gert and Daisy'). Warner played the cockney soldier-compere of this army camp theatre, flirting with his 'littel gel', Joan Winters, and reading out a letter from his 'bruvver' Sid

---

[17] Siân Nicholas, 'Policing Tonal Boundaries: Constructing the Nazi/German Enemy on the Wartime BBC', in Willibald Steinmetz (ed.), *Political Languages in the Age of Extremes* (Oxford: Oxford University Press, 2011), 186–9.

[18] Programme Organiser to DPP, 19 July 1943, BBC WAC R19/941/3, and Siân Nicholas, *The Echo of War: Home Front Propaganda and the Wartime BBC, 1939–45* (Manchester: Manchester University Press), 161–2.

[19] For Hamburg listening, see LR/98, 8 March 1940, BBC WAC R9/14; see also Briggs, *War of Words*, 140–59.

[20] Rose Macaulay, *The Spectator*, 20 October 1939, 538.

'somewhere in France'. He gave Britain its first wartime catchphrases, 'Mind my bike' and 'blue pencil', a reference to the censored parts of Sid's letters that doubled as a useful substitute for forbidden expletives (e.g. 'Not blue-pencil likely').[21] *Garrison Theatre* ran from late 1939 to January 1941, except for a break for a stage tour over the summer of 1940. By 1942 Jack Warner was considered within the BBC to be 'almost as famous' as Arthur Askey.[22]

Programmes aimed at actual servicemen raised questions of their own. From very early in the war, the BBC Home Service had broadcast concerts for and by the British Expeditionary Force in France, meeting criticism of the low standards of the latter by arguing, 'It is the business of the BBC ... to mirror as faithfully as possible "the spirit of the troops".[23] By early 1940 an animated defence of the cultural tastes of the armed forces had reached the pages of *The Listener*:

> I think you will find that this Army is more highbrow than is usually supposed ...
> An awful lot of Tipperary and here's-luck-to-the-boys-in-khaki gets turned out by dance bands and the Press, and though, of course, we don't know how it goes down at home, it is pretty nauseating here.[24]

The launch of the BBC Forces Programme in February 1940 as a 'light' alternative to the Home Service was thus both a declaration of intent – to meet the genuine entertainment needs of servicemen – and a challenge – to find out what would cheer up listeners across the country to the new service, whether in camps, factories, civil defence units and homes.[25]

As the nation became more militarized and more and more of the population found itself mobilized into war service, the *Garrison Theatre* model of canteen comedy made way for its literal manifestation. *Works Wonders* (from 1940) and *Workers' Playtime* (from 1941) pioneered the broadcasting of lunchtime Variety concerts live from factory canteens around the country, the former showcasing local amateur talent, the latter featuring recognized acts. A programme for Anti-Aircraft units, *Ack-Ack Beer-Beer* (1940–4), also featured home-grown comedy acts, entertaining both the live audience and audiences in factories, army camps, civil defence units and homes across the country.

---

[21] See Foster and Furst, *Radio Comedy*, 48–50. Military and government censors – and BBC script editors – traditionally used blue-coloured pencils.
[22] See Variety Booking Manager to Director of Variety, 16 January 1942, BBC WAC RCONT 1: Jack Warner, File 2.
[23] *Radio Times*, 15 October 1939, 43.
[24] *The Listener*, 15 February 1940, 308, also quoted in Dibbs, *Radio Fun*, 121.
[25] For the impact of the BBC Forces Programme, see Siân Nicholas, 'The People's Radio: The BBC and Its Audience 1939–45', in Nick Hayes and Jeff Hill (eds.), *Millions Like Us? British Culture in the Second World War* (Liverpool: Liverpool University Press, 1999), 70–1.

A sign of the recovery of the BBC's own morale in early April 1940 was *Come Out To Play*, with musical stars Jessie Matthews and Sonny Hale, a topical satire on its early wartime programming: the uninformative news, the endless Theatre Organ interludes and the tinny entertainment. Perhaps a further sign of confidence was the increasing number of radio critics bemoaning that the BBC had sacrificed sophisticated entertainment in favour of vulgar majority taste. In fact, a survey by the BBC Listener Research Department found that 80 per cent of those questioned believed that BBC Variety programmes were *not* too vulgar and a quarter felt they were not vulgar *enough*.[26] In May 1940 Mass-Observation likewise found very strong public feeling against the so-called 'puritan' attitude to radio comedy (viz. working-class male respondent, aged 35: 'It'll kill more people than bombs if they stop broadcasting it').[27] John Watt, too, was unrepentant, announcing in July 1940 that BBC Variety 'aimed to entertain the 82 per cent of the British public earning less than £4 per week.'[28]

A policy document circulated by the BBC Listener Research Department in August 1940 laid out bluntly the kinds of programmes that the 'average listener' wanted. Its definition of the 'average listener' was, in its own way, revolutionary: provincial, blue-collar, elementary-school educated, with 'all right' morale but without much faith in politicians – and more likely to be female than male. Its prescription for Variety was prescient, arguing for at least one show per week that would be 'common currency in the street and in the air raid shelter, in camps, in billets, or on leave, in the pub and in the senior common room … [helping to] bind the nation together as a community'.[29]

The Variety Department's move in February 1941 from Bristol to Bangor, north Wales ('Variety Valley', as the *Daily Sketch* somewhat condescendingly described it[30]), brought an increase in personnel, influx of new talent, and a greater element of self-confidence. Following the entry of the United States into the war in late 1941, the BBC began importing several iconic American comedy shows (with the advertisements removed) into its Forces schedules, featuring stars such as Bob Hope, Jack Benny and Bing Crosby. The BBC also championed its comedy efforts against the alleged bad influence of both wartime music hall and the Services' own entertainment organization ENSA.[31] However, criticism

---

[26] See for instance LR/97, 4 March 1940; Robert Silvey to CP, 28 February 1941. BBC WAC R9/15/1.
[27] Mass-Observation File Report FR/149, 28 May 1940.
[28] 'Shows in "Slab"', *Liverpool Echo*, 15 July 1940.
[29] 'Broadcasting Policy', BBC Listener Research Department, 27 August 1940, BBC WAC R9/15/1.
[30] 'BBC's New Variety Drive', *Daily Sketch*, 12 December 1942.
[31] Dibbs, *Radio Fun*, 66–7.

of the poverty of BBC comedy remained a running theme in the entertainment columns of the press, with any new initiatives treated with scepticism. When, for instance, in late 1942 Watt announced a new 'Variety Offensive' for the New Year, several newspapers attributed the move to the BBC's need to meet the demands of American forces in the UK. ('Not, you note, to improve them for you millions whose licences pay for the BBC. You would have gone on getting the same old tripe.')[32]

Comedy for and about the Forces also ran its own risks, notably the sensibilities of senior military staff regarding the dignity of the Services. *Ack-Ack Beer-Beer*, for instance, caused a serious rift with Army representatives after an improvisational talent quiz featured a soldier who had sung *Roll Out the Barrel* 'in the manner of a duck'.[33] More seriously, in 1941 BBC comedians were advised to drop (invariably sexist) jokes about the ATS and Land Girls, for fear they were discouraging female mobilization.[34] In November 1942, the BBC Controller of Programmes Basil Nicolls issued a directive adding to the list of prohibited topics for comedy, references to '"Blimp" colonels, alcoholic mayors, languid subalterns, and troops who drop their aitches'[35] – though like jokes about Hitler, this was hard to enforce. More positively, with so much Variety now being rebroadcast to troops on the BBC Overseas Services, pejorative ethnic terms in comedy routines were now routinely discouraged.[36]

In February 1944 the Forces Programme joined with the General Overseas Service of the BBC (which had been running its own Forces entertainment schedule) to become the General Forces Programme. This meant that one common service united British forces around the world – and not just British but Empire/Commonwealth and Allied forces – as well as home audiences. The impact of this on BBC comedy was significant. New shows available to home audiences included the hugely popular *Variety Bandbox* and *Merry Go Round*, a Forces-based Variety show that on successive weeks featured Army, Navy and RAF comedy shows from, respectively, 'Studio Stand Easy', with Sergeant Charlie Chester, 'HMS Waterlogged' with RN Sub-Lieutenant Eric Barker, and 'RAF Station Much Binding in the Marsh', with Flight-Lieutenant Richard Murdoch

---

[32] *The People*, 29 November 1942; see too 'US Stars to Pep Up BBC Shows', *Daily Express*, 25 November 1942.
[33] DPP to DV, 22 April 1943, BBC WAC R19/9.
[34] See for instance Frere to BBC, 30 August 1941, BBC WAC R34/727/1.
[35] 'The Modern Army', directive from CP, 28 November 1942, BBC WAC R34/275/1, quoted in Dibbs, *Radio Fun*, 93.
[36] Dibbs, *Radio Fun*, 146–7.

(late of *Band Waggon*) and Wing Commander Kenneth Horne (talent-spotted by the BBC organizing an edition of *Ack-Ack Beer-Beer* at his Anti-Aircraft station). The Home Front and front line now shared a common comedy experience.

'English' humour

One striking feature of wartime radio is the number of pre-war Variety programmes that continued during the war, particularly those already rooted in a sense of nostalgia and tradition. *The Tavern in the Town* and *The Pig and Whistle* (with Charles 'Laughing Policeman' Penrose), for instance, both depicted the comfort of a traditional English pub. From February 1941 a new show, *The Happidrome*, broadcast on Sunday nights from the Grand Theatre, Llandudno, presented an old-fashioned 'family' Variety show before a live audience of war workers and service personnel, featuring acts by established variety stars interspersed with sketches involving the fictional goings-on of the theatre management team.[37] Accounted by some the highest-rated entertainment programme of the war, its appeal was attributed to its unashamed old-fashionedness, its 'English hearty obviousness of humour, and a hearty obviousness of sentiment'[38] (no one picked up on the paradox that it was being broadcast from Wales), its deliberate evocation of happier times, and its avoidance of jokes about the war.[39] Meanwhile, Lancastrian comic Robb Wilton, already famous as Mr Muddlecombe, J. P., unveiled a new character, the hapless elderly Home Guard recruit mocked by his wife and frustrated by the world at large, but muddling through all the same.[40] His monologues, invariably beginning, 'The day war broke out …', made him the second most popular wartime radio comedian after Tommy Handley. Other popular throwbacks to a peacetime 'Englishness' were *Old Mother Riley* (1941–2), *Here in Hogsnorton* (1943), 'a scintillating survey of hebdomadal hearsay' with Gillie Potter,[41] and *The Will Hay Programme* (1944–5), featuring the music-hall and film comedy star in his favourite role as a bumbling headmaster.

These programmes divided critics: some praised them, others compared them unfavourably to the slickness and energy of American radio shows featuring Bob Hope, Jack Benny or Edgar Bergen and Charlie McCarthy that were starting to appear on the BBC Forces Programme, and that – once the American GIs

[37] Foster and Furst, *Radio Comedy*, 63–5.
[38] Grace Wyndham Goldie, *The Listener*, 26 June 1941, 924.
[39] Nicholas, *Echo of War*, 130.
[40] Eric Midwinter, 'Wilton, Robb', *Oxford Dictionary of National Biography*.
[41] Foster and Furst, *Radio Comedy*, 69.

started arriving in force – could be heard by those able to tune into the UK-based American Forces Network. Yet although it became the fashion to compare British comedy unfavourably with American, when scheduled against each other, the audience for Will Hay beat that for Jack Benny by a ratio of three to one.[42] Indeed, the most popular American comedians in Britain during the war remained the cast of a home-grown comedy series, *Hi-Gang!*, Bebe Daniels, Ben Lyon and Vic Oliver (Winston Churchill's American son-in-law), who famously broadcast their show from London throughout the Blitz and after.[43]

Perhaps the most surprising – and in its way most 'British' – hit of the war was *The Brains Trust*, a unique bridging of elite and popular culture that from 1941 became a national radio sensation. Each week, three resident panellists plus two guests drawn from politics, academia or the arts, answered questions of fact and opinion sent in by listeners. These ranged from the philosophical ('Can you define Civilisation?'), the serious ('My son is a prisoner of war. I can send him one book, which should it be?') to the comical ('How does a fly land on the ceiling?') Recorded 'as live' to ensure spontaneity, the programme defied all predictions to become one of the most popular radio entertainments of the war, and the three original panellists, Julian Huxley, Secretary of the Zoological Society of London, Cyril Joad, Professor of Philosophy and Psychology at Birkbeck College, London, and retired seafarer Commander A. B. Campbell, became national celebrities. The programme provided information, entertainment (Campbell, asked to name the most beautiful word in the English language, answered 'paraffin'), and occasionally offence (Joad's answer to a question on the respective merits of Confucious and Plato, for instance, that cited the Confucian aphorism, 'What economy is it to go to bed in order to save candlelight if the result be twins?', prompted an outraged question in the House of Commons[44]). There was nothing quite like it on the radio before or since.

Comedy as propaganda

It was inevitable that the Ministry of Information, and other government ministries, would recognize the possibilities of using comedians and Variety shows to disseminate Home Front propaganda messages. The most successful

---

[42] Maurice Gorham, *Sound and Fury: Twenty-One Years at the BBC* (London: Percival Marshall, 1948), 171.
[43] Nicholas, *Echo of War*, 172.
[44] See *HC Deb*, 378, col 209, 25 February 1942. For more on *The Brains Trust* see Howard Thomas, *Britain's Brains Trust* (London: Chapman and Hall, 1944).

example of the use of comedy for propaganda purposes was probably the cockney housewives Gert and Daisy, Elsie and Doris Waters' longstanding music hall characters, who launched the government's Food Economy campaign in April 1940 with a fortnight of daily five-minute early morning programmes, *Feed the Brute*, that became the basis of the wartime food and cookery programme *The Kitchen Front*. Although *The Kitchen Front* built its reputation largely on the seriousness and authority with which it gave food advice, humour played a valuable part, the programme's most famous presenter, the BBC announcer Freddie Grisewood, cultivating an air of amiable masculine fecklessness in the kitchen, while familiar pre-war comedy characters such as Mrs Feather and Grandma Buggins – and on occasion Gert and Daisy themselves – made regular guest appearances.[45]

In general, John Watt opposed the self-conscious 'infiltration' of propaganda into comedy, believing it merely antagonized audiences.[46] Unfortunately, comedy plugs by variety stars had enormous cachet among Ministerial liaison officers, and Variety producers spent much of their time either trying to fend off demands to incorporate more propaganda messages into their scripts, or, as in the case of the government's 1942 Fuel Economy campaign, making mischief by referring every song lyric mentioning firesides to the Ministry of Fuel and Power for approval.[47]

ITMA: universal gratification

Much has been written about *ITMA (It's That Man Again)* and its wartime appeal.[48] 'The most famous and popular radio comedy series ever,'[49] its hold on wartime Britain was so strong and so deep that it bears closer discussion. Written by Ted Kavanagh, produced by Francis Worsley and starring Liverpudlian comic Tommy Handley, it debuted on the BBC in the summer of 1939, as an attempt to

---

[45] See Nicholas, *Echo of War*, 76–85.
[46] Dibbs, *Radio Fun*, 127–8. See too Nicholas, *Echo of War*, 72, 130.
[47] Nicholas, *Echo of War*, 87.
[48] See Francis Worsley, *ITMA: 1939-1948* (London: Vox Mundi Ltd., 1948); P.J. Kavanagh, *The ITMA Years* (London: Woburn Press, 1974); Foster and Furst, *Radio Comedy*, 27–47; Nicholas, *Echo of War*, 130–2; Briggs, *War of Words*, 564–7; Angus Calder, *The People's War: Britain 1939–45* (London: Jonathan Cape, 1969), 360–2; also Topic Collection 'Radio', Box 3B, Mass Observation Archive. Peter Black, *The Biggest Aspidistra in the World: A Personal Celebration of 50 Years of the BBC* (London: BBC, 1972), 110–20, provides an especially evocative account of the programme's appeal.
[49] Denis Gifford, *The Golden Age of Radio* (London: B.T. Batsford Ltd., 1985), 133.

capture *Band Waggon*'s audience for quick-fire patter and absurdist situations.[50] The original idea was to set it in a government ministry, the Ministry of Universal Gratification and call it *MUG*, but the location was switched to a broadcasting ship loosely modelled on Radio Luxembourg, with the title *It's That Man Again*, a reference to Handley but with added topical resonance, being the phrase adopted by the *Daily Express* to headline Hitler's successive territorial demands.[51] (Thus the very title of the show, which relied as no other on catchphrases, originated as a catchphrase itself.) The first programmes were, however, only a moderate success and gave little indication of the fame that was to come.

In September 1939, Kavanagh, Worsley and Handley reassembled at Bristol and came up with a new setting for the series that would both spoof the war and provide comic relief from the anxieties of the time. Since one of the most frustrating features of the Phoney War was the sudden proliferation of new government ministries with wholly mysterious responsibilities, the new series was set in the Ministry of Aggravation and Mysteries, c/o the Office of Twerps, with Handley its newly appointed Minister.

The new series opener gives a taste of the wordplay that would become a defining feature of the programme:

> Hello Folks! It's Mein Kampf again! Sorry, I should say: Hello, Folks! It's That MAN again! That was a Goebbled version a bit doctored. I usually go all goosey when I can't follow my proper-gander.[52]

Regular characters at this point included secretary Dolly (played by Vera Lennox), charlady Mrs Tickle (Maurice Denham) and the civil servant Fusspot (Jack Train). From the second episode the programme always included an appearance by the elusive enemy spy Funf. Each programme followed a similar pattern. Handley would be trying to set up a new Ministerial initiative of varying absurdity and would be constantly dogged by his minions and their various problems. At some point Funf's voice would interrupt and utter dark threats, initially just over the telephone, then from increasingly improbable locations: a desk drawer, an envelope, a pie. There were musical interludes from a resident band, and a parody commercial from 'Radio Fakenburg'. The comedy

---

[50] See Worsley, *ITMA*, and Kavanagh, *The ITMA Years*. The programme's original model was apparently the American Burns and Allen show – though ironically, as Asa Briggs notes, *ITMA*'s 'Englishness' became seen as its outstanding characteristic. Asa Briggs, *The History of Broadcasting in the United Kingdom, Vol II: The Golden Age of Wireless* (London: Oxford University Press, 1965), 118.
[51] Kavanagh, *The ITMA Years*, 16.
[52] Worsley, *ITMA*, 9.

relied heavily on characters, wordplay and catchphrases (Funf's 'This is FUNF speaking', Mrs Tickle's 'I always do the best for my gentlemen' and Handley's 'I wish I had as many shillings') but also parodied the way that the state intruded on people's lives. In November 1939 the ministry was evacuated to the country, and in the series finale in February 1940 its rural haven was taken over by the Army and the residents despatched in caravans to find a new home, with Funf in pursuit. Over the summer of 1940 the cast toured with a stage version, after which half its cast were called up.

It was over a year before *ITMA* returned to the air, during the summer of 1941. Broadcast now from Bangor, the programme followed the wider trend in BBC comedy to abandon direct parody of wartime conditions and reflect the war experience in other ways. Since the public were currently being urged to take 'Holidays at Home', *ITMA* set out to 'give people the holiday they were missing', abandoning the Ministry of Aggravation for a shabby and inefficient seaside resort called Foaming-At-The-Mouth, with Handley as the Mayor; the series was nominally titled *It's That Sand Again*.

It is this series that established the *ITMA* formula proper. With the bigger cast available at Bangor, the number of regular characters greatly increased. The storylines became even less important: little more than a pretext for an endless procession of characters through Handley's office door, each character with his or her own catchphrase. This series gave the programme Sam Scram, Handley's American henchman ('Boss, boss, sump'n terrible's happened!'), Ali Oop, a dubious Arab pedlar ('You buy nice post-cards'?; 'I go – I come back'), the Commercial Traveller ('*Good* morning, *nice* day'), Claude and Cecil, the brokers' men, who spoke in rhyming couplets and endlessly deferred to each other ('After you, Claude', 'No, after *you*, Cecil'), and the Diver (with his doleful 'Don't forget the Diver, sir', and 'I'm going down now sir'). The following series, which began that autumn, introduced Handley's new Foreign Secretary, Signor So-So (a flamboyant Italian with a shaky grasp of English), and possibly the greatest star of the programme after Handley himself, Mrs Mopp (Dorothy Summers), an ebullient cockney charlady, whose opening line 'Can I do you now, sir', her ever more improbable gifts of food for Handley ('I made this for you, sir'), her dialogue laden with almost-but-not-quite double-entendres, and her sign-off 'Ta-Ta for now' (soon shortened to 'TTFN' and answered by Handley with increasingly convoluted and absurd acronyms of his own), became some of the most inventive and hilarious elements of the show.

In subsequent series the setting remained the seaside, with the resort successively hosting a war factory managed by Handley (no one ever found out what it was producing), then as the war news improved, a spa, then a hotel, then a holiday camp, before the show decamped in late 1943 to run a farm at 'Much Fiddling'. Funf returned in 1942, alongside a new character, the permanently inebriated Colonel Chinstrap – just two ranks higher than Nicoll's prohibited 'alcoholic major'- with his catchphrase 'I don't mind if I do', and the programme was relayed for the first time to British troops in the Middle East and North Africa, shortly before the Battle of El Alamein.[53] In 1943 it became the first radio show to give a Royal Command Performance, on the occasion of Princess Elizabeth's birthday,[54] and was given the accolade of a fixed annual autumn-to-spring run, an unprecedented 35–40 weekly shows a year, and an extraordinary departure from the conventional BBC policy of taking programmes off air 'before audiences tired of them' (a fate that successively befell *Garrison Theatre*, *In Town Tonight* and *Hi-Gang!*) *ITMA* became a stage show, a cartoon strip and a successful feature film in which Handley bought a bombed-out London theatre with the Foaming-At-The-Mouth municipal funds and created chaos trying to run a stage school and produce a musical while staying out of the reaches of his creditors. While the plot was rudimentary, the film gave the most famous *ITMA* characters (all played by their radio performers) convincing visible form, including Sam Scram (frenetic), Ali Oop (lascivious), Claude and Cecil (distinctly camp), the Commercial Traveller (disconcertingly anarchic), Mrs Mopp (glorious in a musical set piece), and, in the film's final joke, the Diver; it also featured incidental jokes about gas masks, the blackout and food rationing, a fleeting reference to Churchill, dancing girls and two musical numbers.[55] In early 1944 *ITMA* also broadcast three special Forces shows, starting with a celebrated Naval Edition live from Scapa Flow.[56] By that autumn some 40 per cent of the population was listening in every Thursday evening on the Home Service, with a Sunday repeat on the Forces Programme gaining audiences of up to 20 per cent.[57]

Was *ITMA* as popular as people remember? All available evidence confirms that as early as the spring of 1940 it was already part of everyday life and language.

---

[53] Foster and Furst, *Radio Comedy*, 37.
[54] Apparently, when Handley explained after the performance that *ITMA* was about to take its summer break, the Queen replied 'I see. You go – you come back'. Black, *Biggest Aspidistra*, 117.
[55] *ITMA* (Walter Forde, Gainsborough Pictures, GB, 1943).
[56] For more on the Forces' Editions, see Worsley, *ITMA*, 36–44.
[57] Figures sampled from BBC Listening Barometers September–November 1944. BBC WAC General Listening Barometers Vol, 11 (July–December 1944). The opening show of the new autumn series (Thursday 21 September) was listened to by almost half the population of the UK (48.3 per cent) with 23.8 per cent tuning into its Sunday repeat. Even assuming repeat listeners, this is a genuinely unprecedented programme reach.

As Tom Harrisson, co-founder of Mass-Observation, who clearly adored the show, wrote in the *New Statesman* in February 1940:

> On the train from Streatham, at two stops the porter greets the guard, 'It's that man again'. A boy rings me, and starts in a terrifying voice, 'This is Funf speaking'. I go to Golders Green pantomime, and hear the simple remark, 'O Mr Funf' bring the house down. Twice I hear working people in pubs stay out of the blue, 'I wish I had as many shillings'. And I overheard a woman in the street say, 'I never go out on Thursdays if I can help it. That's when Itma [sic] is on.'[58]

More remarkable was how intellectuals queued up to praise the programme. Harrisson himself claimed that 'the whole construction of the programme is the nearest thing that the BBC has ever done to surrealism', and sought in his *Observer* radio column to pin down its appeal:

> Written down, it doesn't sound anything special. Perhaps that is the definition of first-class broadcasting – looking dead on paper. Yet I have listened to Itma in every kind of surrounding, on a Corvette, and in a tenement, among miners on strike and with three professors on vacation; I have never known it to fail. All over Britain to-day you may hear people using Handleyisms. RAF pilots seeing a perfect target say to each other over the RT, … 'After you, Claude' – 'No, after *you*, Cecil'. Children with painted faces, wrapped in curtains, begging the tradition of pennies for the May Queen on Merseyside, got me every time with 'Don't forget the diver, sir, don't forget the diver', Lovers love to start their 'phone calls in hollow voice – 'This is Funf speaking'.
>
> I estimate that over these past difficult months, Tommy Handley has contributed more than most Cabinet Ministers towards our morale, without mentioning the war (taboo on Itma) …. What is the secret of Itma's success at so many levels of intelligence. The producer, Francis Worsley, and the comedian, Tommy Handley, assume that their enormous audience don't need to have every joke dished out flat on the plate. And Handley has mastered the magnetic quality of radio – which gives to the few who know how, a unique opportunity to establish intimacy with millions …. Itma has built up a feature truly based on sound, on the interplay and cut in of words the double time of rapid wordfire, so that the listener loses the feeling of listening, floats on a cloud of idle laughter.[59]

The 'rapid wordfire' was correct – Kavanagh apparently aimed to get a hundred jokes into the twenty minutes of dialogue in each show.[60] But the war was

---

[58] Tom Harrisson, draft of article for *New Statesman*, 1 February 1940, Topic Collection 'Radio', Box 3B, Mass-Observation Archive.
[59] Tom Harrisson, 'Radio II', draft of article for *The Observer*, 11 May 1942, FR/1252, Mass-Observation Archive.
[60] Foster and Furst, *Radio Comedy*, 28.

certainly not 'taboo' on *ITMA* – rather, it was the ever-present background that underpinned the humour and that gave the show the chance to demonstrate its topicality, with its scripts finalized sometimes only the day before transmission. The fall of Mussolini in July 1943, for instance, saw the following inserted into the script:

> Sam Scram (rushing in): Boss, Boss, something *wonderful's* happened!
> Tommy: I know. They've got a room ready for him in the Isle of Man![61]

while the Soviet advance in spring 1944 prompted the exchange:

> Signor So-So: Well, Mistair Handlebar, as the French say – Au Revoir!
> Tommy: And as the Russians *now* say – O-dessa![62]

But one of the programme's main strengths was that it rarely addressed the war *directly* – its comedy was rooted in a world that happened to be at war, with the everyday problems associated with wartime restrictions mined for easily identifiable humour. Jokes were made about rationing, red tape, the blackout and 'Careless Talk'. Funf was a joke German spy. The programme's satirical edge was blunt, its irreverence essentially benign.

There were, inevitably, attempts to exploit *ITMA*'s popularity for propaganda ends, such as a 'fuel economy' song, *Polly Take That Kettle Off*, in November 1942 – though the programme more usually made fun of than formally endorsed government campaigns (e.g., 'Do you know what you can do with a carrot?' 'Yes'[63]). Mrs Mopp also appeared in several wartime public information films on clothing care sponsored by Persil washing powder – though on screen, being instructed how to properly wash and dry woollens by a somewhat officious lady instructor, she appeared subdued and lacking her radio persona's subversive energy.[64] She also made a guest appearance on *The Kitchen Front* on Boxing Day 1944. However, the *ITMA* characters did not comfortably exist outside their own universe – listeners were apparently unsure whether the recipe she gave was a serious one or meant as a joke.[65]

---

[61] Worsley, *ITMA*, 34.
[62] Ibid., 43.
[63] Foster and Furst, *Radio Comedy*, 36.
[64] 'Mrs Mopp Asks Why' (1943), https://player.bfi.org.uk/free/film/watch-mrs-mopp-asks-why-1943-online; see also 'Mrs Mopp's Birthday' (1942), https://player.bfi.org.uk/free/film/watch-mrs-mopps-birthday-1942-online, and 'Mrs Mopp Finds Out' (1943).
[65] 'Christmas Programmes 1944', LR/3166, BBC WAC R9/9/9.

ITMA provided war-weary listeners with an exhilarating quick-fire mix of puns, topical allusions and free association, a cast of easily recognizable but benignly treated cultural and ethnic stereotypes, and a delight in playing games with the English language. It was inclusive – to the extent that a cast with never more than two female members at a time can be – and in Tommy Handley it had a host who embodied a positive and provincial classlessness that was unique for its time. But, as noted both then and since, what *ITMA* provided above all was a common vocabulary and common set of catchphrases to frame listeners' wartime lives. To Harrisson's anecdotes can be added the small boy buried under rubble after the Baedecker Raid on Bath who called out to an ARP Warden 'Can you do me now sir?',[66] or the reported deathbed final words, 'TTFN'.[67] It was therefore wholly appropriate that *ITMA* was given pride of place in the Victory broadcasts on 10 May 1945, with a victory edition *V-ITMA*. Tommy Handley had started the war singing *Who Is That Man Who Looks Like Charlie Chaplin?* He ended it leading the cast in a chorus of *We're Glad We Walked Behind the Man Who Smoked The Big Cigar*.

Conclusions

During the war the BBC broadcast more, and more popular, comedy than ever before. Comedy was used initially to reflect the mood of a nation simply coming to terms with being at war. As the war continued, it was used to shrink the enemy down to size, to shore up a nostalgic world of comic pubs and familiar characters, to represent and entertain war work and war workers in and out of uniform and to conjure fantastical worlds through fast word-play and ingenious sound effects.

In his analysis of wartime radio, radio critic (and wartime listener) Peter Black noted, 'Suddenly the wireless began to sound like the nation talking to itself.'[68] One can see this in the wider range of accents evident in Variety broadcasts, in the ways in which working-class comics were no longer the butt but at the centre of jokes. One can also see it in how so many BBC Variety shows were based around the conceit of 'putting on a show': from *Works Wonders* and *Ack-Ack Beer-Beer* to *Merry-Go Round* and even *Happidrome*.

---

[66] Worsley, *ITMA*, 21.
[67] Kavanagh, *The ITMA Years*, 37.
[68] Black, *Biggest Aspidistra*, 95.

But the nation also imported the wireless into its own conversation. Radio humour gave people a common reference point, something to talk about that wasn't the news, something to bind them closer together. Separated families felt closer because they knew they were all listening and laughing to the same radio shows. Virtual strangers at work, or in shelters, could swap catch-phrases.

Comedy, as Andy Medhurst has noted, is perhaps above all about *belonging*:

> Comedy is a brief embrace in a threatening world, a moment of unity in a lifetime of fissures, a haven against insecurity … a chance to affirm that you exist and that you matter. Comedy's consoling fantasy is that however difficult life might be, however, much forces way beyond your control try to rip you to pieces, there can still be moments where – right here, right now – you can join those who are like you in a celebratory rite of communal recognition.[69]

Wartime humour on the radio was less about the jokes themselves (few of which are now remembered, and perhaps fewer understood) than the sense of belonging that they created, the common vocabulary they provided and the common cultural environment they fostered. *ITMA* was the archetypal example: a mix of the familiar (the characters) and the wildly unpredictable (the plots), it parodied the absurdities of wartime life, but never got too painfully close to the war itself, and provided people with a point of conversation. But whether it was Jack Warner's 'Mind my Bike', Dorothy Summers' 'Can I do you now, sir?', Robb Wilton's 'The day war broke out' – or the Brains Trusters Huxley, Joad and Campbell's respective opening gambits, 'Surely …'; 'It depends what you mean by …', and 'When I was in …', they all brought people together in a shared experience.

Elements within the BBC hierarchy were clearly slightly baffled at the comic sensibilities of their audiences. Michael Standing, wartime Head of Outside Broadcasts and Watt's post-war successor as Director of Variety, deplored the standard of the amateur performers on *Works Wonders*, but noted that 'the public takes them to their hearts because they're wearing overalls'.[70] John Watt himself expressed some bemusement at the need to tone down ethnic slurs in comedy routines ('even in fun').[71] When announcing the Christmas 1944 edition of *The Kitchen Front*, BBC Director of Talks, George Barnes, felt it necessary to explain to senior staff that Mrs Mopp was 'a character out of a

---

[69] Medhurst, *A National Joke*, 19.
[70] Dibbs, *Radio Fun*, Chapter 5.
[71] Watt, *Radio Variety*, viii.

programme called ITMA'.[72] As the war drew to a close it became fashionable with surprising speed to deplore the poor quality of wartime radio comedy (excepting *ITMA*) and the simplistic comforts it had offered: once peace came, BBC Variety would have to 'pull up its socks and concentrate sternly on quality rather than quantity'.[73]

However, the BBC's wartime culture of comedy survived the war. True, the peace-time 'demilitarized' spin-offs from *Merry-Go-Round*, *Waterlogged Spa*, *Much Binding in the Marsh* and *Stand Easy*, reverted to a staider peacetime idiom. *Hi-Gang!* evolved into the more domesticated *Life With the Lyons*. Although *ITMA* continued to lead the way, with successive and ever more surreal series (including stints in 'Tomtopia', a far-flung outpost of Empire; a Scottish castle; a return to ministerial government; and a sojourn in 'Henry Hall, the tramps' guesthouse'), it came to an end, abruptly, when on 9 January 1949, after 310 shows and in the middle of its fourteenth series, Tommy Handley died suddenly of a stroke. No one even considered that the programme might continue without him. The nation grieved as one as it had formerly laughed. Thousands of mourners lined his funeral route, thousands more attended memorial services at Liverpool Cathedral and St Paul's Cathedral. As Black notes, 'never before had so many people felt sharply, with a sense of heavy personal loss, the death of a man they had never seen'.[74]

However, the anarchic spirit of the best of wartime radio comedy carried on. *Take It From Here* (1948–60), written by Frank Muir and Denis Norden, respectively a wartime RAF photographer and wireless operator, replaced *ITMA* in the schedules, and similarly framed much of its comedy around appalling puns and deliberately bad jokes. *The Goon Show* (1951–60), whose stars Harry Secombe (a veteran of 'Studio Stand Easy') and Spike Milligan had first met while serving in the Western Desert, took aural slapstick to new and ever more surreal levels. Former Wing-Commander Kenneth Horne, once of *Ack-Ack, Beer-Beer* and *Merry-Go-Round*, would in *Beyond Our Ken* (1958–64) and then *Round the Horne* (1965–8) take the wartime template of character- and catchphrase-driven

---

[72] Barnes memorandum, 1 November 1944, BBC WAC R51/285/5.
[73] Philip Hope-Wallace, *The Listener*, 29 March 1945, 360.
[74] Black, *Biggest Aspidistra*, 119. For the extraordinary public response to Handley's death, see Siân Nicholas, 'Now the War Is over: Negotiating the BBC's Wartime Legacy in Post-War Britain', in Jamie Medhurst, Siân Nicholas and Tom O'Malley (eds.), *Broadcasting in the UK and US in the 1950S: Historical Perspective*s (Newcastle: Cambridge Scholars, 2016), 9–28, 20–2; Topic Collection 'Radio', Box 4D, Mass-Observation Archive; and the reports in all newspapers of his death and funeral.

radio comedy into undreamed-of levels of wordplay and innuendo.[75] If the post-war decades were the 'Golden Age of Radio Comedy',[76] they drew on a template forged by the wartime BBC Variety Department.

Bibliography

Peter Black, *The Biggest Aspidistra in the World: A Personal Celebration of 50 Years of the BBC* (London: BBC, 1972).
Asa Briggs, *The History of Broadcasting in the United Kingdom, Vol II: The Golden Age of Wireless* (London: Oxford University Press, 1965).
Asa Briggs, *The History of Broadcasting in the United Kingdom, Vol III: The War of Words* (London: Oxford University Press, 1970).
BBC Written Archives Centre, Caversham, Reading.
BFI Player, https://bfi.org.uk.
Angus Calder, *The People's War* (London: Jonathan Cape, 1969).
Andrew Crisell, *An Introductory History of British Broadcasting* (London: Routledge, 1997).
Martin Dibbs, *Radio Fun and the BBC Variety Department 1922-67: Comedy and Popular Music on Air* (Basingstoke: Palgrave Macmillan, 2019).
James Dyrenforth and Max Kester, *Adolf in Blunderland* (London: Frederick Muller, 1939).
Andy Foster and Steve Furst, *Radio Comedy 1938-1968* (London: Virgin Publishing, 1996).
Denis Gifford, *The Golden Age of Radio* (London: B.T. Batsford Ltd., 1985).
Eric Midwinter, 'Wilton, Robb', *Oxford Dictionary of National Biography*.
Maurice Gorham, *Sound and Fury: Twenty-One Years at the BBC* (London: Percival Marshall, 1948).
P.J. Kavanagh (ed.), *The ITMA Years* (London: Woburn Press, 1974).
The Listener.
Mass-Observation Archive, University of Sussex, and Mass-Observation Online.
Andy Medhurst, *A National Joke: Popular Comedy and English Cultural Identities* (London: Routledge, 2007).
Siân Nicholas, *The Echo of War: Home Front Propaganda and the Wartime BBC, 1939-45* (Manchester: Manchester University Press, 1996).
Siân Nicholas, 'The People's Radio: The BBC and Its Audience, 1939-45', in Nick Hayes and Jeff Hill (eds.), *Millions Like Us? British Culture in the Second World War* (Liverpool: Liverpool University Press, 1999), 62-92.

---

[75] For detailed and evocative accounts of all these and more post-war BBC comedy series, see Foster and Furst, *Radio Comedy*, passim.
[76] See Dibbs, *Radio Fun*, Chapter 6; Andrew Crisell, *An Introductory History of British Broadcasting* (London: Routledge, 1997), Chapter 4.

Siân Nicholas, 'Now the War Is Over: Negotiating the BBC's Wartime Legacy in Post-War Britain', in Jamie Medhurst, Siân Nicholas and Tom O'Malley (eds.), *Broadcasting in the UK and US in the 1950s: Historical Perspectives* (Newcastle: Cambridge Scholars, 2016), 9–28.

Siân Nicholas, 'Policing Tonal Boundaries: Constructing the Nazi/German Enemy on the Wartime BBC', in Willibald Steinmetz (ed.), *Political Languages in the Age of Extremes* (Oxford: Oxford University Press, 2011), 169–94.

Siân Nicholas, 'Potter, Gillie', *Oxford Dictionary of National Biography*.

J.C.W. Reith, *Broadcast over Britain* (London: Hodder and Stoughton, 1924).

Howard Thomas, *Britain's Brains Trust* (London: Chapman and Hall, 1944).

John Watt (ed.), *Radio Variety* (London: J.M. Dent and Sons Ltd., 1939).

Francis Worsley, *ITMA: 1939–1948* (London: Vox Mundi Ltd., 1948).

5

'I couldn't get a parrot, dear, so I brought a wren!': The British Cartoon Archive and wartime visual culture

Juliette Pattinson

In a wartime illustration by noted cartoonist Giles, two old, short, rotund, bearded men are depicted on guard at the Tower of London holding pike staffs and wearing the distinctive uniform of the Yeoman Guards. They inform two young GIs, recognizable by their oversized jackets, side caps and casual posture of slouching with their hands in trouser pockets, 'Beefeaters? We ain't beefeaters? We live on spam like everybody else.'[1] Joke cartoons such as this, which are reliant on the audience's appreciation of current events and attitudes, distil all the complexities and distinctive features of the social and political landscape into a single graphic drawing. Lawrence Streicher, the first scholar to argue for a conceptual approach to cartoons, noted in 1965 that they are 'a way of catching at a glance the meaning of an event, a person in the news, or a pictorial summary of a current power constellation'.[2] Indeed, a cartoon is more likely to be scanned and the meaning of the visual metaphor immediately absorbed than a lengthy editorial or a column article read and digested.[3] Moreover, as these illustrations have resonance with popular opinion, they encapsulate the spirit of the period. Joke cartoons are particularly useful to the historian of the Second World War as they enable us to examine attitudes towards universal social policies such as rationing and the blackout as well as gauge contemporary gender politics.

My thanks go to Pip Gregory (University of Kent) and Linsey Robb for commenting on the article.

[1] British Cartoon Archive (hitherto BCA), CG/1/4/2/1/73/17, *Laughs on the Home Front*, Compiled by S. Evelyn Thomas (1943) 45.
[2] Lawrence Streicher, 'David Low and the Sociology of Caricature', *Comparative Studies in Society and History*, 8, no. 1 (1965), 1–23.
[3] These were features appreciated by Northcliff when he set up the *Daily Mail*. Dennis Griffiths, *Fleet Street: Five Hundred Years of the Press* (London: British Library, 2006), 145.

Not all cartoons are humorous, however. In addition to joke cartoons, there are cartoons of opinion, which are principally pictorial illustrations of current attitudes in which humour may or may not be a constitutive part.[4] They portray foreign affairs, domestic politics and social themes and depend on the audience's recognition of specific individuals and current news. Political cartoons, such as those by the prolific cartoonist David Low who drew over 13,000 illustrations, often had no hint of humour, as exemplified by the poignant example from December 1942 featuring a cattle truck marked 'JEWS to the slaughter house'.[5] The true impact of cartoons on the audience is invariably impossible to know. With this example however, it is evident that the sentiment it expressed resonated widely and at the highest levels: just three days after publication, eleven governments issued a joint declaration condemning 'in the strongest possible terms this bestial policy of cold-blooded extermination' against Jews and made a 'solemn resolution to ensure that those responsible for these crimes shall not escape retribution'.[6] Cartoons of opinion such as this are explicit propaganda pieces, designed to unify the audience in opposition to an identified foe, whereas joke cartoons are less blatantly propaganda and serve to offer temporary respite from the horrors of total war. This chapter seeks to emphasize the importance of visual culture to an understanding of the British attitude to war through an examination of both cartoons of opinion and joke cartoons. Such cartoons are a rich and fascinating source that enables the historian of the Second World War to examine the ways in which the British public responded to wartime events.

Cartoons have a long history, with early examples of humorous drawings discovered on tombs, papyrus, terracotta figurines, vases and walls in Ancient Egypt, Rome and Greece.[7] Centuries later, innovations in technology resulted in cartoons becoming increasingly more sophisticated and more affordable. The technique of etching, which was developed in the 1500s and involved the inscription of cross-hatched lines onto wax-covered copper plates dipped into acid to produce the effect of background shadows, was replaced around 1800 by lithography, wherein images and text could be duplicated through the

---

[4] Thomas Milton Kemnitz, 'The Cartoon as a Historical Source', *The Journal of Interdisciplinary History*, 4, no. 1 (1973), 81–93. Here 82.
[5] David Low, 'I've settled the fate of the Jews' – "and of Germans", *Evening Standard*, 14 December 1942. See also David Low, *The World at War* (Harmondsworth: Penguin, 1942).
[6] Antony Eden, HC Deb 17 December 1942 vol 385 cc2082-7. The eleven governments were Belgium, Czechoslovakia, Greece, Luxemburg, the Netherlands, Norway, Poland, the United States, the UK, the Soviet Union and Yugoslavia, as well as de Gaulle's French National Committee.
[7] Rania M.R. Saleh, 'Political Cartoons in Egypt', *International Journal of Comic Art*, 9, no. 2 (2007), 187–225.

application of ink to stone surfaces marked with wax crayon. Drawings were sold individually at exorbitant cost and were thus attainable only by the wealthiest of collectors until the launch of a number of affordable satirical publications. Following the success of 'Cartoon No.1 – Substance and Shadow' in July 1843, the *Punch* centrepiece thereafter was called a 'cartoon' as were, subsequently, all line drawings.[8]

Cartoons are an important part of the historian's toolkit, preserving social attitudes and stereotypes that were in circulation at a given time. Writing in 1973, Thomas Milton Kemnitz notes:

> The cartoon has much to offer the historian concerned with public opinion and popular attitudes .... Their value to historians lies in what they reveal about the societies that produced and circulated them ... Joke cartoons ... will provide a rich lode of evidence when historians approach humor as an important and revealing facet of society.[9]

Since then, the value of cartoons as pieces of evidence has been widely recognized. They are regarded by Lucy Caswell as shaping opinion as well as reflecting it, by Mariam Ginman and Sara von Ungern-Sternberg as an effective method of social communication with significant 'impact power' to engage users and by Linus Abraham as offering 'deep reflection' rather than just simply 'passing chuckles' on social issues.[10] They serve multiple functions: as entertainment, to make us laugh; as aggression reducers, providing space to vent; as agenda-setters, honing in on the most important issues of the day; and as framers to distil complex issues into a single image. They are a window into the past[11]: we can decode them for their content, examining both the language in the caption as well as the symbols in the illustration. We can think about the artist, the publication and their intended audience. And we can reflect on their proposed function. Frank Palmeri, however, advises caution, noting that they are not a straightforward 'transparent medium' and they ought not to be read purely for what their overt

---

[8] The original meaning of the word, which comes from the Italian *cartone* and dates to the seventeenth century, referred not to the satirical illustration as in the modern understanding of the word, but to the large sheet of paper on which preliminary sketches were made for a painting. Roy Douglas, 'Cartoons and the Historian', *Historian*, 102 (Summer 2009), 12–18.

[9] Kemnitz, 'The Cartoon as a Historical Source', 86, 81, 83.

[10] Lucy Shelton Caswell, 'Drawing Swords: War in American Editorial Cartoons', *American Journalism*, 21, no. 2 (2004), 13–45; Mariam Ginman and Sara von Ungern-sternberg, 'Cartoons as Information', *Journal of Information Science*, 29, no. 1 (2003), 69–77; Linus Abraham, 'Effectiveness of Cartoons as a Uniquely Visual Medium for Orienting Social Issues', *Journalism and Communication Monographs*, 11, no. 2 (2009), 117–65.

[11] Peter Burke, *Eyewitnessing: The Uses of Images as Historical Evidence* (New York: Cornell University Press, 2001).

message implies.¹² Their meaning is not always self-evident and, as Richard Scully and Marian Quartly note, cartoons neither passively reflect reality nor are passively absorbed by readers.¹³ They object to the 'casual deployment' of a single cartoon extracted from its context and urge the need for a critical reading of the sequence of images of a portfolio, which are always interdependent. These are not value-neutral objective facts but subjective opinion pieces designed to influence.

In the twentieth century, cartoons that featured in British illustrated magazines and newspapers contained strong messages about patriotism, duty and justice. Specific characters replaced abstract symbols of nation such as Britannia and the British Lion: Poy's Cuthbert the cowardly rabbit represented those evading their patriotic duty by hiding in the 'funk holes' of Whitehall in their government posts or in a 'cushy bed' to avoid 'the comb' during the First World War, while Bairnfather's Old Bill, a walrus-moustached, pipe-smoking older Tommy, considered the main enemy to be British Army officers, rather than the Hun.¹⁴ Of the more than 700 different figures drawn by David Low during the inter-war and wartime period perhaps the most recognizable are Joan Bull with her union jack waistcoat and Colonel Blimp, a pompous overweight man with a walrus moustache who made over 300 appearances from April 1934 onwards and was made into a wartime feature film.¹⁵ During the Second World War, cartoons featured a host of ordinary Home Front characters that were very much in keeping with this being a 'people's war', as well as political figures exaggerated to comic effect.¹⁶ One such example was Sidney Strube's Little Man, who embodied a less jingoistic and, to borrow Sonya Rose's term, more temperate mode of masculinity.¹⁷

---

[12] Frank Palmeri, 'The Cartoon: The Image as Critique', in Sarah Barber and Corinna Peniston-Bird (eds.), *History beyond the Text: A Student's Guide to Approaching Alternative Sources* (London: Taylor & Francis, 2009), 32–48. Here 32.

[13] Richard Scully and Marian Quartly, 'Using Cartoons as Historical Evidence', in Richard Scully and Marian Quartly (eds.), *Drawing the Line: Using Cartoons as Historical Evidence* (Clayton: Monash University Press, 2009), 1–13. Here 1.

[14] Francis M. Miley and Andrew F. Read, 'Cartoons as Alternative Accounting: Front-line Supply in the First World War', *Accounting History Review*, 24, no. 2–3 (2014), 161–89.

[15] *The Life and Death of Colonel Blimp* (1943), Dirs. Michael Powell and Emeric Pressburger.

[16] The notion of a 'people's war' was articulated both during the war and subsequently by some historians, albeit recently often critically, to denote that as a result of experiences such as rationing, bombardment and conscription, that this conflict to an unprecedented extent impacted upon all sectors of society and that there was a strong sense of national unity and social cohesion with everyone 'all in it together' and 'doing their bit'. Angus Calder, *The People's War: Britain 1939–1945* (London: Jonathan Cape, 1969).

[17] Sonya O. Rose, *Which People's War? National Identity and Citizenship in Wartime Britain, 1939–1945* (Oxford: Oxford University Press, 2003).

While cartoons are frequently short-lived, designed to be of the moment and then 'condemned to the waste-basket by sundown', many have survived.[18] This is partly due to the British Cartoon Archive, housed at the University of Kent's Special Collections and Archives in the Templeman Library, which is a rich repository of over a century of British cartooning.[19] Runs of *Punch* and *Private Eye* are housed, as well as the work of more than 300 cartoonists. These include contemporary graphic illustrators such as Steve Bell (*Guardian*), the 'saucy postcard' art of Donald McGill, as well as wartime artists such as Poy (Percy Fearon) (*Evening News* and *Daily Mail*), Sidney Strube (*Daily Express*), David Low (*Evening Standard*) and Carl Giles (*Daily Express*). Over 200,000 items are held, including pamphlets, artwork, books, letters, material culture and pocket cartoons (drawings the width of a single column featuring a topical political joke, introduced at the *Daily Express* by Osbert Lancaster in 1939 when paper shortages resulted in daily newspapers reducing to just four pages). The more popular cartoonists such as Low, Lancaster, Pont (Graham Laidler), Vicky (Victor Weisz) and Strube convinced publishers to print collections of their work. These collections have survived while the originals have often been lost. One such piece of ephemera (Figure 5.1) that has survived in remarkable condition is a cardboard pincushion with three reels of cotton wound around the card which features a surprised Hitler bending over with five pins sticking out of his backside and on the reverse a bemused Mussolini with a hypertrophied bottom.[20] This item literally encapsulates the humourist's role of puncturing conceit and deflating pomposity. The Archive holds a large number of British cartoons that blatantly mocked and belittled the enemy.

This chapter uses four distinct case studies, namely depictions of the enemy, Home Front restrictions, the uniformed woman and the civilian man, to explore the ways in which humorous cartoons both reflected and shaped the wartime mood. It also highlights the importance, but hitherto underutilization, of cartoons as a historical source for understanding the minutiae of wartime life. It is to a brief examination of the humorous representation of the enemy in cartoons of opinion that we first turn before shifting our focus more squarely on to the joke cartoon that was widely circulating on the Home Front.

---

[18] Mark Bryant, *World War II in Cartoons* (London: Gab Street Publishing, 1989), 9.
[19] https://www.cartoons.ac.uk/.
[20] BCA, KEM 18/2 Box 43.

Figure 5.1 Hitler and Mussolini pincushion. Courtesy of Richard and Alexander Marengo, British Cartoon Archive, KEM 18/2 Box 43.

Cartoons of opinion: ridiculing the enemy

Caricature was frequently deployed by graphic illustrators, serving as a shorthand to identify immediately recognizable political figures. Ridiculing their appearance and mannerisms undermined the spectre of malevolent power: despots could not possibly have a sense of humour after all. A familiar example of this style is Fougasse's (Cyril Kenneth Bird) popular poster series 'Careless Talk Costs Lives', which featured the distinctive moustache, side parting and brown uniform of Hitler, whose face adorned tea-room walls and public house beer pumps and flasks and who appeared unexpectedly from behind telephone boxes, underneath restaurant tables, out of windows and from within paintings. He was sometimes accompanied by an oversized bemedalled Göring in his Luftwaffe uniform. These propaganda posters were designed to use humour to remind the public to be discrete in order to influence behaviour.

While not all political cartoons of opinion were humorous as previously noted, those that were, were often anti-authoritarian and explicitly satirized high-ranking Nazi officials for comic effect. Drawings included in a collection of Soviet cartoonist Boris Efimov's work, published in 1944 by a London publishing house and subsequently archived at the British Cartoon Archive, consistently ridiculed Goebbels's height. Under the title 'The Colossus of Aryan thought', with the caption 'full-length portrait of "Reichminister of Propaganda"

Dr Goebbels', a diminutive Goebbels, held up to the microphone by Hitler, has swastikas blasting out of his mouth and his face is distorted with anger.[21] Similarly, a 1941 Efimov cartoon, captioned 'Pictorial Presentation of the True Aryan', noted 'According to Fascist race-theory the genuine Aryan must be blond like Hitler', which is juxtaposed with a caricature of a black-haired, dark-skinned Hitler wearing rather camp high-heeled boots. Equally, he ought to be 'slim like Göring', which contrasts with the parody of him as morbidly obese in his highly decorated uniform and a bright red face as if he is about to suffer a heart attack and 'beautiful like Goebbels', who assumes the appearance of a tiny Mickey Mouse standing on a stool, with an elongated skull, receding hairline and green skin. By making national leaders the butt of his humour, ascribing deficiencies and embellishing them to comic effect, Efimov, like Fougasse, turned the to-be-feared into the ridiculous thus removing the sting.

Drawings by Kimon Evan Marengo, a Cairo-born Anglo-Greek cartoonist whose artwork, under the pen name KEM, appeared in the *Daily Herald* and the *Daily Telegraph*, also used this device.[22] While working for the Ministry of Information (the domestic propaganda branch of the Government) and the Political Warfare Executive (a secret service that spread propaganda and disinformation to the enemy using rumour campaigns, leaflet drops, radio broadcasts and clandestine publications), KEM produced a storyboard (Figure 5.2), now held by the British Cartoon Archive, comprising rudimentary line drawings in pen for an animated film entitled *Adolf and His Donkey Benito*.[23] Hitler is depicted as maniacal and wildly gesticulating, shouting 'I belong to a superior race ... I am a super man. I shall rule the world.' Having saluted and shouted 'Heil Adolf!', he turns around, points at himself and says 'that's me'. It is a deliberately ludicrous, over-the-top depiction, not dissimilar to that seen in more recent representations such as *Jojo Rabbit* (2019).[24] The hyperbole is recognized for what it is, which accentuates the humour and serves to neutralize the threat of tyranny that he embodied. Hitler is thwarted in his attempt to conquer the world as various modes of transport, including car, aeroplane, ship and horse, are each unavailable. A braying donkey is a crude anthropomorphic representation, replete with blackshirt, of the Italian leader: 'Benito, the greatest

---

[21] BCA, NC 1763.W3, Boris Efimov, *Hitler and His Gang: Cartoons by Boris Efimov* (London: Alliance Press, 1944), 9.

[22] Will Dyson of the *Herald* did this repeatedly in the First World War, although his focus was invariably domestic enemies (including profiteers) rather than foreign ones.

[23] BCA, KEM 7. On behalf of the PWE, KEM produced an Arabic-language cartoon booklet of the same title featuring eighteen black-and-white illustrations which was disseminated in a British-controlled publication in Bahrain in 1942. The National Archives, FO 898/128, 'Propaganda Activities, Leaflet Translations (Arabic)'.

[24] *Jojo Rabbit* (2019), Dir. Taika Waititi.

donkey in the Mediterranean!' They agree to work together to conquer the world, while secretly plotting to overthrow the other once victory is secured: 'I'll kick him so hard that he won't dare to lift his head again'; 'I'll see that this donkey gets his due'. Victory eludes them as they are left seasick and unable to cross the Mediterranean Sea, a reference to Allied victories in that theatre of war including Taranto in November 1940 and Cape Matapan in March 1941. KEM deployed this same image of Benito the inept donkey in his 1941 Christmas card, distributed among friends and business contacts: subtitled 'Mare ... mostrum', a play on 'our sea', it depicts the donkey trying to scramble onto the wreckage of a boat, with a leg and an ear in bandage and his trident broken.[25]

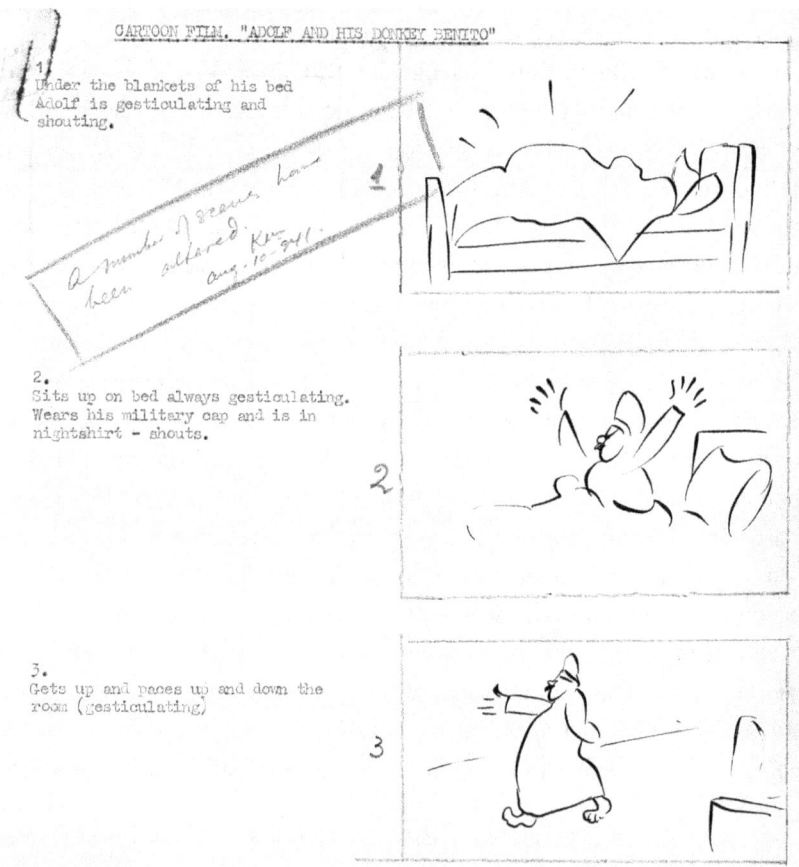

Figure 5.2 Storyboard for *Adolf and His Donkey Benito*. Courtesy of Richard and Alexander Marengo, British Cartoon Archive, KEM 7.

[25] BCA, KEM Christmas Cards Box 4.

A further example of mocking the enemy's national leaders through an animalistic depiction is KEM's 1943 Christmas card.[26] He drew an inflated Churchill sucking on his iconic cigar, Stalin smoking his pipe and Roosevelt with a cigarette holder, each with their claw-like hands poised to wring the neck of a scrawny, bald Hitlerite bird, which is shedding its feathers in panic. The heraldic eagle which had represented the German nation had been replaced by something resembling a plucked turkey.[27] The insinuation was that Germany was on the run in various theatres of war. Having considered some humorous examples of the political cartoon of opinion that derided the enemy, let us now turn our attention to the joke cartoon.

Joke cartoons: satirizing the Home Front

While cartoons of opinion frequently feature immediately identifiable political figures, joke cartoons on the other hand rarely refer to specific individuals; they tend to depict composites that embody stereotyped stock figures: the hen-pecked husband, the archaic elderly gentleman, the battle-axe, the voluptuous temptress, the dumb blonde. These one-dimensional caricatures also serve to perpetuate cultural stereotypes.[28] Unlike political cartoons, there is a colloquial feel to these illustrations as they generally include dialogue by a featured character that lends an informality and accessibility to the cartoon. The 'Careless Talk Costs Lives' series referred to above is a case in point: the colourful minimalist drawings of gossipy middle-aged women on the bus or taking afternoon tea, verbose older men at the bar, in a gentleman's club, in a telephone box or on the train, chatty couples out for dinner or walking the dog and indiscreet young servicemen talking in the street are surreptitiously overheard by Nazi leaders as they conspiratorially note '… but for Heaven's sake don't say I told you!', '… but of course it mustn't go any further', 'Heaven's no … I wouldn't tell a soul!', 'Of course there's no harm in your knowing'. The colloquial language, combined with the ordinary everyday characters that were a staple of the people's war, drives the humour in the joke cartoon. This section examines the comic sketches and humorous text produced about daily life on the Home Front. Such cartoons are a medium of communication, one which conveys its message more speedily than a film, a radio

[26] BCA, KEM Christmas Cards Box 4.
[27] Various cartoonists had depicted the German eagle as plucked and pathetic during the First World War.
[28] Michael Pickering, *Stereotyping: The Politics of Representation* (Basingstoke: Palgrave, 2001).

broadcast or a piece of prose. And unlike a joke (a short story which unfolds with a punch line, the comic ending anticipated by the listener), a cartoon's humour is immediately apparent, the text and illustration working in tandem to constitute the joke. Indeed, the interaction of the caption with the drawing is what creates the humour – one without the other would simply not work.

This mix of verbal and visual humour is apparent in a 'world famous humour series' used in the remainder of this chapter. S. Evelyn Thomas compiled throughout the war and in the immediate aftermath a series of twenty volumes featuring black-and-white cartoons that had appeared in various publications, including *Punch*, *Blighty* and *London Opinion*, with new added material such as short gags and longer stories. They sold for 1 shilling 3 pence (the equivalent today of about £2.50), 1 shilling 6 pence (£3) or 2 shillings 6 pence (£5).[29] Taking on board Scully and Quartly's urge to examine the entire portfolio of work rather than a single cartoon, these twenty anthologies housed at the British Cartoon Archive have been closely examined, the contents of which have been carefully selected by Thomas to serve a particular function.[30] With no sales figures available it is difficult to note how popular these compilations were, or to discern exactly who was reading them, although a poster advertising the full series noted 'many millions sold'. They were likely to have been shared widely, so readership would have been much higher than actual sales. The male editor selected cartoons drawn by male illustrators who likely had a largely male audience in mind. Indeed, much of the material is gentle sexual innuendo. For example, 'During a heavy air raid on London, a Warden ran up to the entrance of a public shelter, peered in and called out: "Are there any expectant mothers in there?" After a brief pause, a feminine voice replied: "Hard to say, we've only been down here a few minutes."'[31]

The front cover image of *Laughs on the Home Front* by Giles sets the tone for the contents: a man tasked with camouflaging a tank is distracted by two attractive women wearing short dresses with cinched–in waists and revealing shapely legs. As they walk past him in the hangar, he unwittingly spray-paints

---

[29] BCA, CG/1/4/2/1/73/5, *Humours of ARP*; CG/1/4/2/1/73/13, *Laughs with the RAF*; CG/1/4/2/1/73/10, *Laughs with the Forces*; CG/1/4/2/1/73/17, *Laughs on the Home Front*; CG/1/4/2/1/73/14, *Laughs with the Workers*; CG/1/4/2/1/73/4, *Good Humour Annual*; CG/3/1/1/77/12, *Laughs with the Navy*; CG/1/3/2/2, *RAF Parade*; CG/1/4/2/1/73/1, *Good Humour magazine*; CG/1/4/2/1/73/16, *More Laughs with the Forces*; CG/1/4/2/1/73/11, *Laughs with the Law*; CG/1/4/2/1/73/8, *Laughs While you Travel*; CG/1/4/2/1/73/15, *Many Happy Returns*; CG/1/4/2/1/73/9, *Laughs with the Busy Bodies*; CG/1/4/2/1/73/6, *Laughs Along the Lines*; CG/2/3/1/31/1, *Laughs around the Land*.

[30] Scully and Quartly, 'Using Cartoons as Historical Evidence', 1.

[31] BCA, *Laughs on the Home Front*, 2.

the foreman instead. Such compilations offered their readers a pleasing diversion and could be picked up for a quick perusal on a break from work. Humour took many forms in these publications: there were quips, riddles, doggerel, aphorisms, wit, word-play, spoonerisms, mispronunciations, catchwords, puns, slogans, irony, satire, allusion, parody, limericks and rhymes. They contain observational humour, incongruous juxtaposition, slapstick, hyperbole and pastiche. The humour within the publications had to resonate with a very broad-based audience and was intended to be inoffensive and cathartic.

Humour revels in the moment. Indeed, cartoonists took inspiration from everyday wartime life: mundane regulations and new ways of living which were stoically endured became the source of inspiration including the blackout, gasmasks, rationing and air raid shelters. In turn, cartoons provided temporary relief from the routine, the boredom, frustration, tension and anxiety. 'However, black the black-out, however weak our tea, there is always a bright side', noted Evelyn Thomas in the preface to *Humours of ARP*.[32] Topicality was thus a key part of their success. An example of timely observational comedy is Lawrence Siggs's cartoon published in *Lilliput* magazine, which references the Spitfire fund, in which pots and pans were donated. On a factory conveyor band, a plane is disassembled and turned back into household items: 'I know what it is – somebody's reversed the confounded band.'[33] The recognizable everyday recycling habit, in which over five million tons of scrap metal were collected, is reconfigured for comic effect.[34]

Wartime strictures were often satirized by humourists. A *Punch* cartoon references widespread food shortages by depicting a waiter informing a diner who is perusing a menu, 'May I strongly recommend the boiled beef and carrots, Sir? We've run out of everything else.'[35] The comedy here is derived from the wry recognition of a near universal comic script, a familiarity that is lampooned: rationing and shortages were common currency which meant that everybody would 'get the joke'. Another *Punch* cartoon alludes to the self-sufficiency drive of 'Digging for Victory' and the turning over of gardens to edible produce. With the front lawn brimming with a variety of vegetables, an office worker is compelled to use a winch and pulley contraption to get from the front door

---

[32] BCA, CG/1/4/2/1/73/5, *Humours of ARP*, 1.
[33] BCA, *Laughs on the Home Front*, 33.
[34] Ministry of Information, *What Britain Has Done, 1939–1945: A Selection of Outstanding Facts and Figures* (Ministry of Information, 1945), 122.
[35] David Langdon, 'May I Strongly Recommend the Boiled Beef and Carrots, Sir? We've Run out of Everything Else', *Punch*, 202, no. 5270, 4 March 1942. Also featured in *Laughs on the Home Front*, 21.

of his house, where his wife waves him off to work, to the pavement where he tells a bemused gent in a bowler hat, 'Yes, I'm devoting every inch of space to food production this year.'[36] The cartoon picks up on the absurdities of everyday life imposed under conditions of total war, as well as invokes cartoonist Heath Robinson's farcically complex gadgets.[37]

It was not only food that was in short supply: clothes rationing was introduced in June 1941, limiting the number of new clothes that could be purchased. This was to reduce pressure on the clothing and retail industries which had experienced significant decreases in staff numbers as employees were directed into war-work and were prioritizing the manufacture of uniforms. The government launched a 'Make Do and Mend' campaign to encourage frugality. The impact of such restrictions was satirized in visual form. Tom Cottrell's cartoon for *Blighty*, the official armed services magazine in the First World War that was relaunched during the Second World War and on whose editorial board Cottrell served, features a housewife holding a pair of black trousers, standing in front of a table laden with needle, thread and scissors, and a petulant seaman. He is wearing belted drainpipe trousers with neither turn-ups nor a zip and is bulging out of his tight tunic with the sleeves half way up his forearms, revealing oversized hands covered with anchor tattoos. 'I cut your baggy pants down to the new "utility" size, and save eight coupons by making myself some "slacks" out of the waste material, and you carry on like a lunatic. I wish your shipmates could see you now!'[38] The Utility clothing scheme referred to in the caption was introduced in 1942 and ensured that fabric was used sparingly with minimal frills. The number of pockets, shirt lengths and the size of lapels were all restricted, double-breasted suits were replaced by single-breasted ones and trouser turn-ups and double cuffs were prohibited, saving annually about five million square metres of cotton. However, this scheme was not popular and the seaman's irritable expression speaks to that frustration. Cartoons presented an opportunity to express frustration, to gripe against new regulations in a way that did not threaten to destabilize or demoralize.

All of these examples reveal that humour is dependent on shared understanding between the humourist and the audience.[39] The cartoonist starts

---

[36] A.E Beard, 'Yes, I'm Devoting Every Inch of Space to Food Production This Year', *Punch*, 200, no. 5223, 23 April 1941. Also featured in *Laughs on the Home Front*, 22.

[37] Cecil Hunt, *Heath Robinson's Home Front: How to Make Do and Mend in Style* (Oxford: Bodleian, 2015).

[38] BCA, *Laughs with the Navy*, 39.

[39] Scott McCloud, *Understanding Comics: The Invisible Art* (New York: HarperCollins, 1994), 24–59, 94–117.

from the presumption that their audience will know the meaning instantly and are able to apply to their reading the necessary background information to fill in the gaps. An example of this is a Giles cartoon depicting a train station. The audience immediately gleans from various visual clues that the setting for the drawing is a rural Welsh village: although only the first few letters of the station sign are visible, the place name begins 'Llwa', still entirely legible despite being crossed out to hinder the enemy in case of invasion. Leeks have been planted in the foreground, the pastoral backdrop of steep valleys is littered with sheep, and a woman, clutching a pig under one arm and a basket and sack under the other, is dressed in the traditional rural Welsh costume (a gown, underskirt, shawl, apron and broad-rimmed tall hat) worn by wives and daughters of farmers going to market to sell their produce. The station master, who points to a board asking 'Is your journey really necessary?', notes 'Well Mrs Evans – is it?'[40] To work, cartoons like this one have to be comprehensible to the audience, who bring to the drawing their own awareness of particular assumptions. The audience derives satisfaction from understanding the illustration. Some cartoons that I examined in preparation for writing this chapter I simply failed to comprehend; so much goes unsaid and I did not have the requisite knowledge or contextual frames of reference needed to decode them. In the remainder of this chapter I want to explore the cartoon as the battleground of gender politics by analysing depictions of the uniformed woman and the civilian man.

The masculinized woman and the hyper feminine soldier: drawing the uniformed woman

Britain went further than any other nation in conscripting 'womanpower'. The Registration for Employment Order in 1941 prompted David Low to draw a cartoon of opinion for the *Evening Standard* featuring the Minister of Labour waiting with flowers underneath a clock tower as if to embark on a blind date.[41] Additionally, the passing of the National Service (No. 2) Act compelled single women aged between twenty and thirty to undertake war work. Women entered industry, the services or civilian defence in large numbers. As the war developed into a protracted total war, the age range was later extended and married women were also liable for conscription depending on the age of their dependents. Of

---

[40] BCA, *Laughs on the Home Front*, 5.
[41] David Low, 'Ernie Bevin Meets His Girl', *Evening Standard*, 19 March 1941.

the 16 million women aged between fourteen and fifty-nine, 7.1 million had been mobilized by June 1944, 467,000 of whom joined the auxiliary services.[42] The uniformed servicewoman, who donned the khaki uniform of the Auxiliary Territorial Service or the blue uniform of the Women's Auxiliary Air Force and Women's Royal Naval Service, and the overalled female industrial worker were signifiers of changing times and were powerful symbols of modernity. This, after all, was a total war in which all resources were fully mobilized, including womanpower. The adoption of clothing previously tagged as male, such as uniform and overalls, and the new skills developed by women were a rich seam for cartoonists to mine.

In the First World War, the appropriation of clothing worn typically by men meant that uniformed women were regarded as subversive, defying established gender distinctions and 'burlesquing our sex'.[43] Accordingly, she was often met with hostility, accused of 'apeing the bearing of soldiers', dishonouring the king's uniform and negating her own femininity by 'glor[ying] in her grotesque and spurious manhood'.[44] Such concerns about the defeminizing consequences of uniform did not animate commentators in the same way in the Second World War, who generally saw the servicewoman as a model of patriotic femininity. Indeed, manufacturers recognized the selling power of the uniformed woman and used her image to sell products such as Weetabix breakfast cereal and Macleans toothpaste.[45] However, the perception of the servicewoman as either a promiscuous heterosexual on the hunt for a soldier, or as a 'mannish', 'Amazonian' lesbian, who wished to wear men's clothing and behave in a manner more typically regarded as male, that Lucy Noakes identifies in the First World War, persisted into the Second and fuelled the imaginations of cartoonists.[46] Because of the adoption of male clothing and occasional performances of manliness, some cartoonists inferred something about uniformed women's sexual identities. A quip that was published in *Laughs with the Navy* noted, 'Two pretty Wrens met in the street and kissed affectionately. Two sailors on leave observed the

---

[42] *What Britain Has Done, 1939–1945*, 13.
[43] 'Matron', *Morning Post*, 19 July 1915.
[44] 'Women in Khaki', *Ladies Pictorial: A Fashion and Society Paper for the Home,* 21 August 1915. Krisztina Robert 'All That Is Best of the Modern Woman'? Representations of Female Auxiliaries in British Popular Culture, 1914–1919', in Jessica Meyer (ed.), *British Popular Culture and the First World War* (Leiden: Brill, 2008), 71–93.
[45] 'Keep War workers fighting fit. On a man's job and equal to it' and 'Did you Maclean your teeth today? Yes, I keep it up' both feature WAAF barrage balloonists.
[46] Lucy Noakes, '"A Disgrace to the Country They Belong to": The Sexualisation of Female Soldiers in First World War Britain', *Revue: Literature, History of Ideas, Images and Societies of the English Speaking World*, 6, no. 4 (2008), 11–26.

encounter, so one of them turned to his friend and said morosely: "you know, that's another thing I don't approve about this ruddy war." "Wocher mean?" asked the other. "Women always doin' men's work'" was the cryptic reply.[47]

Clothing is so distinctly gendered that women's adoption of martial uniform increasingly distanced them from conventional female attire and visually aligned them with men in the armed services, and thereby served to both militarize and masculinize its female wearers. The woman who adopted male dress was, notes Alison Oram in her analysis of the media representation of women who passed as men, the 'focus for contemporary puzzling over gender'.[48] The masculinizing effects of donning uniform, rather than a cause for alarm as in the First World War, provided ripe material for cartoonists working during the later war who revelled in poking fun at the possibilities for gender disruption. Cartoons illuminated underlying attitudes and gently rebuked women's donning of military attire, depicting martial women in big boots and short back and sides.[49] Pitts's drawing published in monthly magazine *London Opinion and Today* (Figure 5.3) portrays a self-assured, socially elite woman in her sixties in ATS uniform sporting a moustache and a monocle, is lighting her own cigarette, holding an alcoholic drink and is leaning manfully against the fireplace. 'The army HAS made a difference to you, dear', notes her husband.[50] This new mode of wartime femininity, made possible by the appropriation of menswear, is suggestive of what Jack Halberstam calls 'female masculinity' in that the cartoon depicts a merging of gender characteristics while simultaneously maintaining the status quo of binary sexes.[51] The privileged background, referenced in the cartoon by the portrait of a medalled older man and the husband's white bow tie and tails, reassured and alleviated any concerns about the challenges to normative femininity.

The masculinized uniformed woman was a common motif in the Jane cartoon strip that appeared in the *Daily Mirror* between 1932 and 1959. Jane mistakenly calls a uniformed woman named Betty 'sir', while Thelma, the wife of a Colonel to whom Jane becomes chauffeur, is an overweight battle-axe in uniform.[52] In

---

[47] BCA, *Laughs with the Navy*, 47.
[48] Alison Oram, *Her Husband Was a Woman! Women's Gender-Crossing in Modern British Popular Culture* (London: Routledge, 2007), 37.
[49] BCA, CG/3/1/1/77/12, *Laughs with the Navy*, 'I hear, Lieutenant, that you were speaking lightly of a man's name in the mess to-night', 34.
[50] BCA, *Laughs on the Home Front*, 3.
[51] Jack Halberstam, *Female Masculinity* (Durham, NC: Duke University Press, 1998). Halberstam's concept has been critiqued for validating the very binary it strives to deconstruct.
[52] BCA, 2/79/D, Norman Pett, *Jane at War: The Original and Unexpurgated Adventures of the British Secret Weapons of World War Two. Jane of the Daily Mirror* (London: Wolfe Publishing Ltd., 1976), 10 September 1939; 11 September 1939.

Figure 5.3 British Cartoon Archive, CG/1/4/2/1/73/17, *Laughs on the Home Front*. Compiled by S. Evelyn Thomas (1943), 3.

contrast to Betty and Thelma, Jane is in no danger of being defeminized by donning martial dress upon joining the WAAF. Rather, her skirt flies up for inspection by the male Commodore.[53]

While the masculinized woman in khaki was a common feature in cartoons, so, too, was the hyper feminine wearer of uniform, as symbolized by Jane. *Men Only*, a pocket-sized humorous magazine launched in 1935 with the first editorial proudly asserting, 'We don't want women readers. We won't have

---

[53] BCA, 2/79/D, Norman Pett, *Jane at War*, 10 October 1940.

women readers' and containing articles on 'current male topics', fiction, jokes, advertisements and black and white plates of female nudes, featured a cartoon of an attractive young woman rebelling against regulations. The cartoon recasts the uniformed body in highly feminine terms: she has a narrow waist, slender legs and a uniform skirt hitched up high above the knees to reveal glimpses of the petticoat underneath and is berated by a featureless tall, thin older woman with her skirt at regulation length while another woman, with a thick waist and plump calves, looks on disapprovingly: 'But suppose we ALL wore our skirts above the – er – "Plimsoll Line" as it were!'[54] This depiction emphasized the continuity of normative gender relations, working to smooth over anxieties about female masculinization by representing the 'innate' femininity beneath the uniform. Simultaneously it spoke to patronizing concerns about frivolous, vain women undertaking vital war work. Another cartoon features a glamorous young recruit of the Women's Royal Naval Service (WRNS) wearing non-regulation skirt and hair length. A middle-aged seaman has his arm wrapped around her and informs his perplexed wife, 'I Couldn't Get a parrot, Dear, so I Brought a Wren!'[55] Affectionately called wrens, members of the WRNS were the subject of disparaging comments that alluded to the perceived promiscuity of servicewomen, such as 'Up with the lark, to bed with a wren'.[56]

It was not only the adoption of uniform that fuelled cartoonists' imaginations: servicewomen's militarization through martial training was also a rich source of humour and the focus of several comic illustrations. A Frank Reynolds cartoon published in *Punch* for example depicts a young woman in smart military uniform in a domestic setting performing an offensive manoeuvre on her father. He is hoisted over her back as if to be thrown down on to the floor, his bald head trapped underneath her arm and his pipe falling to the ground as she tightly squeezes his wrist. She enthusiastically exclaims to two female onlookers, 'Look, Mummy! This is the one they teach us!'[57]

While the servicewoman was often depicted for comic effect as either displaying manly tendencies or appearing hyper feminine, the young woman

---

[54] BCA, *Laughs with the Navy*, 10. Devised by British shipping reformer Samuel Plimsoll in the 1860s following the loss of a number of ships due to overloading, the Plimsoll line is a circle with a horizontal line through it on a merchant ship's hull marking the maximum depth to which it could be safely immersed when loaded with cargo. It was made law in Britain in 1876 and adopted by over fifty maritime countries in 1930.
[55] BCA, *Laughs with the Navy*, 42.
[56] They were not the only ones to be the butt of such jokes: ATS and WAAF members were 'officers' groundsheets' while members of the Women's Land Army 'worked with their backs to the land'.
[57] Frank Reynolds, 'Look, Mummy! This Is the One They Teach Us!', *Punch*, 17 June 1942, 202 no. 5286. Also featured in BCA, *Laughs on the Home Front*, 8.

out of uniform permitted a wider range of representations. She was the ditzy war worker, as in a cartoon that featured a young woman worriedly looking at a huge pile of shell cases while the foreman asks her 'Have you any idea in which one you think you might have dropped your engagement ring, Miss Pringle?'[58] She was the feminine industrial worker flexing her impressively muscular biceps and quipping that she and her husband no longer argue.[59] She was the confident young woman irately complaining on the telephone, 'You know perfectly well what calibre I ordered', when confronted with a delivery of large artillery shell cases for a fairground shooting attraction.[60] She was the young sultry fifth columnist, depicted by Giles in July 1944 with a somewhat French appearance.[61] Alternatively, she was the heavily made-up temptress, as frequently drawn by Scottish cartoonist Arthur Ferrier, whose pin-ups of leggy blondes proved popular with readers of a range of illustrated publications.[62] As with the saucy seaside postcard, popular in the 1930s, with their pun-filled, tongue-in-cheek bawdy humour and double entendres and featuring hen-pecked scrawny husbands and busty women, the mild sexual innuendo of wartime cartoons speak to a culture that firmly regulated sex but which simultaneously was witnessing a loosening of the strict moral code.[63] As George Orwell noted of McGill's work, 'these pictures lift the lid off a very widespread repression.'[64] Yet this was only ever a temporary release, and one in which sexual inhibitions were by no means tested. While considered daring in the 1940s, these illustrations appear extremely tame to modern audiences.

The emasculated man: drawing the older civilian male

Like the woman who pushed against conventional gender boundaries by serving in the military, the man who remained on the Home Front offered myriad opportunities for humour. This is because of the potent societal expectation that

---

[58] BCA, *Laughs on the Home Front*, 47.
[59] BCA, CG/1/4/2/1/73/14, *Laughs with the Workers*, 'I only wish I'd had a job like this years ago. My husband and I never quarrel now', 30.
[60] BCA, *Laughs on the Home Front*, 25. First appeared in *Blighty*.
[61] BCA, CG/2/1/1/237/20, *The Journalist* (1944), 'PSSTT! She's been reading the Sunday Pic!' This British newspaper had been featuring sensationalist tales of pro-Nazi female snipers in Occupied France.
[62] The *Sunday Pictorial*, for example, published his titillating glamour drawings under the heading 'Our Dumb Blonde' between 1939 and 1946. BCA, *Laughs on the Home Front*, 43.
[63] See George Orwell, 'The Art of Donald McGill', in *Collected Essays, Journalism and Letters Volume 2* (London: Heinemann, 1961).
[64] Orwell, 'The Art of Donald McGill', 188.

men of conscription age would enter the services. Indeed, the serviceman was held in very high regard. The primacy of the uniformed man, what R. W. Connell would term 'hegemonic masculinity', positioned him hierarchically above other forms of maleness.[65] Servicemen were often depicted in cartoons in a hyper masculine way, with the stereotype of the sailor as a ladies man deployed frequently. In a Tom Cottrell illustration for example, two burly sailors are in a pub, one of whom is drinking with a woman and the other is surrounded by four attentive civilian women, each holding a small glass of port. The humour is derived from turning around the well-known maritime phrase, with the quip 'His idea is a port in every girl!'[66] Much of what makes this cartoon work, at least to contemporary audiences, if not current ones, is the element of surprise. Scholars of humour call this incongruity[67]: the humour lies in the dissonance between what is expected by the reader and what they see. The ambiguity deliberately leads the audience in one direction and then bamboozles them with the unanticipated. It is in the double meaning that the humour can be found. While there are glimpses of the civilian man depicted in a similarly caddish way, the humour is generated by the assumption that the audience will ascribe a somewhat lesser status to the man on the Home Front. A 1941 *Punch* cartoon for example shows a street scene in which a well-dressed woman says to her male companion dressed in ARP uniform, '... and I suppose you've got a girl in every air-raid shelter?'[68]

There was much less cultural disapprobation of civilian men in the Second World War than the earlier war, in which the masculinity of the civilian man aged within the call-up range was relentlessly challenged by cartoonists and concerns about 'shirkers' 'hiding' and lying low were rife.[69] In the Second World War, there was much wider appreciation of the importance of skilled labour in fighting a protracted war.[70] Accordingly, humorous depictions of the civilian man in the later war were invariably portraying those over the age of conscription. Representations of the Home Front male in poster series such as 'Dig for Victory' and 'Coughs and Sneezes Spread Diseases' frequently depicted the civilian man as middle-aged or elderly and rather comically as either puny or

[65] R. W. Connell, *Masculinities* (Cambridge: Polity Press, 1995).
[66] BCA, *Laughs with the Navy*, 44.
[67] Simon Critchley, *On Humour* (London: Routledge, 2002), 2–3.
[68] '... and I suppose you've got a girl in every air-raid shelter?', *Punch*, 30 April 1941, 200 no. 5224. Also featured in BCA, *Laughs on the Home Front*, 40.
[69] BCA, PF0001-0842, Poy, 'Sketch Map of the Funk Hole of London', *Evening News*, 27 October 1916; Juliette Pattinson, '"Shirkers", "Scrimjacks" and "Scrimshanks"?: British Civilian Masculinity and Reserved Occupations, 1914–45', *Gender and History*, 28, no. 3 (2016), 709–27. Here 714.
[70] Juliette Pattinson, Arthur McIvor and Linsey Robb, *Men in Reserve: British Civilian Masculinities in the Second World War* (Manchester: Manchester University Press, 2017).

rotund, while cartoons often drew him wearing glasses and with a bald head.⁷¹ The fragile positioning of the older male civilian, portrayed as a somewhat pitiful figure, is evident in a *Punch* cartoon (Figure 5.4). Two disapproving middle-aged women are observing a queue in which a short bald man is being crushed by twelve sturdy women who loom large over him, the umbrella of one pressing into his cheek. One notes, 'Pore lil' feller – I told Emily when she went into munitions he'd never make a shopper.'⁷²

In a twist on the notion of women as a reserve army of labour that in wartime are brought into the labour market to fill the vacuum left by men who joined the services, satirists depicted men having to step into the void created by women departing the home and moving into new roles. Male domesticity was a frequent source of amusement, with civilian men shown knitting, laying the table,

PUNCH *or The London Charivari* September 3 1941

"Pore lil' feller—I told Emily when she went into munitions that he'd never make a shopper."

Figure 5.4 'Pore lil' feller – I told Emily when she went into munitions he'd never make a shopper', *Punch*, 3 September 1941, 201: no. 5243, 218. Courtesy of TopFoto.

---

⁷¹ See, for example, BCA, CG/1/4/2/1/73/14, *Laughs with the Workers*, 'Cleaning a Railway Engine', 4.
⁷² 'Pore lil' feller – I told Emily when she went into Munitions he'd never make a shopper', *Punch*, 3 September 1941, 201, no. 5243, 218. Also featured in BCA, *Laughs on the Home Front*, 7.

washing the dishes and cooking.⁷³ With his daughter in the ATS, a father dons a flowery apron and attempts to follow a recipe, mistaking the instruction to 'beat' the contents of the saucepan as a recommendation to leave the kitchen: 'It said, "Bring to the boil and THEN BEAT IT for five minutes" – and when I got back it was burnt to a cinder!'⁷⁴ This cartoon played upon the view that subverting conventional gender roles posed a challenge to the 'natural' division between the sexes and resulted in chaos and emasculation. The humour is derived from the fact that it is the daughter who is fulfilling patriotic service by donning uniform and serving in the armed forces. The blurring of conventional gender roles was a frequent trope in visual humour, which points to the recognition of deep-rooted anxieties surrounding gender disruption.

Female war workers had the potential to render the civilian male worker's masculinity unstable, their presence a continual reminder that women had been drafted to undertake similar work. Concurrent with the increasing numbers of women within the labour force was their entry into industries, which were previously male-dominated, their increased wages, newly acquired skills, heightened sense of self-worth and the recognition of their value in wartime film and print media. Moreover, many of the women who moved into industry were older and married, a consequence of legislation. Indeed, by June 1943, 26 per cent of women workers were aged between thirty-five and forty-four and three million wives and widows were in employment.⁷⁵ The influx of women into industrial work was a source of amusement for satirists as they had the potential to undermine civilian masculinity. Many cartoons depict women in work environments that were previously male. Some feature female industrial workers but the comedy is derived elsewhere, suggesting (as many film shorts do, such as the 1942 *They Keep the Wheels Turning*) that later in the war women's entry into previously male spaces had become accepted.⁷⁶ This is the case in a cartoon in *Blighty* by P. Millar, which depicts a rotund, bald, moustachioed Colonel Blimp-like figure in pinstripe trousers and spats standing at a workbench among male and female shopfloor workers. One man jokes, 'It's the guv'nor. He says there's more money made working in the factory than owning it nowadays –!' The inclusion of the young female worker in the foreground serves

---

⁷³ BCA, CG/1/4/2/1/73/14, *Laughs with the Workers*, 'She told me last Friday morning, just before she went to work', 6; 'I hope you don't mind, dear – I've brought a friend home to dinner', 7; 'I hope this is not giving you any post-war ideas!', CG/1/4/2/1/73/16, *More Laughs with the Forces*, 16.
⁷⁴ BCA, *Laughs on the Home Front*, 45.
⁷⁵ Penny Summerfield, *Women Workers in the Second World War: Production and Patriarchy in Conflict* (London: Routledge, 1989).
⁷⁶ *They Keep the Wheels Turning* (1942), Dir. Francis Searle.

no humorous purpose (unless it subtly implies that first young women entered the shop floor and now employers are taking the men's jobs).[77] More typical, however, is the presence of women driving the humour. Another Millar cartoon depicts a harried-looking man sweating profusely as he is simultaneously nagged by an older woman, the archetypal battle-axe, on one side of him and a heavily made-up harridan on the other. A hammer, spanner and vice as well as boxes of nuts, bolts and screws are clearly visible around the workstation to reinforce the message of him being trapped. One of his co-workers notes, 'He wants to be shifted – he's got his mother-in-law on one side and his wife on the other!'[78] While the threats to masculinity posed by female dilutees are depicted in visual form for comic effect, in reality, many skilled men continued to work in all-male spaces. Moreover, in retrospective oral history interviews, they emphasize their workplace dominance over temporary female workers who lacked the training and received less pay in undertaking work processes that had been fragmented and deskilled.[79]

Conclusion

This examination of visual humour on the Home Front has focused on two types of illustration, opinion and joke cartoons, and has used four case studies to consider how humorous drawings both reflected and shaped the cultural mood, assimilating and repackaging for popular consumption current affairs and social attitudes. Caricatures of recognizable national figures, that punctured inflated claims to global dominance and racial supremacy, served to disarm the public's fear in a seemingly invincible enemy, enabling the maintenance of strong morale. Joke cartoons distracted the public momentarily from the tedium and frustrations of Home Front restrictions wrought by the prosecution of a protracted conflict and provided an important safety valve. Moreover, the pressures building as a consequence of the shifting gender landscape, brought about by a total war in which all resources were mobilized, were released by the lampooning of the female war worker, in particular the uniformed woman, and the civilian man. As noted in the preface to one of the compilations, 'nothing helps to keep up that morale as much as the gift of seeing the lighter side of the

---

[77] BCA, *Laughs on the Home Front*, 8.
[78] BCA, *Laughs on the Home Front*, 37.
[79] Pattinson, McIvor and Robb, *Men in Reserve*.

darkest situation.'[80] Together, these fascinating case studies reveal the richness of visual culture, a hitherto underutilized source, in aiding understandings of the British Home Front.

Bibliography

British Cartoon Archive

CG/1/4/2/1/73/5, *Humours of ARP*, Compiled by S. Evelyn Thomas (1941).
CG/1/4/2/1/73/10, *Laughs with the Forces*, Compiled by S. Evelyn Thomas (1942).
CG/1/4/2/1/73/13, *Laughs with the RAF*, Compiled by S. Evelyn Thomas (1942).
CG/1/4/2/1/73/4, *Good Humour Annual*, Compiled by S. Evelyn Thomas (1943).
CG/1/4/2/1/73/17, *Laughs on the Home Front*, Compiled by S. Evelyn Thomas (1943).
CG/1/4/2/1/73/14, *Laughs with the Workers*, Compiled by S. Evelyn Thomas (1943).
CG/1/4/2/1/73/1, *Good Humour magazine*, Compiled by S. Evelyn Thomas (1944).
CG/1/3/1/1/77/12, *Laughs with the Navy*, Compiled by S. Evelyn Thomas (1944).
CG/1/3/2/2, *RAF Parade*, Compiled by S. Evelyn Thomas (1944).
CG/1/4/2/1/73/16, *More Laughs with the Forces*, Compiled by S. Evelyn Thomas (1945).
CG/1/4/2/1/73/8, *Laughs while You Travel*, Compiled by S. Evelyn Thomas (1946).
CG/1/4/2/1/73/11, *Laughs with the Law*, Compiled by S. Evelyn Thomas (1946).
CG/1/4/2/1/73/9, *Laughs with the Busy Bodies*, Compiled by S. Evelyn Thomas (1947).
CG/1/4/2/1/73/15, *Many Happy Returns*, Compiled by S. Evelyn Thomas (1947).
CG/1/4/2/1/73/6, *Laughs along the Lines*, Compiled by S. Evelyn Thomas (undated).
CG/2/3/1/31/1, *Laughs around the Land*, Compiled by S. Evelyn Thomas (undated).
CG/2/1/1/237/20, *The Journalist* (1944).
KEM 18/2 Box 43.
KEM 7.
KEM Christmas Cards Box 4.
NC 1763.W3, Boris Efimov, *Hitler and His Gang: Cartoons by Boris Efimov* (London: Alliance Press, 1944).
PF0001-0842, Poy, 'Sketch Map of the Funk Hole of London', *Evening News*, 27 October 1916.
2/79/D, Norman Pett, *Jane at War: The Original and Unexpurgated Adventures of the British Secret Weapons of World War Two. Jane of the Daily Mirror* (London: Wolfe Publishing Ltd., 1976).

---

[80] BCA, CG/1/4/2/1/73/5, *Humours of ARP*, 1.

Miscellaneous

Antony Eden, HC Deb, 17 December 1942 vol 385 cc2082-7.
David Low, *The World at War* (Harmondsworth: Penguin, 1942).
Jojo Rabbit (2019), Dir. Taika Waititi.
'Matron', *Morning Post*, 19 July 1915.
National Archives, FO 898/128, 'Propaganda Activities, Leaflet Translations (Arabic)'.
The Life and Death of Colonel Blimp (1943), Dir. Michael Powell and Emeric Pressburger.
The Ministry of Information, *What Britain Has Done, 1939-1945: A Selection of Outstanding Facts and Figures* (Ministry of Information, 1945).
They Keep the Wheels Turning (1942), Dir. Francis Searle.
'Women in Khaki', *Ladies Pictorial: A Fashion and Society Paper for the Home*, 21 August 1915.

Secondary Sources

Linus Abraham, 'Effectiveness of Cartoons as a Uniquely Visual Medium for Orienting Social Issues', *Journalism and Communication Monographs*, 11, no. 2 (2009), 117-65.
Mark Bryant, *World War II in Cartoons* (London: Gab Street Publishing, 1989).
Peter Burke, *Eyewitnessing: The Uses of Images as Historical Evidence* (New York: Cornell University Press, 2001).
Angus Calder, *The People's War: Britain 1939-1945* (London: Jonathan Cape, 1969).
Lucy Shelton Caswell, 'Drawing Swords: War in American Editorial Cartoons', *American Journalism*, 21, no. 2 (2004), 13-45.
R. W. Connell, *Masculinities* (Cambridge: Polity Press, 1995).
Simon Critchley, *On Humour* (London: Routledge, 2002).
Roy Douglas, 'Cartoons and the Historian', *Historian*, 102 (Summer 2009), 12-18.
Mariam Ginman and Sara von Ungern-Sternberg, 'Cartoons as Information', *Journal of Information Science*, 29, no. 1 (2003), 69-77.
Dennis Griffiths, *Fleet Street: Five Hundred Years of the Press* (London: British Library, 2006).
Jack Halberstam, *Female Masculinity* (Durham, NC: Duke University Press, 1998).
Cecil Hunt, *Heath Robinson's Home Front: How to Make Do and Mend in Style* (Oxford: Bodleian, 2015).
Scott McCloud, *Understanding Comics: The Invisible Art* (New York: HarperCollins, 1994).
Francis M. Miley and Andrew F. Read, 'Cartoons as Alternative Accounting: Front-line Supply in the First World War', *Accounting History Review*, 24, no. 2-3 (2014), 161-89.
Thomas Milton Kemnitz, 'The Cartoon as a Historical Source', *The Journal of Interdisciplinary History*, 4, no. 1 (1973), 81-93.
Walter Nash, *The Language of Humour* (London: Longman, 1985).

Lucy Noakes, '"A Disgrace to the Country they Belong to": The Sexualisation of Female Soldiers in First World War Britain', *Revue: Literature, History of Ideas, Images and Societies of the English Speaking World*, 6, no. 4 (2008), 11–26.

Alison Oram, *Her Husband Was a Woman! Women's Gender-Crossing in Modern British Popular Culture* (London: Routledge, 2007).

George Orwell, 'The Art of Donald McGill', in *Collected Essays, Journalism and Letters Volume 2* (London: Heinemann, 1961).

Frank Palmeri, 'The Cartoon: The Image as Critique', in Sarah Barber and Corinna Peniston-Bird (eds.), *History beyond the Text: A Student's Guide to Approaching Alternative Sources* (London: Taylor & Francis, 2009), 32–48.

Juliette Pattinson, '"Shirkers", "Scrimjacks" and "Scrimshanks"?: British Civilian Masculinity and Reserved Occupations, 1914–45', *Gender and History*, 28, no. 3 (2016), 709–27.

Juliette Pattinson, Arthur McIvor and Linsey Robb, *Men in Reserve: British Civilian Masculinities in the Second World War* (Manchester: Manchester University Press, 2017).

Michael Pickering, *Stereotyping: The Politics of Representation* (Basingstoke: Palgrave, 2001).

Krisztina Robert '"All That Is Best of the Modern Woman"? Representations of Female Auxiliaries in British Popular Culture, 1914–1919', in Jessica Meyer (ed.), *British Popular Culture and the First World War* (Leiden: Brill, 2008), 71–93.

Sonya O. Rose, *Which People's War? National Identity and Citizenship in Wartime Britain, 1939–1945* (Oxford: Oxford University Press, 2003).

Rania M.R. Saleh, 'Political Cartoons in Egypt', *International Journal of Comic Art*, 9, no. 2 (2007), 187–225.

Richard Scully and Marian Quartly, 'Using Cartoons as Historical Evidence', in Richard Scully and Marian Quartly (eds.), *Drawing the Line: Using Cartoons as Historical Evidence* (Clayton: Monash University Press, 2009), 1–13.

Lawrence Streicher, 'David Low and the Sociology of Caricature', *Comparative Studies in Society and History*, 8, no. 1 (1965), 1–23.

Penny Summerfield, *Women Workers in the Second World War: Production and Patriarchy in Conflict* (London: Routledge, 1989).

6

"'E's a funny doctor': Dickie Orpen and the visual humour of the Second World War reconstructive surgery ward

Christine Slobogin

Scribbled in spirited, hurried handwriting inside a hardbacked green sketchbook are the words of a patient with a facial wound being treated at Hill End Hospital in St Albans during the Second World War: "'E's a funny doctor … 'E does 'is job, but cripes! It ain't *is* face, is it?'[1] After a nurse had just given him a 'pep talk' on the excellence of the attending physician, here the patient provides a lukewarm commendation of the surgeon's performance within his profession ("E does 'is job'). He also compliments the doctor's sense of humour by calling him 'funny' (although this also could be a pejorative statement about personality or appearance). But overall, this quotation shows that the patient is primarily concerned about the 'funny' surgeon carving apart and reconstructing his face, a highly visible and valued body part. The medical artist recording this interaction was a young woman named Diana 'Dickie' Orpen (1914–2008), who was inspired to work as a surgical illustrator in part by her mentor Henry Tonks (1862–1937), known for his First World War pastel portraits of facially injured servicemen.[2] As a young teenager, Orpen was able to attend two terms at the Slade School of Fine Art, where Tonks was Professor. This access to the Slade was available primarily because of Tonks's connection to her father, the

---

[1] Dickie Orpen, Sketchbook #20, 1942 or 1944, BAPRAS/DSB 20.48, Archives of the British Association of Plastic, Reconstructive and Aesthetic Surgeons.
[2] For more on Henry Tonks's surgical illustrations: Suzannah Biernoff, 'Flesh Poems: Henry Tonks and the Art of Surgery', *Visual Culture in Britain*, 11, no. 1 (10 February 2010), 25–47; Emma Chambers, 'Fragmented Identities: Reading Subjectivity in Henry Tonks' Surgical Portraits', *Art History*, 32, no. 3 (June 2009), 578–607. For more on Dickie Orpen, see Christine Slobogin, 'Dickie Orpen and the Visual Culture of World War II Plastic Surgery in Britain' (PhD diss., Birkbeck, University of London, 2021).

famed portraitist and war artist William Orpen (1878–1931).[3] Dickie Orpen may have overheard this 'funny doctor' conversation in passing or as she drew the patient's pre-operative state, and she likely wrote these words down because she herself found them humorous. The humour in this quotation is apparent in the emphasized regional accent of the patient and in his colourful, doubting protestation ('cripes!') regarding the ability of the doctor to care for a face that is not the practitioner's own. In addition to the humour that Orpen conveys in this interaction, the fear of further facial mutilation is palpable. This short quotation shows the varied emotional registers that permeated the plastic and reconstructive surgery ward of the Second World War: the anxiety surrounding the threat to the face as well as the humour that erupted in unexpected ways in everyday interactions.

Orpen drew images that were used by trainee and visiting surgeons for reference purposes, and practicing surgeons used her drawings to document their progress and to establish and ensure their legacy. Orpen created portrait-like images of patients before their reconstructive surgeries and diagrams and line drawings of the steps of hundreds of operations, as well as sketches of hospital life. While Orpen's surgical illustrations of injury and reconstruction are themselves not humorous, these medical images are juxtaposed and mingled with comical marginalia and stand-alone cartoons throughout her sketchbooks and in her loose sheet drawings, the latter being the more formal, finished images that trainees and surgeons most readily used.

Throughout Orpen's Second World War oeuvre, there are dozens of unexpected flippancies and in-jokes: flirtatious exchanges with surgeons, subtly funny observations of patients and hospital life, and cartoons of tombstones and witches' brooms nestled next to illustrations of life-changing operations. These images of the plastics ward and its staff appear in the hundreds of loose sheets and twenty-six sketchbooks by Orpen that are held in the archives of the British Association of Plastic, Reconstructive and Aesthetic Surgeons (BAPRAS), as well as in the personal papers that Orpen kept until her death. Her cartoons poke fun at high-strung surgeons, corpulent nurses and the daily farces of their demanding workplace and working conditions. In the previous chapter, Juliette Pattinson argues for the revelatory quality of visual culture and cartoons that is often overlooked in histories of humour, war and the Home Front. Orpen's cartoons form another rich collection that, like the British Cartoon Archive at

---

[3] Dickie Orpen, 'Dickie Orpen on Henry Tonks, Her Tutor and Mentor', in Jeanne Woodcraft, Brian Morgan and Angela Eames (eds.), *Dickie Orpen, Surgeons' Artist* (London: The British Association of Plastic, Reconstructive and Aesthetic Surgeons, 2008), 4–5.

the University of Kent, has been neglected in its capacity for revealing truths about the emotional, everyday landscape of the British Home Front.

Because Orpen gave her cartoons as gifts, as we will see, and because she passed notes to colleagues on her sketchbook pages, it is clear that these images, jokes and sketchbooks were not just for scientific purposes or for the private entertainment of Orpen herself; they were for those working with her at Hill End Hospital. While Orpen's humorous images and asides at first appear to be casually scribbled words and cartoons that contrast with the specialist surgical images that make up the majority of her work, they are in fact sympathetically and carefully created forms of visual communication between colleagues. Her images offer insight into the paradoxical atmosphere of the Second World War plastic surgery ward, which was at the same time deadly serious and inescapably playful, as the quotation at the beginning of this chapter illustrates.

Orpen's unique surgical drawings have not yet been written about in a sustained manner, and therefore this chapter adds to the work of historians Emily Mayhew and Simon Millar, to be discussed, on plastic surgery wards in Britain during this period. But this research also contributes to our understanding of the role of humour in the history of health and medicine. While there is much more to be done on the function of jokes and cartoons in the contexts of bodily injury, healing and surgery, humour has been studied to some significant extent in relation to HIV/AIDS. Scholarly work by Daniel Brouwer and Katrien De Moor starts to untangle the difficult relationship between illness and mirth, particularly through the material, camp humour of 'zines' – handcrafted collections of paper, images and text not too unlike Orpen's cartoon collection 'Book of Bucket' or the other magazines that circulated among plastic surgery patients.[4] Beyond this one example of a multivalent subject within the intersection of humour and health, this chapter most directly relates to Jessica Meyer's work on cartoons of male orderlies during the First World War.[5] She interprets these images as representative of the gendered power dynamics within the hospital, showing how visual humour can reveal working conditions and relationships within a medical setting, and her reading influences my analysis of Orpen's drawings.

---

[4] Daniel C. Brouwer, 'Risibility Politics: Camp Humor in HIV/AIDS Zines', in Daniel C. Brouwer and Robert Asen (eds.), *Public Modalities: Rhetoric, Culture, Media, and the Shape of Public Life* (Tuscaloosa: University of Alabama Press, 2010), 290–39; Katrien De Moor, 'Diseased Pariahs and Difficult Patients: Humour and Sick Role Subversions in Queer HIV/AIDS Narratives', *Cultural Studies*, 19, no. 6 (November 2005), 737–54.

[5] Jessica Meyer, 'From Slackers in Khaki to Knights of the Red Cross: Cultural Representations of RAMC Other Ranks', in *An Equal Burden: The Men of the Royal Army Medical Corps in the First World War* (Oxford: Oxford University Press, 2019), 152–85.

Orpen's work provides a rare visual and observational window into the ways in which humour was employed as a tool for medical staff to maintain their own morale in a difficult wartime environment. Like the Royal Navy humour that Frances Houghton analyses in her chapter in this volume, Orpen's overlooked visual jokes were made specifically for the wartime community within which she laboured; Orpen primarily satirized her colleagues and her own working conditions. Rather than being a humour that was consumed by the British public, these cartoons by Orpen were circulated within a smaller community. They were made for a specialized surgical audience, but they served a purpose common to much British wartime humour: they rallied, strengthened community, and lightened the dour mood of war. Orpen's visual humour was a bonding experience, as were some of the short films analysed by Linsey Robb in this volume. By comically exaggerating elements of her working life in art, Orpen provided the release of laughter for herself and her colleagues – as Houghton states, these cartoons could 'take the jagged edge off'. By showing the involvement of surgeons, surgical artists, nurses and anaesthetists in this humour, an analysis of Orpen's drawings and cartoons adds to the extant knowledge of the communal humorous environs and coping mechanisms employed in similar reconstructive surgery wards elsewhere in England during the Second World War. This chapter also shows how surgical illustration, before the field was fully professionalized, was not just objective, scientific documentation; illustrators could add their own observations of their subjective experience of the hospital. The conclusion can be drawn that Orpen's purpose in the surgical ward went beyond the creation of visual medical knowledge.

The humorous context of Second World War plastic surgery wards

Orpen's drawings, and the visual and material culture at other plastics wards operating during the Second World War, demonstrate the need for those within these wards to interpret and frame their experiences in a humorous and convivial manner. Three of the major sites of plastic and reconstructive surgery during the Second World War were Ward III at Queen Victoria Hospital in East Grinstead, Rooksdown House at Park Prewett Hospital in Basingstoke, and Hill End Hospital in St Albans, where Orpen worked.[6] Patients' groups formed at two of

---

[6] A fourth site was run by Thomas Pomfret Kilner in Roehampton. Zachary Cope (ed.), *Surgery* (London: Her Majesty's Stationery Office, 1953), 325.

these hospitals in the 1940s: the Guinea Pig Club at Queen Victoria Hospital and the Rooksdown Club at Park Prewett Hospital. Technically, members of hospital staff and frequent hospital visitors could join the Guinea Pig Club as well, but the main purpose of the group was to unite patients.[7] Historians Emily Mayhew and Simon Millar have written about how humour and camaraderie were used to keep up the morale of Second World War facial injury and burns patients in Queen Victoria and Park Prewett Hospitals, respectively.[8] Orpen's cartoons tie the work of these historians to Hill End, and to the role that humour played amongst employees. Harold Gillies (1882–1960), arguably the most prominent twentieth-century plastic surgeon in Britain, noted that his ward, Rooksdown House, had a particular 'spirit' and an 'aura of its own', and that everyone there had 'high morale'.[9] Millar, however, shows that depression was an issue.[10] Gillies mitigated this for patients through activities, outings, visits to pubs and shops and emotional support from staff.[11] These rehabilitation tactics – many of which were also in place at other plastic surgery wards – combined for a relaxed and genial spirit that helped the patients' psychological improvement as well as their physical recovery.[12] In a documentary film produced by the Realist Film Unit, Gillies discusses how the mental well-being of his plastic surgery patients is just as important as their physical health, and that he and his team members 'must think of rehabilitation of [a patient's] mind' as well as their body.[13] An environment focused on humour and mental health was also important at Queen Victoria Hospital, run by Archibald McIndoe (1900–60). A 1948 *Time* magazine article quoted the 'lighthearted lyrics' of a comical song written by facial injury patients treated by McIndoe, noting the surgeon's 'success in salvaging minds as well as faces'.[14]

---

[7] Group Captain [Tom] Gleave, 'Group Captain Tells All: Founder Member on Club's Inauguration', *The Guinea Pig* (1944), 4. LBY E.81/320.1, Imperial War Museum Archive.
[8] Simon Robert Millar, 'Rooksdown House and the Rooksdown Club: A Study into the Rehabilitation of Facially Disfigured Servicemen and Civilians Following the Second World War' (PhD diss., Institute of Historical Research, University of London, 2015); Emily Mayhew, *The Guinea Pig Club: Archibald McIndoe and the RAF in World War II* (Barnsley: Greenhill Books, 2018).
[9] Harold Gillies and D. Ralph Millard, *The Principles and Art of Plastic Surgery*, vol. 2 (London: Butterworth & Co., 1956), 438.
[10] Millar, 'Rooksdown House and the Rooksdown Club', 220.
[11] For more on Harold Gillies: Reginald Pound, *Gillies, Surgeon Extraordinary* (London: Michael Joseph, 1964); Murray C. Meikle, *Reconstructing Faces: The Art and Wartime Surgery of Gillies, Pickerill, McIndoe and Mowlem* (Dunedin, NZ: Otago University Press, 2013).
[12] Millar, 'Rooksdown House and the Rooksdown Club', 237, 243, 293.
[13] Harold Gillies, narr., *Plastic Surgery in Wartime*, Dir. Frank Sainsbury, prod. John Taylor, Realist Film Unit, 1941.
[14] 'Medicine: The Man Who Makes Faces', *Time*, 27 September 1948, accessed 5 March 2021, http://content.time.com/time/subscriber/article/0,33009,780038,00.html.

The magazines that the Rooksdown Club and the Guinea Pig Club produced, called *The Guinea Pig* and the *Rooksdown Pie* or *Rooksdown Club Magazine*, link this focus on mental rehabilitation to the importance of surgical visual and material culture like Orpen's within the process of companionate healing. These magazines included cartoons and stories that joked about difficult physical and social conditions. These patient groups were aided and encouraged in their activities after the war by each group's first president, the head surgeons Gillies and McIndoe, the 'funny doctors' who helped to influence the communal atmosphere of the surgical wards. Humour, like that which appears written and illustrated throughout Orpen's sketchbooks, played a role in the relationships within these clubs, their activities and the general attitude of the plastics wards populated by club members.

Writing about the psychological purpose of humour, Sigmund Freud explains how humour can diminish feelings of danger or pain like those experienced by patients of reconstructive surgery: the 'principal thing is the intention which humour fulfils … Its meaning is: "Look here! This is all this seemingly dangerous world amounts to. Child's play – the very thing to jest about!"' Freud describes humour as a diversion from fear or difficulty: 'humour has in it a *liberating* element', meaning that it can free an individual from their personal traumas or pains, making them 'impervious to wounds dealt by the outside world'.[15] While here Freud alludes to spoken humour, philosopher Patrick Maynard argues that comics (which he states act as 'visual jokes') have a function similar to that of verbal jokes: their purpose is 'not to entertain but to induce a less serious state of mind: thus to affect, even shift, our states of mind'.[16] Cartoons in patients' group magazines, like *The Spirit of the Sty* (Figure 6.1), or doodles like Orpen's, can fulfil this function of palliative release. This role of both verbal and visual humour can justify the prevalence of jokes, particularly dark jokes, in wartime – shown throughout this edited volume.

The Spirit of the Sty exemplifies how cartoons were used to 'induce a less serious state of mind' by depicting the humour and congenial atmosphere of the plastics ward – something that Orpen's images do as well. The artist Henry Standen was a Queen Victoria Hospital patient and a member of the Guinea Pig Club. He depicts the patients primarily with smiling faces, and beyond the occasional crossed bandages or cast, this cartoon does not obviously reference the severe facial injuries or bodily burns that placed the patients on this ward in

---

[15] Sigmund Freud, 'Humour', *International Journal of Psycho-Analysis*, 9 (January 1928), 2, 5.
[16] Patrick Maynard, 'What's so Funny? Comic Content in Depiction', in Aaron Meskin and Roy T. Cook (eds.), *The Art of Comics: A Philosophical Approach* (Chichester: Wiley-Blackwell, 2012), 106.

Figure 6.1 'The Spirit of the Sty'. Courtesy of the Guinea Pig Club.

the first place. Details of this image suggest the immature humour and prank-playing of schoolboys: one patient even aims a slingshot at another who is visibly annoying his wardmates with his trombone playing. Images like this in *The Guinea Pig*, like many of Orpen's cartoons, exaggerate the behaviours and features of the pictured individuals while also contextualizing the surgical ward as a place of fun and humour, of 'courage, confidence and cheerfulness', as one American newspaper described McIndoe's ward.[17]

While these clubs and the images and materials that they produced helped the morale of the plastic surgery patients, the mental state of hospital staff who

---

[17] 'Scars of Battle Now Overcome: Plastic Surgeon Stresses Restoration of Confidence', *Middletown Times Herald*, 23 October 1941, 2.

cared for these individuals was also protected in various ways. Hill End Hospital, where Orpen worked, had clubs comprised of medical students, nurses and staff for cricket, hockey and table tennis (among other sports), as well as debating, choral and dramatic societies. The St Bartholomew's Hospital Journal, which reported on affairs at Hill End, where St Bart's was evacuated during the war, states that these clubs and groups were 'an important factor in keeping the party happy in the rather out of the way spot in which the Hospital is placed'.[18] (Hill End was a forty-minute walk from the centre of St Albans, which itself was outside of exciting London.) According to the St Bart's journal, there was even an unofficial 'Hill End Cartoonist' taking a course at the hospital and drawing morale-boosting images, successful in catching even 'the most unsuspecting member of the Senior Staff' with 'his uncanny pen and ink'.[19] These stories, clubs and events reported in the hospital journal, and the cartoons published within it, show that keeping up morale was necessary for all of those at the hospital, not just the facially injured who were members of the aforementioned patients' clubs. Orpen's drawings, like those by the unnamed 'Hill End Cartoonist', aided in this endeavour.

'With Corporal Bucket's compliments': Dickie Orpen's 'Book of Bucket'

Orpen created humorous imagery in several formats: she produced a collection of drawings called 'Book of Bucket' for her colleagues, doodled in her sketchbooks, included some cartoons and comments in her more formal loose sheets and she kept additional drawings in her personal papers. Orpen had relative freedom to annotate many of the core medical images that were to be used for documentation and for reference. The modern-day viewer may expect surgical illustration to be strictly professional, but specialist expectations for surgical artists in Britain were not formalized until the late 1940s. The Medical Artists' Association of Great Britain (MAA) was founded in 1949, after Orpen had finished working at Hill End and had moved to present-day Malawi with her new husband. As noted by historian of the MAA Patricia Archer, there was not a network for

---

[18] 'Hill End: At Hill End and Cell Barnes Hospitals', *St Bartholomew's Hospital Journal*, 3, no. 2 (1 November 1941), 24–5. Soc. 15084 d.29 753251476. 1941–42, Bodleian Libraries.

[19] *St Bartholomew's Hospital Journal*, 3, no. 4 (1 January 1942), 76. Soc. 15084 d.29 753251476. 1941–42, Bodleian Libraries.

medical artists prior to this.[20] Without a professional body, consistent training or standardized job descriptions, surgical illustration during the Second World War was a field fluid enough to allow for personalized improvisation.

One main group of Orpen's humorous material, 'Book of Bucket', is fundamental to understanding the culture in which Orpen and the Hill End staff worked. 'Book of Bucket' is a collection of thirty drawings depicting Orpen's colleagues; the images within are at times irreverent, caricaturing nurses and orderlies, and at times tender, showing trainee surgeons nervous on their first day of work. The plastic surgeon and Orpen's friend John Barron wrote in 1986 to the founder of the BAPRAS archive to explain 'Book of Bucket':

> The origin of 'Bucket' in the book of Bucket is as follows:– The artist and the author of the book was Dickie Orpen who was our war-time artist and she spent most of her time in the theatre with us. There came a 'flu' epidemic which smote the theatre orderlies and Dickie undertook many of their duties such as cleaning floors, adjusting lights, etc. and was often to be seen carting buckets of dirty water from the theatre to the so-called 'sluice'. So the rude surgeons dubbed her 'bucket' which remained her nom de plume for a long time so when she decided to get one back on us by doing the sketches she called it 'The Book of Bucket'.[21]

The drawings point out some of the less flattering aspects of employees' personalities and appearances and the more difficult or frustrating elements of working at Hill End during the war, but they were meant to be taken in good fun by all involved. While she kept the original drawings for herself along with two copies, Orpen gifted a duplicate to Barron on Christmas 1945, 'With Corporal Bucket's compliments'.[22]

Corporal Bucket appears in several of these cartoons as an avatar for Orpen herself. While this character is a plump male orderly, it is obvious that he stands in for the surgical illustrator, an alter ego resulting from the necessity of taking over ill colleagues' duties. The identity of this figure is changeable, as the name switches from Corporal Bucket, to Buckett, to Buckets. *Portrait of Corporal Buckett* (Figure 6.2, top right) includes the moniker 'Cpl Dickie Bonaparte Buckett'. This image shows the character climbing a spindly ladder, which leans against a tall colleague, to adjust a large overhead light. This height contrast and

---

[20] Patricia Archer, 'A History of the Medical Artists' Association of Great Britain 1949–1997' (PhD diss., University College, London, 1998), 153.
[21] John N. Barron, Correspondence to Antony F. Wallace, 22 August 1986, BAPRAS/A/IMAGES/142, Archives of the British Association of Plastic, Reconstructive and Aesthetic Surgeons.
[22] Copy of John Barron's Cartoon Book, BAPRAS/A/IMAGES/142, Archives of the British Association of Plastic, Reconstructive and Aesthetic Surgeons.

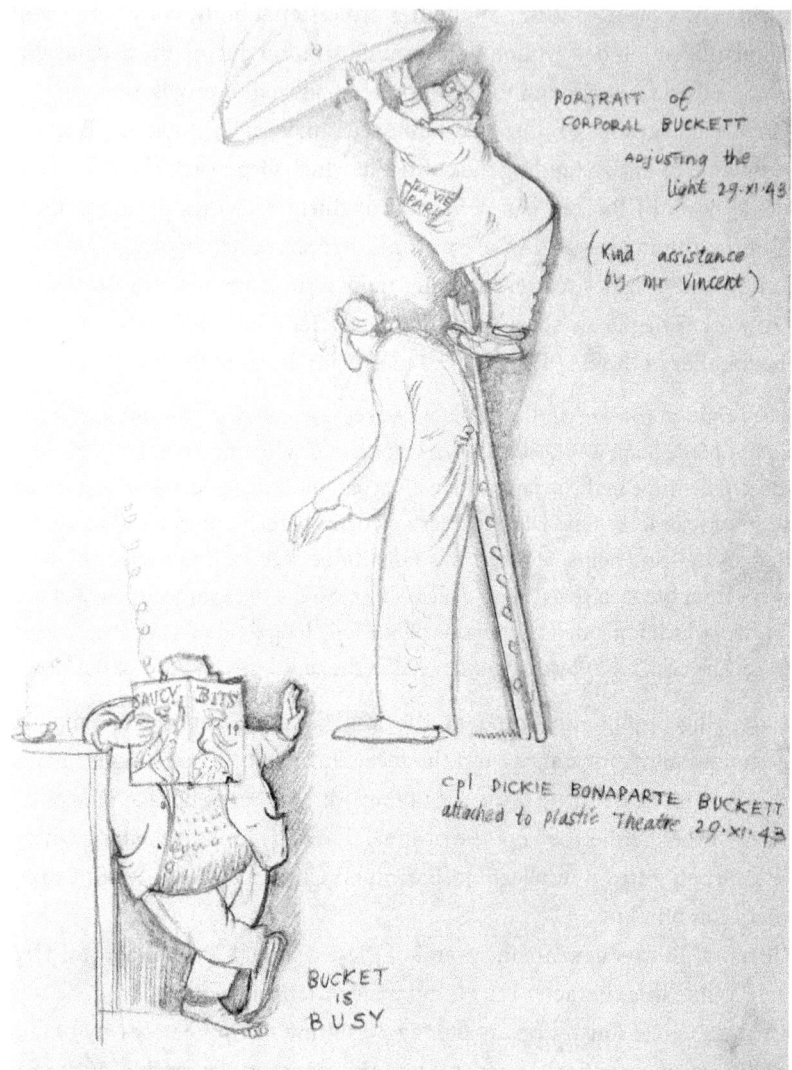

Figure 6.2 'Portrait of Corporal Buckett' and 'Bucket is Busy' from Dickie Orpen's personal papers. Courtesy of Bill Olivier.

the use of the name 'Bonaparte' – after the historical figure often derided as 'the little corporal' in British culture – emphasizes the ridiculousness and humour in Bucket's (Orpen's) short stature, which is highlighted in several of her other cartoons. As evidenced by the many French asides in her sketchbooks, Orpen was a Francophile, and a publication called *La Vie Paris* or *La Vie Parisienne* protrudes from Bucket's pocket, an element of Orpen's personality transposed onto her caricature.²³ On the same page, in another cartoon called *Bucket is Busy* (Figure 6.2, bottom left), Bucket avoids work while smoking, drinking tea and looking at a magazine called *Saucy Bits*: an imagined erotic publication perhaps less in line with Orpen's usual reading material. This second composition is humorous because of the contrast with Orpen's real personality and because of the character's relaxed naughtiness; Bucket (or Orpen) is looking at a bawdy magazine when he (or she) should be helping in the high-pressured, life-or-death situations occurring on the ward, like some of the orderlies shown avoiding work in cartoons analysed by Meyer.²⁴ Within this one page, we can see the tension between Bucket as a true-to-life satirical stand-in for Orpen and as a wholly fictional comical character. The artist substitutes this Bucket figure, low in the hospital hierarchy as an orderly and low in the military hierarchy as a 'corporal', for herself when she wants to depict the dirtier, less prestigious or less pleasant tasks throughout the ward.

Bucket appears 'still busier' in another cartoon (Figure 6.3) in which he is tentatively lifting up the bottom of an infant patient upon the operating table, revealing *Nursery World* peeking out of his pocket. Bucket's discomfort and displeasure is humorously highlighted in how the character, wide-eyed, is pulling his body as far away from the infant's bottom as possible, his surgical mask slipping below the nose. These images of Bucket portray the avoidance or the ridiculousness of work, rather than the difficulty, or the psychological consequences, of labouring on a ward filled with deeply traumatic physical injuries and reconstructions. By choosing to show work on the ward, through the guise of her avatar Bucket, as nothing serious, Orpen creates a narrative that could act as a salve for the realities of the injuries, surgeries, recoveries and tragedies around her and her colleagues.

Orpen's 'Book of Bucket' is subtly challenging of cultural norms, in part because she makes the unusual choice of depicting herself as a male orderly. In these cartoons, Orpen performs a gender other than the one with which she seems to have identified.²⁵ The flexible artistic medium of the cartoon, as well as the casual format of 'Book of Bucket', allowed Orpen to enact this humorous gender performance in a way that she may not have had room to

---

[23] Examples of Orpen using French can be found here: BAPRAS/D 666, BAPRAS/DSB 6.20, BAPRAS/DSB 6.76, and BAPRAS/DSB 12.9, Archives of the British Association of Plastic, Reconstructive and Aesthetic Surgeons.
[24] Meyer, 'From Slackers in Khaki to Knights of the Red Cross', 152–85.
[25] The idea of gender as a performance originates in Judith Butler's work. Judith Butler, *Gender Trouble: Feminism and the Subversion of Identity* (New York: Routledge, 1990).

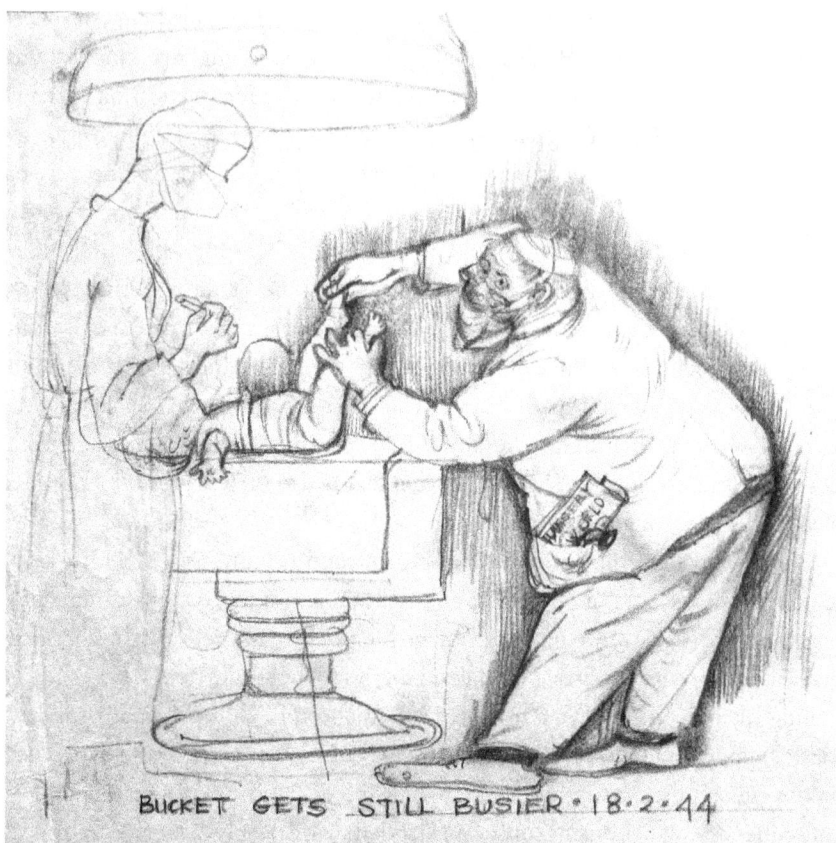

Figure 6.3 'Bucket Gets Still Busier' from Dickie Orpen's personal papers. Courtesy of Bill Olivier.

do in either her surgical drawings or in more formal, published cartoons for wider consumption. Wartime was also perhaps critical to this gender fluidity: Corinna Peniston-Bird and Emma Vickers frame war as a period in which rigid gender roles could be softened, in which what is 'negotiable and flexible' about gender is revealed, and in which genders 'overlapped'.[26] The orderly figure proves a historically canny vehicle for this gender bending: Meyer outlines how there could be an 'ambiguity of [orderlies'] roles as men' and they were sometimes 'unsexed' in First World War representations.[27] It was known that Bucket was

---

[26] Corinna Peniston-Bird and Emma Vickers, introduction to *Gender and the Second World War: The Lessons of War* (London: Palgrave Macmillan, 2017), 1–2, 6. The idea of the 'fuzzy boundaries' of war and the 'overlap' of genders can also be found in a 2018 chapter by Peniston-Bird. Corinna Peniston-Bird, 'Commemorating Invisible Men: Reserved Occupations in Bronze and Steel', in Juliette Pattinson and Linsey Robb (eds.), *Men, Masculinities and Male Culture in the Second World War* (London: Palgrave Macmillan, 2018), 190.

[27] Meyer, 'From Slakers in Khaki to Knights of the Red Cross', 153, 167.

a nickname for Orpen, and these depictions of her as a man could serve as a further masculinization of her already male-coded long-held nickname Dickie, a sort of campy drag performance executed by Orpen with her pencil, in which she fulfils the visual expectations put forth by her names. Another possibility is that Orpen is artistically blending herself into the male-dominated sphere of the hospital. By depicting herself as a man, she aligns herself more with the surgeons, anaesthetists and orderlies. But by depicting herself as an orderly and as a corporal she aligns herself with those at the bottom of the hospital hierarchy.

The gendering of Orpen through her alter ego could be seen to cross a line of propriety typical of 1940s Britain. Equally, some of Orpen's depictions of colleagues could be interpreted as transgressive of workplace hierarchies. Within 'Book of Bucket', the entire surgical team was pulled into the visual jokes, and no member of the team escaped Orpen's witty sketching, from low-ranking orderlies to high-profile surgeons and from drained nurses to dozing anaesthetists. Orpen drew a nurse, Miss Oliver, looking wizened and exhausted in *Sartorial Softening* (Figure 6.4). The wisps of hair peeking out from under her surgical cap suggest that she has aged before her time. Orpen marked the long hours and difficult days onto the nurse's face while still bringing a comic element by exaggerating the bend of her back and neck and by drooping the theatre mask. From the caption 'The Influence of the Crown Film Unit', it can be deduced that publicity or documentary filming was happening at the hospital, adding even more stress to her job. Humour again intersects with the hospital's permeating atmosphere of fatigue in a simple drawing by Orpen of anaesthetists napping at their post. This cartoon is titled *Are They Light or Deep?*, describing two levels of anaesthesia as well as two intensities of slumber. This doodle suggests that workplace exhaustion could knock out these medical professionals as effectively as the drugs that they distributed, something that other staff would have no doubt found amusing.[28]

Surgeons were included as well, perhaps even the unspecified men who gave Orpen the nickname 'Bucket'. One surgeon called George Grey-Turner was lampooned for his large ears in a drawing given the tongue-in-cheek title *Homo Sapiens: species chirurgo-leprecaunus*. The term 'chirurgo' refers to the Latin word

---

[28] The broader issue of workplace exhaustion and long hours in Britain during the Second World War, particularly in industry, has been covered by Peggy Inman, Peter Howlett, and Juliette Pattinson, Arthur McIvor and Linsey Robb. Peggy Inman, 'Hours of Work', in *Labour in the Munitions Industries* (London: Her Majesty's Stationery Office and Longmans, Green and Co., 1957), 288–314; Peter Howlett, *Fighting with Figures: A Statistical Digest of the Second World War* (London: Her Majesty's Stationery Office, 1995), 236; Juliette Pattinson, Arthur McIvor and Linsey Robb, *Men in Reserve: British Civilian Masculinities in the Second World War* (Manchester: Manchester University Press, 2017), 16, 231.

Figure 6.4 'Sartorial Softening' from Dickie Orpen's personal papers. Courtesy of Bill Olivier.

for surgery, and the nod to leprechauns (even though Grey-Turner was English, not Irish) makes the surgeon's ears impossible to ignore. In another example of a caricatured surgeon (Figure 6.5), Rainsford Mowlem (1902–86), the lead plastic surgeon at Hill End Hospital, is depicted as an ape slamming down the telephone against the requests of administrator Dr Kimber, rudely stating that Kimber can go and 'plant cabbages'. These cartoons show the weary, tense states of Orpen's colleagues, but with an unmistakable touch of humour. Orpen has taken the figures who have the most power and prestige within the surgical ward and made them into caricatures, drawing on surgeons' less flattering characteristics such as large ears, simian features or short tempers.

Figure 6.5 'Homo (Mowlemiensis) Sapiens (species Chirugo – Plasticus)' from Dickie Orpen's personal papers. Courtesy of Bill Olivier.

A cartoon called *Maison Minestrone: Conforts Modernes + Chauffage Toutafait Centrale* (roughly translating to 'The House of Minestrone: Modern Comforts and Total Central Heating') shows Orpen finalizing a drawing in a desolate workroom (Figure 6.6). In Orpen's cynical, hyperbolic satirizing of her workspace, a sizeable hole in the floor dominates the foreground. Rats and a spider skulk in the room's corners and snow builds up against the windowpane: it is an exaggerated, bleak scene. Like the drawings of Bucket at work (or *not*

Figure 6.6 'Maison Minestrone: Conforts Modernes + Chauffage Toutafait Centrale' from Dickie Orpen's personal papers. Courtesy of Bill Olivier.

at work) and the image of Mowlem being thwarted by hospital administration, this image ridicules Hill End Hospital working conditions. A sign above Orpen's desk reads 'Per Ardua Ad Asylum', which translates to 'through adversity to the asylum'. 'Per Ardua Ad Astra' ('through adversity to the stars') was the motto of the Royal Air Force, whose members suffered greatly during the war from disfiguring facial injury and burns that required plastic reconstruction. Orpen uses her morbid wit here to twist the RAF's motto, showing that through difficulty, many of these men did not reach the stars but instead ended up in plastics wards. Hill End was originally a psychiatric 'asylum': it was founded in 1899 as the Hertfordshire County Mental Hospital, but was renamed 'Hill End' in 1936.[29] When Mowlem's plastics ward was set up there and when most of St Bartholomew's Hospital was evacuated to Hill End to anticipate casualties from aerial bombardment, the asylum patients were moved elsewhere, and their beds were filled with patients requiring plastic surgery.[30] Orpen cleverly uses her visual humour to parody her working conditions and to suggest that instead of being an 'asylum' literally, Hill End became one in the sense of the bedlam of surgical trauma, reconstruction and recovery.

Caricatures, relationships and tube pedicles: further visual humour by Orpen

Like 'Book of Bucket', Orpen's sketchbooks contain abundant clues to her working conditions. They reveal some of the frustrating elements of her position and they exhibit the convivial, joking atmosphere fostered at Hill End. The members of the plastics team spent many hours of the week together, partially evidenced by the working hours and overtime that Orpen noted in her sketchbooks. In one example of this, from November 1943, Orpen worked almost twelve hours overtime during a fourteen-day period.[31] The inaugural issue of *The Guinea Pig* states that the spirit of the plastic surgery ward at Queen Victoria Hospital was created not only by the 'brotherhood' of casualties, but by 'the Surgeons, the Doctors, the Sisters and Nurses. They shared their life in the Ward to the full.'[32] This is similar to how the team at Rooksdown House was described, and Orpen's sketchbooks and 'Book of Bucket' also depict employees 'sharing their lives' at Hill End.

In Sketchbook #2, Orpen draws a female hospital worker from behind in platform heels, 'UMBRAGE' written across her backside.[33] Diagrams of mattress sutures, a technique for closing skin wounds, float on the page above and to the

---

[29] 'Hospital Records Database: Hill End Hospital, St Albans', The National Archives, accessed 8 November 2019, http://www.nationalarchives.gov.uk/hospitalrecords/details.asp?id=415&page=27.
[30] Meikle, *Reconstructing Faces*, 158.
[31] Dickie Orpen, Sketchbook #16, November 1943, BAPRAS/DSB 16.1, Archives of the British Association of Plastic, Reconstructive and Aesthetic Surgeons.
[32] Gleave, 'Group Captain Tells All', 3.
[33] Dickie Orpen, Sketchbook #2, 30 October 1942, BAPRAS/DSB 3.2, Archives of the British Association of Plastic, Reconstructive and Aesthetic Surgeons.

right of the figure. There is no other identifying information, but this cartoon was likely inspired by a negative interaction between Orpen and this woman. In contrast, there are hints of a particularly close friendship between Orpen and the surgeon Oliver Mansfield. Also in Sketchbook #2, there is a minimalist caricature of Mansfield as 'the country squire'.[34] Twelve sketchbooks and a year after the 'country squire' sketch was made, a humorous and rudimentary cartoon of an old man appears, labelled as being drawn by Mansfield. On the inside back cover of Sketchbook #7, which at first appears blank, messages between Orpen and presumably another member of staff have been erased. In the erased text, Orpen responds 'Go away will you behave yourself please' to the other person's mention of some 'moody' conversation 'coming down'.[35] The interaction could have been between Orpen and a friend like Mansfield, or perhaps a love interest at the hospital. These pieces of ephemeral archival evidence suggest, like Orpen's gifting of the 'Book of Bucket' to her colleagues and superiors, that Orpen's visual humour was interactive and visible to surgeons and other co-workers in the plastics ward. Her sketchbooks as spaces for humorous release were open to her colleagues.

A caricature in Sketchbook #6 depicts the head of the ward. Mowlem is shown wide-eyed with a cigarette dangling from his mouth (Figure 6.7). The wrinkles on Mowlem's forehead in this image, combined with his round eyes and tense jaw, confirm the stressed characterization of him from the 'Book of Bucket' cartoon depicting the surgeon as a monkey (Figure 6.5). According to Orpen's sketchbook and 'Book of Bucket' images, Mowlem was an uptight leader with a cigarette always handy, either showing tension in every wrinkle and muscle of his face in the former or animalistic and fed up in the latter. This supports a contemporary's description of Mowlem as a 'sprightly person with a sharp, decisive mind' who was 'allergic to bureaucracy' (such as that represented by the administrator Dr Kimber) and 'direct and outspoken'.[36] Like some of Orpen's other drawings, this caricature of Mowlem is not an overly positive representation. But the description of Mowlem's personality suggests that, like any good caricaturist, Orpen simply exaggerated already extant features of the people around her. Orpen's drawings provide a better understanding of the

---

[34] Dickie Orpen, Sketchbook #2, October–November 1942, BAPRAS/DSB 3.16, Archives of the British Association of Plastic, Reconstructive and Aesthetic Surgeons.
[35] Dickie Orpen, Sketchbook #7, January–February 1943, BAPRAS/DSB 7.74, Archives of the British Association of Plastic, Reconstructive and Aesthetic Surgeons.
[36] Benjamin K. Rank, *Heads and Hands: An Era of Plastic Surgery* (London: Gower Medical Publishing, 1987), 23.

Figure 6.7 BAPRAS/DSB 6.5. Courtesy of The Collection of Plastic, Reconstructive and Aesthetic Surgeons.

individual characters of Hill End as well as the relationships between them and the way that workers like Orpen viewed their superiors. This page (Figure 6.7) demonstrates how in this ward the personal shared space with the professional; Orpen's caricature of Mowlem is entangled with her 'real' surgical work, the drawings of an injured hand.

A third source of cartoons and doodles, in addition to the sketchbooks and 'Book of Bucket', is Orpen's loose sheet drawings. As the more finalized surgical images that were used most readily for documentation and for the instruction of visiting surgeons, these papers might seem least likely to contain humour transgressing its boundaries to merge with 'serious' surgical drawings. And yet Orpen's subjectively comical experience of the plastics operating theatre and ward emerges here as well. For example, she labelled one particularly small Thiersch Graft – a technique that uses just the top layers of the skin to form a small, thin, hairless graft – 'tiny tots', certainly not professional medical language.[37] A more extensive humorous aside in Orpen's loose sheet drawings appears in the form of a cartoon of a black cat and a witch's broom alongside working surgeons, jarring because of the morbid suggestion that these surgeons are acting as witches in their dark magic of reconstruction. This image is paired with the text 'double, double toil and trouble' and is nestled into the top right corner of a page dominated by a skin flap being placed onto the injured arm of a patient, a positioning similar to how Orpen's sketchbook caricature of Mowlem (Figure 6.7) lives in the corner of a page monopolized by a hand surgery. These loose sheets provide examples of how Orpen's humour, as well as the implicit humour of those working with her, was approvingly enmeshed with the everyday injuries and labours of the surgical ward.

One particularly prominent feature, often made humorous by surgeons and patients alike, was the tube pedicle: a sculpture of flesh used to create new ears or noses. In the tube pedicle procedure, skin that was to be grafted was rolled into a tube to prevent infection. Often starting at the inside of the thigh, both ends of the tube are attached to the body to ensure blood flow before one is removed and reattached to the body closer to the injury. This is repeated until the tip of the tube pedicle meets the wound. The tube pedicle is also called a 'waltzing' or 'walking stick' pedicle because of the way in which the flesh is slowly transferred from the donor site to the area of reconstruction. The unsightly cylinder of skin became a ubiquitous tool for facial reconstruction after it was popularized by Gillies during the First World War in Sidcup, where, in his words, 'the wards soon resembled the jungles of Burma, teeming with dangling pedicles'. He continues with his humorous perspective on tube pedicles in the same publication, writing:

> If all the tube pedicles that I have made and those my assistants have made were laid end to end, by calculations at two and a half pedicles per week, they would

[37] Dickie Orpen, 1 November 1944, BAPRAS/D 32, Archives of the British Association of Plastic, Reconstructive and Aesthetic Surgeons. T. Pomfret Kilner, 'The Thiersch Graft. Its Preparation and Uses', *Post-Graduate Medical Journal*, 10 (May 1934), 176–81.

string like sausages from Buckingham Palace down the Mall, straight on through the Admiralty Arch to Trafalgar Square and half-way up Nelson's monument. It is my ambition that before my last pedicle is made we will reach the top of this famous pinnacle with at least one pedicle left to go into the Admiral's palate.[38]

Several of Orpen's cartoons also focus on the tube pedicle, making it, as Gillies does, something ridiculously grotesque rather than frightening. Orpen illustrates a convergence of religion and humour in a drawing of the stages of a combination tube pedicle/skin flap being transposed; she depicts a basin of holy water 'christening' one of the structures with the name 'Angus' on 13 January 1943 at 2:55 pm.[39] Again Orpen's humour chimes with that of the 'funny doctors', as Gillies also had a tendency of naming tube pedicles. He even held funerals for pedicles that failed.[40] Orpen also depicts the 'abortion' (excision) of an extra pedicle from a 'pregnant' one, performed by John Barron at 6:20 pm on 16 July 1945.[41] The religious rite of baptism (held in high esteem by the Catholic Orpen) and the serious procedure of abortion (presumably looked down upon by the devout artist) are performed visually here on a soulless piece of flesh. She creates humour in these images by collapsing the boundaries of the religious and the bodily as well as the serious and the playful.

Conclusion

Orpen's drawings provide a glimpse into the cultivated environment that protected the minds of those repairing the damage of the Second World War. Humour was used to diffuse some of the trauma and fear surrounding the facial injuries of the patients in these plastic surgery wards – such as the one who exclaimed 'cripes!' at the idea of a 'funny doctor' interfering with his face. But Orpen's wartime collection, of which the cartoons analysed here are only a small percentage, reminds its viewers that the war brought camaraderie and enjoyment, alongside exhaustion and perhaps even secondary trauma, to medical professionals. As shown by the patient groups formed at Gillies's Rooksdown House at Park Prewett Hospital and at McIndoe's Ward III at Queen Victoria

---

[38] Gillies and Millard, *The Principles and Art of Plastic Surgery*, vol. 1, 37, 153.
[39] Dickie Orpen, Sketchbook #7, 13 January 1943, BAPRAS/DSB 7.26, Archives of the British Association of Plastic, Reconstructive and Aesthetic Surgeons.
[40] Andrew Bamji, 'Sir Harold Gillies: Surgical Pioneer', *Trauma*, 8, no. 3 (July 2006), 152.
[41] Dickie Orpen, *The Plight of the Pregnant Pedicle*, 1945, from Dickie Orpen's personal papers, courtesy of Bill Olivier.

Hospital, friendship and support were major determinants of recovery. While there was no patient group at the plastics ward at Hill End, Orpen's drawings and cartoons show that there were congenial, humorous connections between staff members.

Today, one can easily picture Second World War surgeons and nurses, like those seen in Hollywood war films, as noble, long-suffering, serious and stoic. But these people joked with one another in wartime just as they did during peace, and Orpen's papers are invaluable visual sources that attest to this. One of Orpen's sketchbook drawings shows a surgeon named Cope leaning down to work on a prone patient; Orpen writes 'war memorial in hoptonwood [sic] stone? No Cope taking a TG [Thiersch Graft]'.[42] The activities that Orpen participated in, observed and drew in the Hill End operating theatres were not those of commemorative sculptures, made out of materials like Hopton Wood stone, that she would have seen after the First World War and that she would have expected to come out of the deaths and tragedies of the Second World War. Rather, Orpen's visual production suggests that it was the everyday and the banal that occurred at Hill End, not the heroic. Therefore, the surgeons, patients, operations and setting were all susceptible to being lampooned or made ridiculous by the artist's pencil. Historians Valerie Holman and Debra Kelly make the same point: 'In time of peace, it may seem that the only ethically correct way of writing about war is to show that its gravity is never forgotten. If, however, we seek to understand what two world wars were like for the millions involved, whether as soldiers or civilians, then humour emerges as a key factor.'[43] Hill End employees used a psychological tool, humour, as well as relationships and interactions with their colleagues, to handle their traumatic daily work. Orpen's drawings played a palliative role, but she did not shy away from exhibiting – in an exaggerated and humorous manner – the toll that this work took on those labouring in the ward. Moving beyond what we know from patient groups, accounts and records, Orpen's evocative Second World War collection acts as an invaluable cultural history source for understanding the complex emotional realities of the British wartime hospital.

---

[42] Dickie Orpen, Sketchbook #17, December 1943, BAPRAS/DSB 17.74, Archives of the British Association of Plastic, Reconstructive and Aesthetic Surgeons.

[43] Valerie Holman and Debra Kelly, 'Introduction. War in the Twentieth Century: The Functioning of Humour in Cultural Representation', *Journal of European Studies*, 31, no. 123 (September 2001), 249.

Bibliography

Patricia Archer, 'A History of the Medical Artists' Association of Great Britain 1949–1997', PhD diss., University College, London, 1998.

Andrew Bamji, 'Sir Harold Gillies: Surgical Pioneer', *Trauma*, 8, no. 3 (July 2006), 143–56.

John N. Barron, Correspondence to Antony F. Wallace, 22 August 1986, BAPRAS/A/IMAGES/142, Archives of the British Association of Plastic, Reconstructive and Aesthetic Surgeons, London.

Suzannah Biernoff, 'Flesh Poems: Henry Tonks and the Art of Surgery', *Visual Culture in Britain*, 11, no. 1 (10 February 2010), 25–47.

Daniel C. Brouwer, 'Risibility Politics: Camp Humor in HIV/AIDS Zines', in Daniel C. Brouwer and Robert Asen (eds.), *Public Modalities: Rhetoric, Culture, Media, and the Shape of Public Life* (Tuscaloosa: University of Alabama Press, 2010), 290–39.

Judith Butler, *Gender Trouble: Feminism and the Subversion of Identity* (New York: Routledge, 1990).

Emma Chambers, 'Fragmented Identities: Reading Subjectivity in Henry Tonks' Surgical Portraits', *Art History*, 32, no. 3 (June 2009), 578–607.

Zachary Cope (ed.), *Surgery* (London: Her Majesty's Stationery Office, 1953).

Copy of John Barron's Cartoon Book, BAPRAS/A/IMAGES/142, Archives of the British Association of Plastic, Reconstructive and Aesthetic Surgeons, London.

Katrien De Moor, 'Diseased Pariahs and Difficult Patients: Humour and Sick Role Subversions in Queer HIV/AIDS Narratives', *Cultural Studies*, 19, no. 6 (November 2005), 737–54.

Sigmund Freud, 'Humour', *International Journal of Psycho-Analysis*, 9 (January 1928), 1–6.

Harold Gillies, narr., *Plastic Surgery in Wartime*, Dir. Frank Sainsbury, prod. John Taylor, Realist Film Unit, 1941.

Harolds Gillies and D. Ralph Millard, Jr., *The Principles and Art of Plastic Surgery*, vols. 1 and 2 (London: Butterworth & Co., 1957).

Group Captain [Tom] Gleave, 'Group Captain Tells All: Founder Member on Club's Inauguration', *The Guinea Pig* (1944), 3–4. LBY E.81/320.1, Imperial War Museum Archive.

'Hill End: At Hill End and Cell Barnes Hospitals', *St Bartholomew's Hospital Journal*, 3, no. 2 (1 November 1941), 24–5. Soc. 15084 d.29. 753251476. 1941–42, Bodleian Libraries.

Valerie Holman and Debra Kelly, 'Introduction. War in the Twentieth Century: The Functioning of Humour in Cultural Representation', *Journal of European Studies*, 31, no. 123 (September 2001), 247–63.

'Hospital Records Database: Hill End Hospital, St Albans', *The National Archives*, accessed 20 November 2020, http://www.nationalarchives.gov.uk/hospitalrecords/details.asp?id=415&page=27.

Peter Howlett, *Fighting with Figures: A Statistical Digest of the Second World War* (London: Her Majesty's Stationery Office, 1995).

Peggy Inman, 'Hours of Work', in *Labour in the Munitions Industries* (London: Her Majesty's Stationery Office and Longmans, Green and Co., 1957), 288–314.

T. Pomfret Kilner, 'The Thiersch Graft. Its Preparation and Uses', *Post-Graduate Medical Journal*, 10 (May 1934), 176–81.

Emily Mayhew, *The Guinea Pig Club: Archibald McIndoe and the RAF in World War II* (Barnsley: Greenhill Books, 2018).

Patrick Maynard, 'What's so Funny? Comic Content in Depiction', in Aaron Meskin and Roy T. Cook (eds.), *The Art of Comics: A Philosophical Approach* (Chichester: Wiley-Blackwell, 2012), 105–24.

'Medicine: The Man Who Makes Faces', *Time*, 27 September 1948, accessed 5 March 2021, http://content.time.com/time/subscriber/article/0,33009,780038,00.html.

Murray C. Meikle, *Reconstructing Faces: The Art and Wartime Surgery of Gillies, Pickerill, McIndoe and Mowlem* (Dunedin, NZ: Otago University Press, 2013).

Jessica Meyer, 'From Slackers in Khaki to Knights of the Red Cross: Cultural Representations of RAMC Other Ranks', in *An Equal Burden: The Men of the Royal Army Medical Corps in the First World War* (Oxford: Oxford University Press, 2019), 152–85.

Middletown Times Herald (Middletown, NY), 'Scars of Battle Now Overcome: Plastic Surgeon Stresses Restoration of Confidence', 23 October 1941, 2.

Simon Robert Millar, 'Rooksdown House and the Rooksdown Club: A Study into the Rehabilitation of Facially Disfigured Servicemen and Civilians Following the Second World War', PhD diss., Institute of Historical Research, University of London, 2015.

Dickie Orpen, 'Dickie Orpen on Henry Tonks, Her Tutor and Mentor', in Jeanne Woodcraft, Brian Morgan and Angela Eames (eds.), *Dickie Orpen, Surgeons' Artist* (London: The British Association of Plastic, Reconstructive, and Aesthetic Surgeons, 2008), 4–5.

Dickie Orpen, 'Book of Bucket', From Dickie Orpen's Personal Papers, courtesy of Bill Olivier.

Dickie Orpen, Loose Sheet Surgical Drawings, 1942–1945, BAPRAS/D, Archives of the British Association of Plastic, Reconstructive and Aesthetic Surgeons.

Dickie Orpen, Sketchbooks, 1942–1945, BAPRAS/DSB, Archives of the British Association of Plastic, Reconstructive and Aesthetic Surgeons.

Juliette Pattinson, Arthur McIvor and Linsey Robb, *Men in Reserve: British Civilian Masculinities in the Second World War* (Manchester: Manchester University Press, 2017).

Corinna Peniston-Bird, 'Commemorating Invisible Men: Reserved Occupations in Bronze and Steel', in Linsey Robb and Juliette Pattinson (eds.), *Men, Masculinities and Male Culture in the Second World War* (London: Palgrave Macmillan, 2018), 189–208.

Corinna Peniston-Bird and Emma Vickers, introduction to *Gender and the Second World War: The Lessons of War* (London: Palgrave Macmillan, 2017), 1–8.

Reginald Pound, *Gillies, Surgeon Extraordinary* (London: Michael Joseph, 1964).

Benjamin K. Rank, *Heads and Hands: An Era of Plastic Surgery* (London: Gower Medical Publishing, 1987).

Slobogin, Christine, 'Dickie Orpen and the Visual Culture of World War II Plastic Surgery in Britain', PhD diss., Birkbeck, University of London, 2021.

St Bartholomew's Hospital Journal 3, no. 4 (1 January 1942), 76. Soc. 15084 d.29 753251476. 1941–42, Bodleian Libraries.

7

Taking 'the jagged edges off': British naval humour during the Second World War

Frances Houghton

British cultural memories of the Second World War have long been dominated by representations of the war at sea as blood-soaked attrition against wind, wave and U-boats. These images became embedded in the nation's cultural repertoire through the unceasing popularity of war films such as *In Which We Serve* (1942) and *The Cruel Sea* (1953), and through a tranche of popular postwar naval fiction by authors including Nicholas Monsarrat, Alistair MacLean, and Douglas Reeman.[1] But the Second World War also saw an amplification of persuasive late nineteenth-century British cultural representations of the lower-deck sailor as a 'Jolly Jack Tar'. This was particularly embodied through actor John Mills's characterization of the kindly, smiling and good-natured Ordinary Seaman 'Shorty' Blake, who meets family tragedy with commendable stoicism in *In Which We Serve*.[2] Cultural stereotypes of wartime naval officers and ratings displaying unflinching 'good humour' in dreadful circumstances therefore became well established through a plethora of war films, novels and memoirs, but little has yet been written about the specific forms and conditions of naval humour that operated above and below decks during the Second World War. Opening up fresh directions in broader historical enquiry into the functioning of military service humour, this chapter asks how British naval humour on the upper deck *worked* during the Second World War. What did naval officers find funny and what does this reveal about a shared naval identity? What forms of humour did the Royal Navy (RN) consume? How were 'inside' jokes produced and circulated around the Fleet? The main purpose of this brand of

[1] *In Which We Serve* Dir. Noël Coward and David Lean (1942) and *The Cruel Sea* Dir. Charles Frend (1953).

[2] Mary Conley, *From Jack Tar to Union Jack: Representing Naval Manhood in the British Empire, 1870–1918* (Manchester: Manchester University Press, 2009).

Service humour was to influence the mood of a closed community of wartime naval personnel; unlike other humorous formats which generated laughter in or about wartime Britain, the Navy's private humour was not generally intended for public consumption. Jokes and cartoons that were shared between the Navy's officers usually remained an 'in-house' affair and were not widely circulated to civilians or designed to speak to the general British public in the ways explored by other chapters in this collection. Nevertheless, naval humour was not completely watertight and, as several other contributors also discuss, occasionally spilled out into a broader cultural arena. Linsey Robb's review of filmic representations of humour emphasizes that laughter was understood as a fundamental means of social connection and bonding in the Services, while Juliette Pattinson's analysis of published cartoons which played on naval stereotypes accentuates the wartime Navy's ability to laugh at itself.

Uncovering the intimate workings of British Service humour in the maritime world, this chapter analyses subjectivity and functionality in officer humour in the wartime Royal Navy. Through exploring how RN officers individually and collectively deployed comedic absurdity to navigate their wartime naval service, the chapter assembles a broad 'humour profile' of the upper decks during the Second World War. As the following analysis demonstrates, this 'humour profile' was fundamentally a self-enclosed circuit of opportunistic, incongruous, 'in-jokes' which relied heavily on the insertion of inappropriate images and dialogue into more formal naval scripts. Popular cartoons produced by Commander JE Broome (RN), who sought to take 'the jagged edges off' the fear and exhaustion experienced by the naval community between 1939 and 1945, and amusing dialogue in the form of witty signals exchanged between ships, are explored throughout this chapter as key forms of 'in-house' naval humour.[3] Whilst these sources have been somewhat overlooked by historians of the war at sea, close analysis reveals that they were valuable mechanisms of creating and distributing wartime naval humour and had much in common.[4] Recovering historical

---

[3] Jack Broome, *Convoy Is to Scatter* (London: William Kimber, 1972), 52. Regrettably, due to difficulties encountered in obtaining images of a publishable quality, these cartoons are not included in this chapter. They are available for viewing in the published memoirs, magazines and archives that are identified in the accompanying footnotes.

[4] Until recently, the scholarship of the Second World War at sea fell largely into the categories of either traditional naval history or popular social histories of the wartime Navy. In the former category, see S.W. Roskill, *The War at Sea 1939–1945*, vols. 1–3 (London: HMSO, 1954–60); John Terraine, *Business in Great Waters: The U-Boat Wars, 1916–1945*, rev. ed. (Barnsley: Pen & Sword Military, 1999); Corelli Barnett, *Engage the Enemy More Closely: The Royal Navy in the Second World War* (London: Hodder & Stoughton, 1991); in the latter category, see Brian Lavery, *In Which They Served: The Royal Navy Officer Experience in the Second World War* (London: Conway, 2008); Glyn Prysor, *Citizen Sailors: The Royal Navy in the Second World War* (London: Viking, 2011).

humour is tricky and there are certainly some obstacles to tracing humour in the wartime RN. One challenge is that many jokes were oral, whilst those that were written down may not be typical of the verbal jokes that circulated. Censorship by officialdom, publishers and self-censorship may have had a restrictive effect on the kinds of jokes that were printed.[5] However, numerous 'jokes' were committed to paper in the form of visual humour such as the cartoons that Broome intended for the particular consumption of naval officers, and in the form of signal communications which were written down and recorded on special message pads in naval ships and shore establishments. These cartoons and signals also feature as meaningful models of wartime naval humour in multiple veterans' memoirs of the Second World War. These sources thus enable the recovery of key types of naval humour that were on offer during the conflict and help to produce new understandings of how that humour was remembered and reflected on by sailors after the war.

Within the wider scholarship, debates about laughter and war are often located within discussions of personal and political power, fixed as dichotomous acts that either support hierarchies or resist authority and powerlessness.[6] Yet as Jan Rüger's study of humour in First World War Berlin observes, laughter is inherently ambiguous. This chapter meets Rüger's call for historians to study the different possible meanings of laughter within diverse contexts, contending that the humour displayed by RN officers during the Second World War embodied a complicated yet broadly harmonious relationship with naval authority. Wartime naval 'upper deck' humour does not fit neatly into power-based models which polarize paradigms of 'support' or 'subversion' of authority in humour forms.[7] This was not a case of naval executive command structures censoriously dictating against sources of potentially 'dangerous' humour to which junior and mid-ranking officers (and the men under their command) might be exposed; nor do we see here any traces of rebellious and antagonistic lower-ranking officer humour that significantly sought to undermine the power of the naval executive. Instead, this chapter complicates the bigger picture, highlighting that senior Admirals in charge of operational command centres were just as likely to seize upon unexpected opportunities to enjoy a bawdy or absurd joke as their junior officers serving 'at the sharp end'. Furthermore, as Davies observes, much wartime humour exists in a 'cultural black market' in which individuals pursue

---

[5] Christie Davies, 'Undertaking the Comparative Study of Humour', in Victor Raskin (ed.), *The Primer of Humor Research* (New York: Mouton de Gruyter, 2008), 158.
[6] Jan Rüger, 'Laughter and War in Berlin', *History Workshop Journal*, 61, no. 7 (2009), 25.
[7] Ibid., 27.

their own amusement. Identifying humour as formal military 'strategy' – that is, a 'planned and co-ordinated activity directed towards the successful resolution of a conflict' – thus overlooks the spontaneity and locality of much of this humour.[8] By interrogating the ways in which naval officers created or took advantage of opportune moments to generate amusement within the wider endeavour of the war at sea, this chapter also critically considers how military humour is 'mobilized' at the intersection of the popular and the institution in wartime.

As anyone who has ever tried to explain why a joke is funny knows, such explanations do not necessarily translate easily outside of the fleeting and unique 'moment' in which the joke is told. Victor Raskin's models of semantic mechanisms of humour offer an important tool to help break down how British naval humour operated during the Second World War and understand why naval officers raised a smile.[9] One model positions humour as a form of release or relief, in which laughter generates a psychological liberation from tension or societal inhibition. In wartime naval humour, this release or relief mechanism was also firmly tethered to Raskin's location of humour in incongruity, which relies on switching social situations around to generate laughter.[10] This chapter synthesizes Raskin's model of 'incongruity' theory with Arthur Koestler's theory of 'bisociation' to unravel wartime naval humour. Defining a 'matrix of thought or behaviour' as 'any ability, habit, or skill, any pattern of ordered behaviour governed by a '*code*' of fixed rules', Koestler proposes that when two independent matrices of thought or behaviour collide with each other, humour is generated from the juxtaposition of previously incompatible thoughts or experiences.[11] Applying this theory to First World War pictorial humour, Pierre Purseigle suggests that war should not be viewed as a passive backdrop against which humour played out but instead supplied its own 'all-encompassing' matrix of thought.[12] In the case of a military institution such as the RN, the vast web of martial rules and regulations that governed all aspects of life in the Service provided a ready-made matrix that was ripe for humour-generating collisions of thought and conduct. Much of wartime naval humour relied on the surprise

---

[8] Christie Davies, 'Humour Is Not a Strategy in War', *Journal of European Studies*, 31, no. 123 (2001), 406.; 395.
[9] Victor Raskin, *Semantic Mechanisms of Humor* (Dordrecht: D. Reidel Publishing Company, 1985), 31.
[10] Ibid., 32.
[11] Arthur Koestler, *The Act of Creation* (London: Arkana, 1989), 51.
[12] Pierre Purseigle, 'Mirroring Societies at War: Pictorial Humour in the British and French Popular Press during the First World War', *Journal of European Studies*, 31, no. 123 (2001), 302.

effect of what Koestler labels 'the bisociative shock', or the ability to cause 'mental jolts' by breaking away from 'stereotyped routines of thought'.[13] During the Second World War, there was considerable scope for opportunistic naval personnel to create their own matrices of incongruous thought and behaviour, which were deliberately intended to collide with more official naval scripts as a means of producing spontaneous laughter.

The role of fellow naval officers as co-creators of laughter is key to understanding wider humour in the wartime RN. Since incongruity-based humour relies upon the audience to identify, perceive and resolve the inconsistency in a joke text, humour is reliant upon contextual cognizance.[14] Situated interpretation is therefore vital for a joke to 'work' and so it becomes essential to consider how humour was both produced and received in the community of naval officers. As Corinna Peniston-Bird and Penny Summerfield note, humour played an effective role in the wider imagined community of the British nation during the Second World War precisely because it was rooted in audience recognition of common cultural references.[15] The naval humour analysed in this chapter was also dependent upon the assumption of instantly and mutually recognizable ideas, behaviours and experiences within the male homosocial community of wartime naval officers. Two common denominators shaped the humour profile created through the mechanisms of these cartoons and signals. First, naval officers of all ages, backgrounds and lengths of service, were required to possess an intimate knowledge of the formal naval language and procedures enshrined in official texts such as the *King's Regulations & Admiralty Instructions* and the vast numbers of Admiralty Fleet Orders which governed the war at sea. All naval officers would therefore have been familiar with the linguistic concision and formality of the 'navalese' script that framed their war. The second common denominator was gender. During the war, only men were eligible to hold commissions in His Majesty's fighting ships and ships' companies also remained all-male. The earthy sexualized humour with which many of the creators of the following joke texts and images imbued their productions suggests that they assumed their audience would be able to recognize shared scripts of adult heterosexual male sexuality. These jokes, however, were not necessarily confined to the upper deck. Although distribution of some of the humour addressed here

---

[13] Koestler, *Act of Creation*, 91–2.
[14] Amy Carrell, 'Historical Views of Humor', in *Primer of Humor*, 312.
[15] Corinna Peniston-Bird and Penny Summerfield, '"Hey, you're dead!": The Multiple Uses of Humour in Representations of British National Defence in the Second World War', *Journal of European Studies*, 31, no. 123 (2001), 413.

was initially restricted to officers because it accompanied classified instructions, a number of Broome's cartoons were later printed in popular journals, whilst the text of non-classified communications was always accessible to designated ratings and the contents of 'interesting' signals travelled rapidly via word of mouth throughout a ship's company. Second World War RN officers were mostly middle-class, but class-based knowledge resources were not necessarily required to locate the humour in these cartoons and signals. Rather, the fundamental knowledge parameters required for full enjoyment of this humour related to understandings of basic naval language/procedure and male sexuality. This turned the cartoons and signals created and exchanged by naval officers into a brand of humour that could be accessed by non-naval personnel, including women, but was intentionally presented as an intimate naval 'in-joke' that could be appreciated by seamen above and below decks.

Naval cartoons

Commander John 'Jack' Egerton Broome keenly appreciated the incongruous in wartime naval humour and perfected the art of 'bisociative shock' in his artwork. Broome was a vastly experienced naval officer, having first seen service as a young midshipman during the First World War and served aboard submarines and surface vessels during the interwar period, before taking up a commission as captain of a destroyer upon the outbreak of the Second World War. After the war, he would achieve public fame for winning a ground-breaking libel case, but he was also well-known throughout the Service during the war for his amusing cartoons and sketches of naval personnel and procedures.[16]

Broome's self-described 'built-in addiction to cartooning and caricature' spanned much of the twentieth century.[17] At Cambridge University during the early 1920s, he became art editor of the student periodical the *Granta*. Throughout the interwar period and during the Second World War, he frequently contributed amusing drawings to *The Sketch* society magazine, serving as editor of that publication between 1947 and 1951. After the war, Broome penned and illustrated humorous books about naval life including *Make a Signal* (1955), *Make Another Signal* (1973) and *Services Wrendered* (1974), an affectionate, if

---

[16] Frances Houghton, 'The Trial of Convoy PQ17 and the Royal Navy in Post-War British Cultural Memory', *Twentieth Century British History*, 31, no. 2 (2020), 197–219.
[17] Broome, *Convoy Is to Scatter*, 22.

satirical, portrayal of the wartime Women's Royal Naval Service (WRNS). When his war memoir, *Convoy Is to Scatter*, was published in 1972, it was illustrated with many of the sketches and cartoons which had enlivened his lengthy naval career. Analysis of Broome's wartime cartoons presents some methodological challenges, as many appear in a variety of lightly altered guises. At least three slightly different versions exist of one saucy cartoon initially published in 1942, depicting an attractive WRNS plotter (also known as a 'Wren') being admired by a male Admiral. Similarly, there are several small differences in content and caption between some of Broome's sketches as they appear in the 1942 Atlantic Convoy Instructions (ACIs), his own memoir and the war memoirs of other naval veterans. It seems probable that these small variations were the result of the sketches being redrawn from memory. Nevertheless, the overall integrity of the sketches remains unchanged, and minor variations in reproductions of Broome's drawings do not detract from the inherent 'bisociative shock' that his work communicates. Although Broome's artistic talents encompassed both civilian and naval realms, for many sailors, the name of Jack Broome was synonymous with tongue-in-cheek cartoons which poked self-appreciative, acerbic fun at the Service. The cartoons that he drew for the enjoyment of fellow naval personnel thus particularly help to uncover a distinctive 'humour profile' of the wartime Royal Navy.

Some eighteen months into the war, the Navy recognized Broome's artistic talents as a distinct asset and harnessed his skills to new developments in the war at sea. The fall of France in June 1940 had provided multiple new opportunities for German U-boats, surface raiders and aircraft to attack transatlantic convoys delivering precious cargoes of food, ammunition and fuel to the British Isles, necessitating critical changes to the ways in which the convoy war was fought. In February 1941, the large operational command centre that organized Atlantic convoys, known as 'Western Approaches Command', was relocated to Derby House in Liverpool. New focus was directed towards devising, revising and teaching convoy procedures to improve safety and efficiency on the dangerous trip across the north Atlantic. Shortly after Western Approaches Command transferred to Liverpool, Broome served for a brief period on the staff there. His skill as a cartoonist, combined with his experience as a seasoned naval officer, were quickly appreciated and in his memoir, he writes of being co-opted by his Chief-of-Staff to inject a 'rich flow of comic relief' into the Navy's war effort.[18] Accordingly, Broome produced a range of entertaining cartoons depicting

---

[18] Ibid., 52.

specific naval challenges at sea. These were accompanied by 'punchlines' in the form of captions that emphasized problematic and desirable behaviour for convoys and their escorts. For example, in 1942, one of Broome's cartoons explicitly warned that constant attention must be maintained to protect against collision whilst navigating incoming and outgoing convoys through poor visibility in fog and darkness. He created a comical sketch of three different convoys clashing unexpectedly and becoming tangled up, accompanied by the humorously understated punchline 'Some Possibility Exists of Convoys Meeting'.[19] As Hempelmann and Samson note, 'Cartoons are understood as a humor-carrying visual/visual verbal picture, containing at least one incongruity that is playfully resolvable in order to understand their punch line.'[20] By using clear visual imagery and few words, a cartoon could speak easily to those with a shaky grasp of English, including foreign merchant sailors from allied nations. Broome and his commanding officers at Western Approaches repeatedly demonstrated a clear understanding of the power of cartoons to communicate vital information simply, expediently and entertainingly to both British and foreign sailors.

Broome also produced a set of posters in 1941 to adorn the large rooms at convoy assembly ports where naval escorts and merchant skippers attended conferences together before sailing. For naval escorts, convoy work was beset with frequent frustrations and challenges. A convoy of forty-five ships covered about five square miles of sea and within this stretch of open water, merchant vessels were prone to breaking down, belching out smoke emissions which revealed the convoy's position to the enemy, or making unduly slow progress and falling behind.[21] Known as 'straggling', the latter practice was viewed by the RN as a cardinal sin because it endangered the entire convoy. In 1941, Broome's response to this eternal frustration was to create a famous poster in which he sketched the aftermath of shipwreck at sea, depicting a group of forlorn sailors packed into two small open rowing boats, one of which has partially overturned, forcing several bedraggled seamen to perch precariously on top.[22] To the right of the image, two sailors cling to a piece of wreckage, whilst others are being pulled from the sea into the lifeboats. Heavy waves batter the survivors and it is

---

[19] Printed in 'Atlantic Convoy Instructions', 1942, ADM 239/344, The National Archives (Hereafter TNA).
[20] Christian F. Hempelmann and Andrea C. Samson, 'Cartoons: Drawn Jokes?', in *Primer of Humor*, 614.
[21] Roskill, *The War at Sea 1939–1945*, vol. 1 (1954), 464.
[22] 'An Extraordinary General Meeting of the Straggler's Club', (1941), PST18881, Imperial War Museum.

evident that their predicament is desperate. The humour of the poster is created through the contrast of this scene with the headline caption, 'An Extraordinary General Meeting of the Straggler's Club'. Within the corporate world, the term 'extraordinary general meeting' commonly refers to an irregular and urgent meeting of shareholders to deal with a crisis situation. By framing the fate of tardy merchantmen in the procedural language of organized business, the sketch generates incongruity through the deliberately exaggerated contrast between the grandiose formality of the text and the caricature of a gaggle of woebegone, tattered survivors in their precarious, watery 'meeting place'.

This satirical poster was intended to be read by naval and merchant navy officers who commanded convoy vessels with both amusement and warning. Satire is designed to hold up folly or vice to ridicule in order to shame groups or individuals into improvement, and this poster extends an implicit invitation for merchant ships who might lag behind to change their behaviour in order to avoid the grim consequences that Broome illustrates. The humour situated in the juxtaposition of caption and content in Broome's satirical illustration is not really intended to entertain the Merchant Navy, in that it creates amusement at the expense of the slow merchant ship. But it does reveal something about the circulation of 'in-jokes' among RN personnel, suggesting that the poster was intended to raise a smile among naval officers who would appreciate Broome's recognition of the shared frustrations of shepherding merchant 'stragglers' across U-boat-infested oceans. Broome returned to the theme of 'straggling' multiple times in his sketches of 1941 and 1942, making quite clear his views on the threat posed by lagging behind.[23]

Broome's artistic talents and intimate knowledge of the convoy war were also deployed in what he described as 'possibly' his 'most useful cartoon assignment'.[24] In April 1941, Western Approaches Command issued their naval officers with a tactical pamphlet which contained new and clear directives to assist close escorts to achieve their key objective of the 'safe and timely arrival' of a convoy. This so-called convoy 'Bible', however, made dull reading. Directed by his Chief of Staff to '"draw something that will make those clots at sea look at the bloody book"', Broome produced a number of humorous sketches which illustrated the convoy instructions.[25] When the pamphlet was reissued in 1942 as 'Atlantic Convoy Instructions' (ACIs), Broome's illustrations remained a staple feature of the

---

[23] These can be found in the 'Atlantic Convoy Instructions' (1942) in the National Archives, London.
[24] Broome, *Convoy Is to Scatter*, 58.
[25] Ibid., 58.

official instructions for conducting the convoy war. Like the 'Stragglers' poster, these cartoons both warned against certain dangerous behaviours at sea, and emphasized the desirability of behaviours which involved good co-operation, speed and comprehension of how U-boat warfare was conducted.

One sketch in the ACIs portrays a survivor waving merrily as he is retrieved from enormous waves by an oilskin-wearing sailor who is balancing precariously on a ship, wielding what appears to be an outsize tea-strainer in order to fish the survivor out of a heavy sea. The presence of the White Ensign flag on the liberating ship identifies the rescuers as RN. A U-boat's periscope comically depicted as an eye on an elongated stalk pokes above the waters, clearly observing proceedings with interest. The sketch accompanied convoy instructions that escorts should not stop to pick up survivors until a thorough search for U-boats had been carried out in order to minimize risks to remaining escort and merchant ships.[26] A different ACIs sketch, captioned simply 'Teamwork!', also emphasizes that the war at sea was a collective endeavour.[27] This cartoon depicts four warships, evenly spaced across the sea, each carrying an outsized central caricature of a sailor on deck. The sailors are drawn as rugged and muscular, wearing the striped jerseys, shorts, knee-length socks and boots of a rugby player, and are competently fielding a small U-boat comically depicted as a rugby ball between them. This alluded to the recent institution of improvements in the convoy escort structure, in which a high premium was placed on welding escorts together to form discrete escort groups, teams of small warships which gained valuable experience of training and fighting together in order to maximize success in identifying, hunting and killing marauding U-boats. Another sketch, captioned as 'Call up his consorts to assist', served as a reminder that U-boats also worked together in teams. From Sept 1940, patrolling U-boats were in radio contact with each other, and if one spotted a convoy, it would report the sighting and wait for other U-boats to join in an attack. As in the previous sketch, the U-boat is drawn as a humorous caricature. On a flat sea, a large sea creature bearing the conning tower and rough outline of a U-boat simultaneously points to a convoy steaming ahead on the horizon, and shouting backwards to small silhouettes that are gathering in pursuit of the convoy, and which can be instantly recognized as other U-boats.[28] The strong elements of caricature in these cartoons are

---

[26] 'Atlantic Convoy Instructions'. Captioned 'ANY quick method of picking up survivors is encouraged' in *Convoy Is to Scatter*, 62.

[27] 'Atlantic Convoy Instructions'. Also captioned as 'A lot depends on the teamwork of an escort group' in *Convoy Is to Scatter*, 61.

[28] 'Atlantic Convoy Instructions'. Also captioned as 'The first U-boat that sights your convoy is bound to tell his friends' in *Convoy Is to Scatter*, 61.

very significant. Overtly ridiculing the enemy, Broome presents the German submarine as an absurd form of sneaky but comical sea-life rather than as a dreaded hunter-killer machine, so robbing the U-boat of some of its sense of menace. By contrast, these cartoons also emphasize the skill and tenacity of the British Navy.

The cartoons that accompanied these convoy instructions were officially sanctioned by the Commander-in-Chief at Western Approaches, Admiral Sir Percy Noble. In 1943, he wrote to express his appreciation of the value of Broome's sketches to wartime naval escort officers. In this letter, Noble reflected that his original decision to approve the illustrations in 1941, on the grounds that they would 'liven up the prosaic text and make it more attractive and human to the many officers who had to study it', had proved well-founded as they had given considerable 'pleasure' to many sailors fighting the Battle of the Atlantic.[29] Broome's cartoons thus complicate the power/resistance dichotomy that Rüger identifies as an enduring feature of scholarship of war and laughter. Whilst some of his work was technically commissioned by the Navy, Broome made it clear that decisions of content and style were his alone. Broome, in fact, enjoyed a reputation throughout the Service for being something of a maverick, and his memoir makes his generally uncompromising attitude towards the Admiralty very clear. He clearly did not perceive himself as fulfilling any official role of naval propagandist:

> It may look as if my appointment to the C-in-C's WA staff was exclusively for cartoon duties ... let me perish the thought by swearing all this drawing was homework, done at night, to the soothing accompaniment of bursting bombs over Liverpool.[30]

Although he produced a number of humorous sketches at the behest of his Chief-of-Staff, his memoir suggests that he viewed this as a personal, extra-curricular favour to his senior officers at Western Approaches and, more importantly, his colleagues at sea. Some evidence of the appreciation which greeted Broome's illustrations is offered by the post-war memoirs of naval officers who served as close convoy escorts during the Second World War. For example, Donald Macintyre reflected that Broome's cartoons had indeed served to 'enliven the otherwise arid pages of the Western Approaches Convoy Instructions'. As a marker of Macintyre's appreciation of the significance of Broome's humorous

---

[29] Letter from Admiral Sir Percy Noble to Jack Broome, 18 September 1943, reproduced in *Convoy Is to Scatter*, 59.
[30] Broome, *Convoy Is to Scatter*, 58.

sketches to RN personnel fighting the Battle of the Atlantic, he included two of his comrade's cartoons to illustrate his own memoir of the grim war at sea.[31] Similarly, Roger Hill, who served in Broome's close escort group on the PQ17 convoy in 1942, also expressed his gratitude for Broome's cheer and wit, describing him as a 'brilliant cartoonist', whose humorous illustrations of the Western Approaches Convoy Instructions 'must have made hundreds of officers read them'.[32]

Broome's artistic skills were clearly recognized as offering multiple opportunities to communicate vital information quickly and easily between seagoing personnel. When custody of a convoy was handed over from one group of naval escorts to another, a mass of documented convoy details was also passed over from the senior officer escorting the convoy to his relief. A staff meeting at Western Approaches in early 1941 raised a need to improve the speed and efficiency of the handover. Once again Broome was instructed to draw something 'to make these long-winded manifests less boring'.[33] This time, his contribution took the form of two coloured postcards which Broome described as 'minor obscenities' due to their use of crude sexual imagery and language to catch attention and to entertain his audience.[34] The first postcard was captioned 'THIS is how the torpedo goes, Miss Snodgrass'. Drawn in the style of popular 1930s bawdy seaside postcards, it depicted an exaggeratedly glamorous naked woman sharing a bath with a burly man, who is clearly intended to represent a sailor.[35] Rudely intruding upon this intimate scene, a furtive caricature of Hitler can be seen leaning out of the toilet bowl to eavesdrop on the lovers' conversation. The second postcard depicts the same man climbing into bed with the woman. This second 'obscenity' explicitly references the 'torpedo' of the first image, containing the punchline: 'It penetrates, Miss Snodgrass, then it explodes'. Again, Hitler lurks under the bed, clearly listening in to this sensitive information. The immortal wartime declaration that 'CARELESS TALK COSTS LIVES' is stamped prominently across both drawings. The 'careless talk costs lives' trope formed a staple feature of wartime security warnings, and these postcards invoke the posters printed by the Ministry of Information to warn British civilians of the dangers of heedless chatter about sensitive information.

---

[31] Donald Macintyre, *U-Boat Killer: Fighting the U-Boats in the Battle of the Atlantic*, rev. ed. (London: Casell, 1999), xii; 84–5.
[32] Roger Hill, *Destroyer Captain* (London: William Kimber, 1975), 36.
[33] Broome, *Convoy Is to Scatter*, 53.
[34] Ibid., 53. Broome maintained that 'Miss Snodgrass' was an entirely fictional character.
[35] Lara Feigel and Alexandra Harris, *Modernism on Sea: Art and Culture at the British Seaside* (Oxford: Peter Lang, 2009).

Broome explained that because of their bearing on 'the ever-important security angle', official approval was willingly granted for the production and distribution of these postcards throughout the Navy.[36] Once again, incongruity abounds in these examples of naval humour, where a matrix of very serious official naval technology and security procedures collides with ribald double entendre of the penis/torpedo imagery, and the obvious absurdity of Hitler listening from inside the toilet and under the bed. These postcards work on the basis of the artist's intention to force the audience to switch between scripts of naval technology and sexual activity in order to generate knowing laughter. Broome recorded that these postcards became highly popular with his fellow seafarers, and were 'liberally distributed across officers' wardrooms throughout the Navy.'[37]

Some of Broome's humorous drawings were also distributed to civilian audiences, although they were evidently composed with the naval officer as chief consumer in mind. For example, one of his most famous cartoons, titled 'Appleton – either the Admiral routes the convoys further south or Snodgrass goes into trousers!', which caricatured gender relations in the Admiralty's new operational command centre in Liverpool, first appeared in the civilian periodical, *The Sketch*, in November 1942.[38] Between February 1941 and November 1942, the new Western Approaches Command was presided over by Admiral Sir Percy Noble, a man whose leadership qualities, wit, warmth and charm were admired throughout the wartime Navy.[39] Noble's domain included a spacious Operations Room which contained a vast floor-to-ceiling wall chart of the Atlantic battlefield known as 'the Plot'. This map provided a picture of the convoy war which showed at a glance the position and route of every convoy, escort group, sunken or damaged vessel, and known U-boat, and was continually updated by WRNS plotters. The backdrop of nimble Wrens continuously bounding up and down ladders to update 'the Plot' was a sight with which all naval visitors to the Operations Room at Derby House were familiar. The scene also tickled Broome's sense of humour, resulting in his popular humorous sketch of 1942. Like many other wartime naval personnel, Broome communicated a fondness for Noble, whom he described as 'our courtly, spick, span and sexy Admiral'.[40] This did not prevent him from affectionately

---

[36] Ibid., 53.
[37] Ibid.
[38] 'Appleton, either the Admiral Routes the Convoys Further South or Snodgrass Goes into Trousers', *The Sketch*, 18 November 1942.
[39] Terraine, *Business in Great Waters*, 305.
[40] Broome, *Convoy Is to Scatter*, 50.

lampooning what he described as the Admiral's 'very personal supervision' of a particularly attractive Wren whom Broome dubbed 'indisputably "Miss Plotter of Western Approaches"'.[41] Whenever this particular Wren was tracking the movements of northern convoys high up on 'the Plot', Broome explained, 'the Admiral was down his stairs and across the operations room like a streak of light' to direct proceedings.[42] The resultant sketched interpretation of Broome's 'personal observation' of the Admiral's appreciation of the visible charms of the young female plotter depicted a glamorous buxom Wren plotting the route of a northerly convoy at the top of her ladder. At face value, she is receiving instructions from the Admiral, who is directing operations from the foot of the ladder. However, on closer inspection, the Wren is wearing a very short skirt that inadvertently reveals the tops of her stockings when she is working at altitude, a view which the Admiral is well placed to appreciate. To the bottom right of the sketch, stand two uniformed WRNS officers, who are chuntering disapprovingly to each other, and their imagined conversation is depicted via the sketch's acidic caption.

Again, Broome deliberately introduces a sense of incongruous humour into his drawings. He generates a collision of matrices in which the situation of a young WRNS plotter acting on legitimate instructions from her senior commanding officer clashes with an alternative situation in which that male commanding officer has temporarily reorganized the operation of the convoy war to afford himself a moment of sexual gratification, derived from the sight of the Wren's underwear as she ascends the ladder. There is also an important contrast between the appearances of the female naval personnel. Whereas the young Wren who has been tasked to alter the northern latitudes of the map is portrayed in a short skirt and tight-fitting blouse which accentuate the overtly sexualized contours of her figure, the uniform of the two older disapproving WRNS officers is more loosely tailored to conceal their form and their skirts reach a 'sensible' mid-calf length. This contrast thus deepens the incongruity of the collision between matrices of naval operations and opportunistic male pleasure-seeking in Broome's sketch.

Unlike Broome's other naval cartoons, this drawing first appeared in *The Sketch* in 1942. *The Sketch* was a weekly publication which ran from 1893 to 1959 as a 'light-hearted sister paper' to *The Illustrated London News*. Primarily a society magazine, its readership was identified as 'cultivated people who in

---

[41] Ibid., 50–2.
[42] Ibid.

their leisure moments look for light reading and amusing pictures, imbued with a high artistic value'.[43] Despite its publication in a civilian periodical, Broome's cartoon created a distinctive and intimate dialogue with naval officers on convoy duties during the early war years. One war memoirist recorded that 'We were delighted' when this drawing appeared in one of the periodicals and was circulated around ships on Arctic convoy escort duty.[44] The cartoon retains the strong sense of naval humour that characterizes Broome's other sketches; it is clear that naval officers would have an intimate 'insider knowledge' of the content of this drawing. The core joke may be broadly understood by a civilian audience, but the fact that this cartoon was based on a recognizable Admiral and room with which many wartime naval officers would be familiar suggests that the sketch operated on a both a private and a public level.

Naval signals

Broome's cartoons employed a distinctively absurd humour that rested on the violation of logic, sense, reality or practicable action. Something very similar can also be identified in the opportunities that ship-to-ship and ship-to-shore communications offered for humour-generating collisions between official and individual scripts in the wartime RN. Indeed, with his keen sense of the absurd and his in-depth knowledge of life within the Service, whilst at Western Approaches, Broome also found himself charged with the task of maintaining and illustrating a kind of 'Scrap Log' of some of the more memorable wartime signals.[45] After the war Broome published two popular edited collections of these signals as *Make a Signal* and *Make Another Signal*.[46]

For much of the war, until the development of voice radio and the installation of radio telephony (R/T) sets on a ship's bridge, short and succinct signals remained the most effective means of ship-to-ship and ship-to-shore communication. Signalling was conducted via a combination of Aldis lamps that flashed messages, flags, semaphore and wireless telegraphy (W/T), and formed the backdrop to day-to-day life on active service. Although much of this communication dealt with routine and technical matters, when radio silence

---

[43] https://www.britishnewspaperarchive.co.uk/titles/the-sketch (accessed 24 April 2021).
[44] R. Ransome Wallis, *Two Red Stripes: A Naval Surgeon at War* (London: Ian Allan, 1973), 72.
[45] Broome, *Convoy Is to Scatter*, 53.
[46] Jack Broome, *Make a Signal* (London: Putnam, 1955); Jack Broome, *Make Another Signal* (London: William Kimber, 1973). In naval parlance, communication between ships and/or shore establishments is described as 'making' a signal.

was not required, it was also usual for 'cheerful and facetious messages' to be passed along.⁴⁷ As a mechanism of communication, the wartime naval signal offered unique and plentiful opportunities to create humour. Like a telegram, each signal was a concise self-contained message; unlike a telegram, they were public and most could be read by any sailor (British or otherwise) with a working knowledge of Morse code or Naval flag codes. Nevertheless, British naval protocol remained extremely strict and only a ship's commanding officer or officer of the watch could order signals to be transmitted. Despite their requisite pithiness of wording and formality of structure, because they recorded the reactions of the 'man on the spot', many signals also communicated the character of their authors. Some naval officers therefore acquired the reputation of 'craftsmen who could compose on a pad the exact phrase to suit the situation. Their signals had power and penetration; they inspired, provoked, amused … with an aptitude all their own.'⁴⁸

In short, the call-and-response form of many naval signals offered ready-made opportunities for humourists to introduce a deliberate switch from two oppositional scripts to make a recipient backtrack and realize that a different interpretation was possible all along. Signals often contained the necessary conflict between different frames of reference that generates incongruity-based laughter. Frequently, during an exchange of signals, one party pretended to misunderstand a word or phrase in order to introduce a suitable incongruity, deliberately subverting official naval language and procedure into a recognizable social or sexual script. Sheer incongruity seems to have resulted in the heightened memorability of a number of signals which naval veterans writing about their experiences after the war chose to include in their accounts of 'what it was like' to fight the war at sea. As Broome noted, occasionally in wartime, the 'flashes from a lamp or crackles from an aerial [are] a gem which is worth preserving', and the inclusion of particularly memorable 'funny' signals exchanged at sea forms a small but well-defined feature of many naval war memoirs.⁴⁹

Many signals that were recounted as amusing incidents at sea were of necessity reconstructed from memory. During the process of researching and writing *Make a Signal* during the early 1950s, Broome was aided by his discovery that the Admiralty archives contained over 200 tons of naval signal logs – the texts of signals – that had been made and received during the Second

---

[47] Hill, *Destroyer Captain*, 45.
[48] Broome, *Make a Signal*, 7.
[49] Ibid., 165.

Taking 'the Jagged Edges Off' 153

World War alone. Within a few short years, however, most of these had been destroyed, and presumably with them the opportunity for veterans to fact-check their recollections.[50] Yet the reconstituted wartime naval signal, as it is exhibited in veteran memoirs, offers an important insight into *remembered* humour of the war at sea. Some reconstructions of signals were slightly distorted by time and memory, whilst others appear distinctly apocryphal, yet this did not dim their humorous cultural currency for the naval war memoirist. One particular anecdote of an entertaining signal made at sea appeared in multiple accounts and offers an instructive insight into the significance that was attached to signals as mechanisms of humour. In Broome's report, it reads thus:

> A Russian convoy, was being steadily shadowed day and night by relays of Blohm and Voss flying boats. The aircraft flew round and round the convoy keeping low on the horizon and well out of range of the escorts' guns. An irritated escort leader told his signalman to make by lamp to the German:
> YOU ARE MAKING ME DIZZY, FOR GOD'S SAKE GO ROUND THE OTHER WAY.
> The signal was read and acknowledged and the flying boat turned round immediately.[51]

The same anecdote was recounted by naval memoirists Graeme Ogden, Roger Hill, and AGF Ditcham.[52] Unfortunately it was not always apparent whether these veterans had personally witnessed the transmission of the critical signal, or were simply repeating an amusing little story that had 'done the rounds' of the wartime Fleet. Arguably, however, the veracity and origin of this particular signal are less important than the evident memorability of the humorous anecdote. The sheer incongruity of an RN officer's signal to order that a shadowing enemy aircraft should switch his direction of travel – and its apparent acceptance by the German pilot – appears to have achieved the status of a kind of 'urban legend' throughout the wartime Navy, a status that was also anchored in the post-war memoirs.

Close textual analysis of the presentation of signals that veterans remembered as amusing and opted to include in their war memoirs highlights the distinctive curation of wartime naval humour in these narratives. For example, in the early part of Denys Rayner's memoir of serving as a convoy escort, he narrated an

[50] Broome, *Convoy Is to Scatter*, 16.
[51] Broome, *Make a Signal*, 188.
[52] Graeme Ogden, *My Sea Lady: An Epic Memoir of the Arctic Convoys*, rev. ed. (London: Bene Factum Publishing, 2013), 123; Hill, *Destroyer Captain*, 45; AGF Ditcham, *A Home on the Rolling Main: A Naval Memoir 1940–1946* (Barnsley: Seaforth Publishing, 2013), 144.

incident involving a muddled exchange of signals. On one occasion, patrolling off Holy Sound in dense fog, a fleet destroyer showed suddenly through the mist:

> 'Quick,' I said to the signalman, 'make to him – "can you tell me where I am?"'
>
> He took up the lamp and passed the signal. Almost at once I could see the reply coming back from the destroyer which was already disappearing from view in the fog. I spelt it out for myself. 'Regret-have-not-known-you-long-enough-to-venture-an-opinion.'
>
> 'That's a very curious reply. What on earth did you make to him?'
>
> It turned out that the signalman had made 'can you tell me *what* I am?'[53]

As a 'stand-alone' anecdote, although certainly incongruous, this incident is mildly amusing at best. However, 'cold reading' does not always do justice to wartime signals that made sailors rock with laughter. Context is key to understanding the emotional importance that was attached to the humorous signal. This is illustrated by the way in which Rayner built his anecdote about the amusing signal into his wider narrative. His signalman's muddle and the destroyer's dry response are integrated into the end of a section of narrative which details at length the appallingly miserable conditions of serving aboard an anti-submarine trawler at Scapa Flow during the autumn and winter of 1939. Keen for his reader not to perceive that sailors spent all their time whinging, Rayner situated this anecdote at this specific point within the text to demonstrate that seamen could 'raise a laugh however bad the conditions'.[54] Similar devices were widely employed throughout other memoirs, in which linear saturation of graphic details about the horrors, miseries and boredoms of naval warfare is unexpectedly disrupted by a recollection of an amusing signal; a moment's light relief for the reader that mirrors the way in which sailors manufactured and seized any available opportunity to generate laughter.

Mistakes in signalling were gleefully seized upon as an immediate source of amusement, and misinterpretation of signals – both intentional and unintentional – was viewed as a staple ingredient of humour in the war at sea. Ditcham recounted an episode in 1943, in which the First Lieutenant of a ship that was new to anchoring at Scapa Flow sent a signal to the First Lieutenant of the destroyer HMS *Scorpion*, enquiring 'What length do you give her?'. *Scorpion*'s Number One returned a bawdy response of 'The full six inches'. In fact, when the original signal was repeated, the new ship had got its Morse code muddled up

---

[53] D. Rayner, *Escort: The Battle of the Atlantic* (London: William Kimber, 1955), 46–7.
[54] Ibid., 45.

and intended to make 'What leave do you give here?'.[55] Both of the signals sent by the new ship pertained to naval technicalities of anchoring up or allocating shore leave but the First Lieutenant of the *Scorpion* clearly seized an opportunity to make others laugh, playing upon the Navy's habit of referring to ships in the feminine to switch scripts from the language of routine naval business to a familiar and overtly macho, phallic jargon. Such communication of sexual jokes was commonly produced by the simple means of switching scripts in exchanges of naval signals, as illustrated by the following anecdote:

> I remembered a day in a full Atlantic gale when a corvette [small warship] had approached close to *Verbena* to pass a long visual signal. She had been flinging herself half out of the water as she came round the corner of the convoy, and we had made to her 'I can see your dome,' (referring to the asdic dome which was fixed to the ship's keel almost beneath the bridge). The reply came back like a flash, 'How indelicate of you to mention it.'[56]

Humorous signals based on similar inappropriately timed bawdiness and intentional misinterpretation of more official scripts were also present all the way up through the ranks of naval command during the Second World War. These too made quite an impression on more junior naval officers, as is illustrated by one memoirist's representation of a ribald signal made by Admiral Cunningham to his old friend Vice-Admiral Sir James Admiral Somerville, when the latter received his second knighthood:

> 'Fancy. Twice a knight at your age.'[57]

Wordplay such as this 'knight/night' joke which could be invested with sexual innuendo and readily understood by all ranks and classes of sailors was very popular in the language of humorous naval signals. But naval scripts could also be used as sexual innuendo in their own right. Upon being invited to spend his leave with the family of a WRNS rating with whom he had become friendly, junior officer Robert Clarkson recounted that his fellow wardroom members sent a telegram to him at the family's residence in London which instructed him to 'Indicate position, course and speed at midnight.' This communication 'mystified' his hostess, who was clearly not acquainted with an instruction that was highly familiar to all officers of the watch at sea. The young naval officer, however, immediately recognized the intended duality of naval and sexualized

---

[55] Ditcham, *Home on the Rolling Main*, 149.
[56] Rayner, *Escort*, 212.
[57] Ditcham, *Home on the Rolling Main*, 44.

meaning in the message, reflecting ruefully that it would have been 'a waste of time to have sent a truthful answer'.[58] A similar subversion of the formality and conciseness of naval scripts to generate amusement was related by medical officer Ralph Ransome Wallis, who served in the cruiser HMS *London*. Standardized abbreviations were often employed in signals exchanged between HM ships in harbour. For example, 'RPC' meant 'Request Pleasure of Company', to which a standard response was 'WMP' ('With Much Pleasure'). Some way into his ship's commission, 'when nobody had enjoyed female company for many months some magazines arrived and in one of them was an advertisement for a mattress. This was a picture of a pretty girl in bed, luxuriously stretching her arms and yawning'.[59] With the presumable intention of using the girl in the advert as a 'pin up', the advertisement was affixed to the noticeboard, with predictable results. In response to its caption of 'Do this tonight', some wag scribbled a 'heartfelt WMP'.[60] As these instances illustrate, seemingly incompatible matrices of naval procedure and male sexuality offered an irresistible opportunity for sailors to trigger laughter-generating collisions between these scripts. The sheer incongruity of yoking together dry 'navalese' language and earthy sexual discourses significantly amplified the humour value of wartime naval signals.

Conclusion

Production and consumption of humour in the RN during the Second World War drew heavily on the concept of 'bisociative shock'. Both the cartoons created by naval officer Jack Broome and amusing naval signals crafted throughout the Fleet attempted to create humour by deliberately injecting a recognizable absurdity into 'stereotyped routines' of naval thought, speech and behaviour. The war memoirs of naval veterans also offer a rich insight into the world of remembered naval humour, demonstrating how these cartoons and signals functioned as important conduits of humour and were received with appreciation throughout the community of wartime naval officers. Memorability of amusing cartoons and signals was clearly rooted in the level of incongruity in the switch between matrices: the greater the 'bisociative shock' that the punchline triggered, the more memorable a cartoon or signal remained.

---

[58] Robert Clarkson, *Headlong into the Sea* (Bishop Auckland: The Pentland Press, 1995), 192.
[59] Ransome Wallis, *Two Red Stripes*, 27–8.
[60] Ibid., 28.

Seafaring humourists thus sought deliberate collisions between professional and personal scripts in the wartime Navy in order to entertain their fellow sailors. The role of the naval audience as collaborators in this humour was integral to its success, and a shared cognizance of mutually recognizable naval and male sexual language and ideas was an important facet of the RN's 'humour profile'. Although the naval humour examined in this chapter would have been generally accessible across gender, civilian and military boundaries, full comprehension was likely to depend on possession of specific masculine and professional naval knowledge resources in order to be able to identify the conscious incongruity of the joke-texts. This distinctively specialized, 'in-Service' brand of humour was thus flavoured with the irresistible richness of an 'inside joke' and a shared sense of emotional intimacy extends through these jokes to connect the community of male wartime naval officers.

The identification and mobilization of these humour resources by Second World War RN officers underline the sheer complexity of humour-production within a wartime military institution. The cartoons and signals examined in this chapter do not fit snugly into the dominant models of 'subversion' versus 'support' that Rüger identifies in relation to humour's relationship with wartime hierarchies of power. Despite the gently subversive nature of twisting 'navalese' scripts into frequently crude sexualized scripts, this was not an overtly rebellious form of humour; indeed the possibilities of using such humour to prosecute the war at sea were also recognized, deployed and even enjoyed by naval 'top brass'. A distinctive degree of individualism was present in decisions to create and deploy jokes in the form of humorous cartoons and signals. Whilst some of Broome's cartoons were certainly commissioned by senior officers on the staff at Western Approaches, his memoir very much represents these men as making a spur-of-the-moment decision to commandeer his particular sense of humour to help fight the convoy war. This mobilization of his artistic talents is presented not as any kind of official Admiralty 'joke policy' but rather as sheer opportunism on the part of several humane and well-respected senior officers, a decision that reflects the spontaneity embedded into the wider 'humour profile' of RN officers.

Yet this humour was enacted within an institutional framework of naval discipline and procedure. Despite the mockery of key figures in the Service and the injection of 'inappropriate' sexual discourse and absurd imagery/captions into 'serious' professional topics, this humour never offered overt resistance to the RN as a military establishment. If Broome's sketches cannot be classified as Admiralty propaganda, neither were they transgressive or prejudicial to discipline. Similarly, whilst witty signals disrupted the horrors of the war at sea for a moment, they did not endanger its prosecution, and a form of tacit consent to remain within the boundaries of professional naval discipline is evident within these mechanisms of humour. There remain further questions to be asked regarding instances of transgressive naval humour, medical naval humour and the 'humour profile' of the lower deck. A much deeper and more comprehensive conversation must also enquire into the performance and consumption of popular humour in the wartime Navy as an agent of psychological resilience, group bonding and unit cohesion. Ultimately, though, as this chapter demonstrates, it is possible to identify a broad 'humour profile' for wartime RN officers that was spontaneous, resourceful, gendered, intimate and above all, consciously incongruous.

Bibliography

Corelli Barnett, *Engage the Enemy More Closely: The Royal Navy in the Second World War* (London: Hodder & Stoughton, 1991).
Jack Broome, *Make a Signal* (London: Putnam, 1955).
Jack Broome, *Convoy Is to Scatter* (London: William Kimber, 1972).
Jack Broome, *Make Another Signal* (London: William Kimber, 1973).
Amy Carrell, 'Historical Views of Humor', in Victor Raskin (ed.), *The Primer of Humor Research* (New York: Mouton de Gruyter, 2008), 303–32.
Robert Clarkson, *Headlong into the Sea* (Bishop Auckland: The Pentland Press, 1995).
Mary Conley, *From Jack Tar to Union Jack: Representing Naval Manhood in the British Empire, 1870–1918* (Manchester, 2009).
Christie Davies, 'Humour Is Not a Strategy in War', *Journal of European Studies*, 31, no. 123 (2001), 395–412.
Christie Davies, 'Undertaking the Comparative Study of Humour', in Victor Raskin (ed.), *The Primer of Humor Research* (New York: Mouton de Gruyter, 2008), 157–82.
AGF Ditcham, *A Home on the Rolling Main: A Naval Memoir 1940–1946* (Barnsley: Seaforth Publishing, 2013).
Lara Feigel and Alexandra Harris, *Modernism on Sea: Art and Culture at the British Seaside* (Oxford: Peter Lang, 2009).
Christian F. Hempelmann and Andrea C. Samson, 'Cartoons: Drawn Jokes?', in Victor Raskin (ed.), *The Primer of Humor Research* (New York: Mouton de Gruyter, 2008), 609–40.
Roger Hill, *Destroyer Captain* (London: William Kimber, 1975).
Frances Houghton, 'The Trial of Convoy PQ17 and the Royal Navy in Post-War British Cultural Memory', *Twentieth Century British History*, 31, no. 2 (2020), 197–219.

Arthur Koestler, *The Act of Creation* (London: Arkana, 1989).
Brian Lavery, *In Which They Served: The Royal Navy Officer Experience in the Second World War* (London: Conway, 2008).
Donald Macintyre, *U-Boat Killer: Fighting the U-Boats in the Battle of the Atlantic*, rev. ed. (London: Cassell, 1999).
Graeme Ogden, *My Sea Lady: An Epic Memoir of the Arctic Convoys*, rev. ed. (London: Bene Factum Publishing, 2013).
Corinna Peniston-Bird and Penny Summerfield, '"Hey, you're dead!": The Multiple Uses of Humour in Representations of British National Defence in the Second World War', *Journal of European Studies*, 31, no. 123 (2001), 413–35.
Glyn Prysor, *Citizen Sailors: The Royal Navy in the Second World War* (London: Viking, 2011).
Pierre Purseigle, 'Mirroring Societies at War: Pictorial Humour in the British and French Popular Press during the First World War', *Journal of European Studies*, 31, no. 123 (2001), 289–328.
R. Ransome Wallis, *Two Red Stripes: A Naval Surgeon at War* (London: Ian Allen, 1973).
Victor Raskin, *Semantic Mechanisms of Humor* (Dordrecht: D. Reidel Publishing Company, 1985).
D. Rayner, *Escort: The Battle of the Atlantic* (London: William Kimber, 1955).
S.W. Roskill, *The War at Sea 1939–1945*, vols. 1–3 (London: HMSO, 1954–60).
Jan Rüger, 'Laughter and War in Berlin', *History Workshop Journal*, 61, no. 7 (2009), 23–43.
John Terraine, *Business in Great Waters: The U-Boat Wars, 1916–1945* (Barnsley: Pen & Sword Military, 2009).

8

'Divided between *ITMA* and a sense of terror': Humour and remembering the war for the BBC People's War Archive

Corinna Peniston-Bird

In contrast with the First World War which is seldom remembered as comic, the Second World War has always been allowed to have had its funny side in Britain. This was true in the war itself where humour could be association with morale as well as escapism – as evidenced, for example, by the renaming of Joseph Lee's cartoon series in the *London Evening News* from 'London Laughs' to 'Smiling Through', and by the popularity of such radio programmes as *ITMA (It's That Man Again)* which littered English vocabulary with its catchphrases throughout its run (1939–49).[1] Humour has remained part of the cultural memory of the war, as the popularity and longevity of the television series, say, *Dad's Army* (1968–77) and *'Allo 'Allo!* (1982–92) suggests.[2] One reason for that accommodation may be that the memory of the Second World War holds greater space for the significance of the experiences of the Home Front, owing to aerial warfare and given the interventions in civilians' lives

---

[1] I would like to thank Joanne Wood, Learning Developer, Lancaster University, whose fascination and support for the writing process and finding one's voice transformed my experience of writing up this research, and the wonderful members of 'Talking about Writing', our joint workshop with the Lancaster University History Department PhD cohort.
    The *ITMA* quote in the title is from Catherine Glenys Rees Hibbert who was in Denton, Lancashire, Article ID (term omitted henceforward): A2079218, BBC People's War, 25 November 2003. Her full comment reads, 'So many nights passed – divided between *ITMA* and a sense of terror.' In the response of Frank Mee, Researcher 241911, to a post on ITMA and the popularity of wartime catchphrases by John Borlase Wilson, A2987021, BBCPW, 9 September 2004, Mee commented 'There was a wartime prediction that "if Hitler invaded during *ITMA* he could have walked right up White Hall without seeing a soul."'
[2] See the British Cartoon Archive for the series, and an introduction to the cartoonist: Joseph Lee, https://www.cartoons.ac.uk/cartoonist-biographies/k-l/josephlee.html, accessed 2 July 2021.

through conscription and rationing.[3] The humour of wartime civilian life was not dissimilar from that of wartime military life, serving to establish national and institutional codes of behaviour, mock the enemy, target those and that deemed antithetical to the war effort, express frustration with state and military bureaucracy, and shore resilience, maintain morale and disarm fear, as distraction as often as commentary.[4] As two audience members watching a disaster film at the cinema comment to each other in a cartoon by Sillince, 'Yes, dear, it DOES help to keep one bright and cheerful these days' – as a train crashes into a ravine from a tall crumbling bridge.[5]

Civilian humour is, however, differently gendered, and it shares more obvious commonalities and continuities with subjects and tropes of Britain at peace. Whereas military humour may require insider status (both in narration and reception), the humour of the Home Front can accommodate nearly all. For the purpose of this study it also has the advantage that it attracts humourists of both genders, in a field in which the male voice often dominates.[6] It does not prioritize the male combatant experience, although the Blitz is ever present, and retrospective accounts incorporate the child's experience of war alongside that of adults of both genders. The focus of this chapter is thus on the mundane in retrospection – not the unimportant, but the ordinary, the immediate and the

---

[3] The author has explored the role of humour in wartime representations of the Home Guard with Penny Summerfield in '"Hey, you're dead!": the Multiple Uses of Humour in Representations of British National Defence in the Second World War', *Journal of European Studies*, 31 (2001), 413–35. See also, for example, Lucy Noakes and Juliette Pattinson (eds.), *British Cultural Memory and the Second World War* (London: Bloomsbury Publishing Plc, 2013). The few references to humour in that collection are largely located within the war or its immediate aftermath.

[4] On humour and English national identity, see Andy Medhurst, *A National Joke: Popular Comedy and English Cultural Identities* (Abingdon: Routledge, 2007). The role of humour amongst the soldiers of the First World War has been discussed, for example in relation to the songs of the Western Front. Edward Madigan argues that mock-heroic humour functioned not only as a coping mechanism, but also provided a basic standard of conduct for soldiers, to which to adhere or aspire. Edward Madigan, '"Sticking to a Hateful Task": Resilience, Humour, and British Understandings of Combatant Courage, 1914–1918', *War in History* (Special Issue on Courage and Cowardice in Wartime), 20, no. 1 (2013), 76–98. For humour amongst the forces in the Second World War, see, for example, Paul Fussell, *Wartime: Understanding and Behavior in the Second World War* (New York: Oxford University Press, 1989) where the emphasis is largely on black humour, or, the unreferenced Alan Weeks, *Cheer Up Mate: Second World Humour* (Stroud: The History Press, 2011). The decreasing popularity of jokes pertaining to the war in Christmas pantomimes is revealed in the Mass-Observation Archive (see Chris Smith's chapter in this volume).

[5] Sillince, *We're All in It* (London: Collins, 1941), 46.

[6] To the present day there are fewer female comedians: see, for example, Michele A. Court's blog: 'Are Women Funny (and other stupid questions)', http://micheleacourt.com/are-women-funny-and-other-stupid-questions/, accessed 28 March 2021. J. B. Priestley dedicates one chapter to feminine humour in his history of English humour, concluding 'What my sex needs is an ample supply of first-rate women, who can look at us and listen to us not without sympathy but are always prepared to laugh at us,' a summary which imagines female agency only in relation to the male. J.B. Priestley, *English Humour* (London: Heinemann, 1976), 138.

practical – although what was mundane in wartime is not necessarily mundane in other times, and vice versa. Pont, who was described by fellow cartoonist David Low as 'a keenly satirical social observer', captured this succinctly in a cartoon showing one frustrated middle-aged woman complaining to another at the breakfast table, 'Must you say "Well, we're still here" every morning?'[7] And as Harold Church, who served in the RAF and became a POW in the war, reflected over six decades later, with excellent comedic rhythm,

> Provided that one has freedom, friendship, enough food and water to prevent starvation, reasonable health, warmth and shelter, nothing else is of major importance, although, in my opinion, a sense of humour is almost essential. Material possessions are irrelevant in achieving contentment. However, it does help to have a toothbrush, a bar of soap, spare underwear and an extra pair of socks.[8]

The British experience of the Second World War brought a panoply of deprivation – of loved ones, of light, of time, of sleep, of unsullied leisure spaces like parks and beaches. On the Home Front, the mundane was rendered a luxury: petrol, oranges, deep baths and un-darned socks.[9] Ingenuity in ensuring self and others were provided for was a weapon of war. Sillince suggested this merging of the civilian/military in his cartoon depicting a smart woman speaking to a moustachioed gentleman in his study, 'General, I'd be delighted if you'd write a foreword to my new book "Strategy and Tactics on the Kitchen Front".'[10] In recollections of the war, ingenuity functions as a proud symbol of resilience only sometimes allowed a whiff of the ridiculous: mashed roast parsnips in 'banana' sandwiches, beetroot juice for lipstick, cardboard tiers masquerading as wedding cake or gravy-browned legs with pencilled seams. My focus here on the less attended (extra)ordinary in retrospection is made possible by a project which generated the archival material at the heart of this chapter. The British Broadcasting Corporation World War II People's War (BBCPW) testimony-gathering project, which ran from June 2003 to January 2006, created an archive of 47,376 wartime reminiscences. Individuals logging on to the BBCPW website were asked to 'contribute your military and Home Front stories. A growing

---

[7] Pont, reproduced in J.B. Priestley, *English Humour*, 195; David Low, *British Cartoonist's Caricaturists and Comic Artists* (London: William Collins of London, 1942), 48.
[8] Harold (Harry) Church, A1950897, BBCPW, 2 November 2003. The easiest way to find the BBCPW sources is to put the Article ID into a search engine.
[9] 'Everyday objects which we took for granted such as hairclips, combs and make-up disappeared off the market as all metal went towards munitions and plastic was not at that time available.' Edith Taylor, A2499519, BBCPW, 7 April 2004.
[10] Sillince, *We're All in It*, 83.

archive of wartime memories. Sign in to add your story or that of your family.'[11] As a result, alongside and within tales of the dramatic and exceptional are the humorous and the mundane, everyday details of everyday lives at war. The humour of retrospection echoes wartime preoccupations, but reflects also the temporal disjunctures between experiences then and retelling now, between the world at war, and contemporary life, the self then and the self now.

While humour is a vibrant research field in history, sociology, anthropology, management and more, its role in retrospection remains under-researched.[12] The most significant exception is the work of the linguist Neal Norrick, including his reflections in *Oral History* on the role of humour in the interview relationship, in narration, in self-reflection and in terms of its relation to memory, specifically 'the role of reassessment of remembered events as a natural narrative source of the dual perspective characteristic of humour'.[13] This chapter addresses similar themes but through a particular case study: the recollection of experiences on the Home Front in the Second World War, with a focus on the temporal dimensions of the interplay between reminiscence, experience and humour.

Humour is a dimension of composure, both of narrative and of self.[14] It provides a template for narrative structures (shaggy dog stories, anecdotes and witticisms, for example). Testimonies are multi-layered, reflecting the subject matter and the speaker, the subjective and the socially-rooted, and their intertwining.[15] For individuals recalling their war, humour anchors cherished memories, revealing character or contribution. In performance, humour also reveals intent to build rapport, or to alienate or distance, not necessarily by offence. Humour is a tool in identity-construction, allowing speakers to present

---

[11] The site requests the following acknowledgement: WW2 People's War is an online archive of wartime memories contributed by members of the public and gathered by the BBC. The archive can be found at bbc.co.uk/ww2peopleswar. Abbreviated as BBCPW, listed after the Article ID. See 'About This Site', https://www.bbc.co.uk/history/ww2peopleswar/about/, accessed 18 April 2021.

[12] In addition to the multi-disciplinary authors cited in this article, see for example the social anthropologist Mary Douglas on the role of the body in spoken communication: Mary Douglas, 'Do Dogs Laugh? A Cross-Cultural Approach to Body Symbolism', *Journal of Psychosomatic Research*, 15, no. 4 (1971), 387–90; Francois Maon, Adam Lindgreen, Joelle Vanhamme, Robert J. Angell and Juliet Memery, *Not All Claps and Cheers* (Milton: Routledge, 2018); Richard Godfrey, 'Soldiering On: Exploring the Role of Humour as a Disciplinary Technology in the Military', *Organization (London, England)*, 23, no. 2 (2016), 164–83. In Lynn Abrams, *Oral History Theory* (London: Routledge, 2010), the only reference to humour in her thorough introduction to oral history is on p. 148, cited below.

[13] Neal R. Norrick, 'Humour in Oral History Interviews', *Oral History*, 34, no. 2 (Autumn 2006), 85–94, here 85.

[14] For the original discussion of composure, see Graham Dawson, *Soldier Heroes: British Adventure, Empire and the Imagining of Masculinities* (London: Routledge, 1994), 22.

[15] For narrative-making in oral history, see Martha Rose Beard, 'Re-thinking Oral History: A Study of Narrative Performance', *Rethinking History*, 21, no. 4 (2017), 529–48.

themselves as wit or numpty. Humour can face outward in performance or social commentary, or inward in self-deprecation; both are relational.[16] The cultural specificity of the British humour of the Second World War remains relatively accessible to modern anglophone audiences, and adults are likely to claim familiarity with certain tropes of wartime experience. Some humour, such as that relating to bodily functions, is relatively timeless: addressees may not have experienced gas mask drill, for example, but it does not require much imagination to understand why 'The boys in the school loved to breathe out in such a way that they made a rather rude noise and set everybody giggling.'[17] The narrator can also choose to explicate, as here in John Cox's rendition of a wartime joke: 'When the Germans fly over, the English duck. When the English fly over the Germans duck. And when the Americans fly over, everyone ducks! (because of friendly fire).'[18] As national friends and enemies, gender relations and constructions of ethnicities and sexual orientations are each reconfigured over time, not all jokes are comfortable for a modern audience. The site trod a fine line between asking individuals to self-police, capturing wartime attitudes and intervening to avoid the explicit: switching out 'blow jobs' to 'sexual favours' in Dudley Cave's narrative, for example.[19]

An interesting historic context to a narrative can act as a justification to tell a story, as too can humour. Mary Heath's anecdote of an air raid, for example, complete with punchline, could equally plausibly be told as one of trauma:

> After one particularly heavy raid over London during the Blitz a 1,000 [lb] bomb landed nearby, deafening us and filling the air of our shelter with thick dust. We had the two aging grandmothers with us and one started to cry. She was upset because her old cat was somewhere around. Dad went to look for the cat so that he could ease her worry. He went to her house across the road and started

---

[16] For genres of humour, see Marta Dynel, 'Beyond a Joke: Types of Conversational Humour', *Language and Linguistics Compass* 3, no. 5 (2009), 1284–99. Daniel Miller and Jolynna Sinanan argued self-deprecating humour is the 'Most English of English Genres', in *Visualising Facebook: A Comparative Perspective* (London: UCL Press, 2017), 125. It is also gendered: I have discussed it in the narratives of women describing unofficial weapons training in C.M. Peniston-Bird, 'Of Hockey Sticks and Sten Guns: British Auxiliaries and Their Weapons in the Second World War', *Women's History Magazine*, Autumn, no. 76 (2014), 13–22.

[17] Contributed by Researcher 240879 featuring Eva Coad, A2205848, BBCPW, 15 January 2004. For an adult version of a similar story, see Rose Edgar, a civil servant in the war, who recalled drill: 'When you breathed out it made a noise like a raspberry. Can you imagine fifty people all breathing out at once! Hilarious!' Rose Edgar, A2637975, BBCPW, 16 May 2004. For more on the childhood experience of the material culture of war, see Gabriel Moshenska, *Material Cultures of Childhood in Second World War Britain* (Abingdon: Routledge, 2019).

[18] Contributed by nottinghamcsv [CSV/BBC Radio Nottingham] featuring John Cox, who served in the Royal Air Force in Sicily, A4487204, BBCPW, 19 July 2005. Bill Barrett listed as many such jokes as he could recall. A2193392, BBCPW, 11 January 2004.

[19] Dudley Cave's narrative was submitted by Peter Tatchell, A2688636, BBCPW, 1 June 2004.

his search. Out back was nothing but a huge awful crater where the bomb had landed. The house was little more than a few timbers and remnants of furniture. He started up what was left of the staircase when another stick of bombs came hurtling down. Dad crouched down and waited for the worse to happen but suddenly found himself upside down with his feet trapped in what was left of the stairs. A scary moment for him, but it had its funny side because the blast had turned on the radio which was pounding out the tune of 'I ain't got no body'. We never did find the poor cat though![20]

The theme tune granted by happenstance to the father's predicament and the picture painted for the external gaze suggest the humour of the surreal, characterized as the latter is by fantastic imagery and incongruous juxtapositions. The surreal is an under-recognized dimension of both the experience and the memory of the war, but humour is a particularly powerful vehicle for its communication.[21] Virginia Graham, the English writer, critic and poet, predicted that the surreality of wartime experience would not travel well through time in her poem 'It's all Very Well Now' in which she imagines herself failing to convince her grandchildren of the value of her war effort: to transport two goats travelling from Camberley across London to catch 'another train, third class, non-smoker of course, to Amberley'.[22] As both Graham and Heath show, however, humour can convey the surreal across time. The anthropologist Henk Driessen discusses how the affinity between humour and the surreal rests on estrangement (*Verfremdung*), in which the unexpected is evoked and familiar subjects are situated in unfamiliar, even shocking, contexts.[23] This is illustrated in Alice Burman's tale, who described how her family prepared for the Blitz in

---

[20] 'Can laugh now!', contributed by Mary Heath, A1145297, BBCPW, 14 August 2003. The song referred to 'I ain't got nobody' of 1914 continues, 'And nobody cares for me'. Modern audiences are likely to be familiar with it in the pairing with 'Just a Gigolo', first recorded by Louis Prima in 1956, and subsequently by a variety of artists including the Village People (1978) and David Lee Roth (1985).

[21] Visual representations of the surreal in the Second World War are explored in the PhD of Lynn Hilditch, 'Wonder and Horror: An Interpretation of Lee Miller's Second World War Photographs as "Surreal Documentary"' (PhD dissertation, University of Liverpool, 2010). The photographs of the Blitz, for example, 'reveal Surrealism's love for quirky or evocative juxtapositions while creating an artistic visual representation of a temporary surreal world of fallen statues and broken typewriters.' (Quotation from abstract.)

[22] Virginia Graham, 'It's all Very Well Now', in Virginia, Graham, *Consider the Years, 1938-1946* (First ed. Jonathan Cape, 1946; London: Persephone Books, 2000), 60–1.

[23] Henk Driessen, 'Humour, Laughter and the Field: Reflections from Anthropology', in Jan Bremner and Herman Roodenburg (eds.), *A Cultural History of Humour* (Cambridge: Polity Press, 1997), 222–41, here 227; see also Freud's exploration of the joke and its dependence on condensation, displacement, double meaning, use of the same material, plays on words, and paradox. Sigmund Freud, *Der Witz Und Seine Beziehung Zum Unbewußten [Jokes and Their Relation to the Unconscious]* (Leipzig and Vienna: Franz Deuticke, 1905).

East London, and recounted how her father had replaced the black sheeting covering the window frames with a second hand carpet.

> After an air raid, [my sister] Doris and I went back to bed to get a little comfortable sleep before the next day's work when Mum came into the room, stood ruminating at the carpeted windows and said, "If I only had a *!!- so and so hoover, I could clean the *!!- windows!"[24]

There is a temporal element of estrangement in reminiscence. Take, for example, a gentle example of wit dependent on linguistic reframing in a tale narrated by Rose Edgar, a civil servant in the war. She shared an encounter with two firemen: '[They asked] where I had been and I said, "Fire watching" They laughed and said "Which one did you watch?" Very funny!'[25] The disjuncture between the expected and the interpreted meaning of words is a staple in humour, but told retrospectively, there is a further dimension. A contemporary audience is unlikely to go 'fire watching' or to choose which of the many fires created by aerial bombardment to watch: it is not a witticism likely to be coined in any contemporary context. To consider the significance of the temporal in greater depth, however, we need to consider further the nature of the archive under scrutiny.

The BBC World War II People's War project sought to gather 25,000 stories, with a target of 30 per cent from the over-60s. The result was an impressive 47,376 stories from 32,000 contributors, with 91 per cent from the over-65s. The remaining 9 per cent was largely made up of friend and family entries on behalf of the very elderly or deceased, suggesting also the significance of the family unit as a location for transmitting memories of the war.[26] Children and close friends could also take this opportunity to eulogize the dead, including with humour: 'Cyril Thomas, my Dad died in 2005. This war memory story was told to me the week he passed – and now I send in onto you to be held on file for others to smile at.'[27] Cyril had literally got 'egg on his face' when three eggs fell on him from the shelf above during an air raid. One goal of the project was to encourage online literacy: at least 43 per cent of contributors had never used a computer

---

[24] Alice Burman née Clarke, A1904771, BBCPW, 21 October 2003.
[25] Rose Edgar, A2637975, BBCPW, 16 May 2004.
[26] See, for example, the descendant who noted 'This series of letters have recently come to light after the death of John Swallow in 1999. They must have been saved up carefully by his parents and have passed down to me with other family papers.' Contributed by Sian W. featuring John Swallow, A1130653, BBCPW, 2 August 2003.
[27] Contributed by his daughter under the name of Cyril Thomas, A6176766, BBCPW, 17 October 2005.

before, and many were supported by children or grandchildren. For example: 'I've just come in to Worcester Library to show my grandson where my story is. He does all the internet stuff.'; 'My Grandad was really interested in the Second World War and he just got a computer a few months ago and I had to show him the BBC People's War and stuff, and get pictures for him.'[28] Because of the goal to encourage digital literacy in the older generations, the age profile of contributors is easier to glean than other identity markers: impressionistically, however, a range of UK geographies, occupations and socio-economic backgrounds are represented, by both genders, but with only a little ethnic and sexual diversity. This is reflected in my citations. My collection strategy began wide, by reading several thousand entries (still only a fraction of the whole) that related to the Home Front, and then subsequently using broad search terms ('rationing', for example, or markers of humour such as 'smile' or 'laugh' and their variants) which led on to more specific searches such as 'false teeth'. The surreal is also an element of academic research!

One factor encouraging the prevalence of the civilian and Home Front experience was the age profile of contributors. To hold memories of the war at the turn of the twenty-first century, individuals needed to have been between one and thirty years old on outbreak of war and most likely fell somewhere in between, meaning that wartime children are well represented on the site. The fact that 91 per cent of contributors were over sixty-five is also significant because individuals over sixty years of age have been shown to have enhanced recall of memories for the period of their life between fourteen and thirty years of age – even when this was not marked by war (the lower end marking the commencement of paid employment for some contributors in this period). This is perhaps because, as the psychologist and academic Douwe Draaisma argues, these years 'shape our personality, determine our identity and guide the course of our life'.[29] From those who were younger children in the war, we read of the novel, the emotionally charged and the sense-based, the life of family and home, school and friends, evacuation and food.[30] The child often co-exists with the adult in the narration. Sheila was five years old when the war

---

[28] Story gathering: Contributing stories – the individuals, https://www.bbc.co.uk/history/ww2peopleswar/about/storygathering_02.shtml.

[29] D. Draaisma cited in Sarah Housden and Jenny Zmroczek, 'Exploring Identity in Later Life through BBC People's War Interviews', *Oral History*, 35, no. 2 (2007), 100–8, citation 104.

[30] The categories are listed here: https://www.bbc.co.uk/history/ww2peopleswar/categories/. Around 17,500 of the 47,000 articles were placed into categories by the BBC editorial staff, and the rest through an automated process based on Bayesian analysis, with an estimated accuracy of 85–90 per cent. Technical Overview of the Archive Build, https://www.bbc.co.uk/history/ww2peopleswar/about/project_12.shtml, accessed 30 March 2021.

broke out. She recalled: 'The only advantage that I could see about the shelters was that it was possible to pass your rice pudding to your neighbour without being seen in the dim light. You may gather I didn't – and still don't – care for rice pudding.'[31]

The submissions were ultimately organized into sixty-four categories. The largest category is childhood and evacuation, with 14,336 stories, while family life attracted 3203 stories and rationing 1295 (in contrast, narratives of service in the Armed Forces total 11,829 and in the auxiliary forces 698).[32] Much of the tone is descriptive, with evidence that elements were researched for accuracy. The connotations of the BBC as an organization are significant here, as the project ascertained:

> Feedback suggests that the BBC name was crucial in giving participants a sense of taking part in something national and significant. The BBC had played a central role for many during wartime, and the trust engendered by memories of this made them proud to be asked to contribute to the website.[33]

Significant to the project's success was also the mobilization of the BBC's local radio and regional TV networks, and the adoption of a collaborative approach: over 2,500 associate centres signed up to the project, providing internet access and training over 2,000 volunteers as story gatherers.[34] Organizations involved included Age Concern, the Royal British Legion, local history organizations and local museums, libraries and archives, as well as schools and youth groups, and more. Reminiscences were gathered 'at grassroots level, in local libraries and museums, and at events such as 1940s tea parties, big band concerts, airshows and steam railway festivals', in towns and more rural locations:

> A herd of cows at Croft Castle, Herefordshire, was very surprised by the sudden arrival in their field of Shropshire's NACRO Net Navigator Bus and Worcestershire County Council Comput@bus. Poking their noses into the buses, the cows found a Girl Guide unit helping local residents add their stories about rural life in wartime.[35]

---

[31] Contributed by epsomandewelllhc featuring Sheila, A2763957; BBCPW, 20 June 2004.
[32] See archive list, reference 29.
[33] Story Gathering: Introduction, at https://www.bbc.co.uk/history/ww2peopleswar/about/storygathering_01.shtml. For the BBC in WWII, see Siân Nicholas, 'The People's Radio: The BBC and Its Audience, 1939-1945', in Nick Hayes and Jeff Hill (eds.), *Millions Like Us?: British Culture in the Second World War* (Liverpool: Liverpool University Press, 1999), 62–92.
[34] For descriptions of the story gathering, see http://www.bbc.co.uk/history/ww2peopleswar/about/storygathering_05.shtml, accessed 3 April 2021.
[35] Story gathering: Contributing stories – the individuals, https://www.bbc.co.uk/history/ww2peopleswar/about/storygathering_02.shtml.

During the story-gathering phase, stories were selected for promotion on the site, chosen for 'particularly vivid storytelling, an unusual theme not covered in other stories, a dramatic or particularly resonant account of the events'.[36] These may well have been instrumental in setting the tone. Furthermore, certain themes helped to trigger further similar memories with cumulative effect, as is evident in comments posted on entries.[37] 'Writing buddies' encouraged further submissions and details in an open way: 'I'd be delighted to hear a wee bit more about yourself' or 'Would you be interested in expanding a bit on your story and include some detail from your experiences?'[38]

Sarah Housden and Jenny Zmroczeck describe how their involvement in reminiscence work with Norfolk Adult Education's Older People's Projects led them to interviewing contributors for the site. They explain the process and how the versions of the stories which subsequently appeared on the website were much truncated 'as words were limited, so transcripts were turned into brief articles which were approved by the contributors'.[39] It is impossible to gauge whether the uploaded narrative had benefitted from a longer interview with an engaged listener, an experience which permits more nuanced recall.[40] Some interviews appear to have been captured quickly in the moment, with wartime vocabulary occasionally misunderstood or mistranscribed, indicating the orality of the original source – WAF for WAAF, for example.[41] Other stories archived on the site were created as written prose, entered by individuals in the privacy of their own homes. Some of these are clearly carefully crafted, not least to convey humour. Some entries are unremittingly sad, for the events described, or the

---

[36] As explained on Site Information, during gathering, these stories were known as Editorial Picks. In the archive, these are Recommended stories, identified by a star icon. ★ https://www.bbc.co.uk/history/ww2peopleswar/about/siteinformation.shtml.

[37] 'Hi Joan. Reading your lovely story reminded me about a snap in my Army Album and as a result I have just posted another article that mentions bananas in Alexandria, see (A3060677).' Ron Goldstein, regarding Joan Stokoe's submission on 'Banana Sandwiches, A2734003, BBCPW, 29 September 2004.

[38] June responded to Carey thanking him for the encouragement, and hoping to send a little more information when she 'can do some thinking as to what to write'. MY WAR EFFORT; 22 December 2003 by Bob Gibb – WW2 Site Helper; https://www.bbc.co.uk/history/ww2peopleswar/user/02/u528602.shtml; Good comes from evil – feedback, 6 January 2004 by Carey – WW2 Site Helper, https://www.bbc.co.uk/history/ww2peopleswar/user/24/u529024.shtml 12 January 2004.

[39] Housden and Zmroczek. 'Exploring Identity in Later Life'.

[40] For the significance of the duration of an interview in moving beyond the dominant cultural narratives, see Corinna M. Peniston-Bird, "All in It Together" and "Backs to the Wall": Relating Patriotism and the People's War in the 21st Century', *Oral History*, 40, no. 2 (2012), 69–80. It becomes particularly obvious when themes and stories are repeated or returned to in the course of a longer interview.

[41] The story 'Happy memories as a WAF' was 'input by Emma McLaughlin of the BBC [Big Yellow] Bus team on behalf of Margaret Hodgett, the author', A3684152, BBCPW, 18 February 2005.

lives lived; a very few submit only a humorous story.⁴² But a substantial number of contributors, whether prose or in dialogue, punctuate their memories with or conclude on the lighter side of the war: 'However, there were some lighter moments ...'⁴³ Contributors used serious/funny framing as prompts to promote recall, and, as Lynn Abrams notes in relation to oral history interviewees, some narrators feel 'a responsibility to tell interesting or humorous stories'.⁴⁴ After relating how desperately homesick his wife had been as an evacuee, Ken Derrick closes 'on a lighter note', for example, by relating her brother's story of not changing his socks for seven weeks when he was evacuated, concluding with the wry punchline, 'No wonder he didn't stay long in his billet'.⁴⁵

There are a wide variety of real and imagined audiences evident in the entries, ranging from friends and family, project interviewers and live audiences including children, to strangers listening to the radio or browsing the archive in the future. The appropriate audience and occasion for humorous retrospective accounts are wider than for narratives of trauma or self-reflection. Such memories can therefore come across as more polished and refined, though not necessarily frozen: Norrick explores the extent to which repeated jokes by the same speaker hold certain anchor points consistently (such as the punchline), but vary the details getting there, adapting to audience.⁴⁶ From a methodological point of view, the fact that many testimonies included at least two if not more voices and were solicited through dialogue is often omitted in the uploaded entries, and thus so too is evidence of the impact of intersubjectivities on their humour. The effects of the gathering techniques on the material generated can only be surmised: the memories triggered by group interactions and chance encounters, the genres of story encouraged or impeded by the physical environment, the domino effects on the type of material generated. Like most oral history transcripts, the uploads also lack the contextualization cues of an oral performance. These are particularly important in setting up the listener to get a joke, such as smiling. Marta Dynel describes the performative nature of anecdotes, for example, of which there are ample examples on the site:

---

[42] See, for example, the memories contributed by Sheila Betty, A Child's War in Hull, A2073214. BBCPW, 23 November 2003.
[43] Mary Goodhand, A3396233, BBCPW, 11 December 2004.
[44] Abrams, *Oral History Theory*, 148.
[45] Ken Derrick, Message 29 July 2003, in response to 'A Happy Evacuee', Evelyn May, A1107901 BBCPW, 13 July 2003.
[46] Neal R. Norrick, 'Retelling Stories in Spontaneous Conversation', *Discourse Processes*, 25, no. 1 (1998), 75–97.

Anecdotes are delivered in a colourful style abounding in witty lexemes and phrasemes, coupled with rich non-verbal expression (the tone of voice, facial expression and gestures), which contribute to the humorous effect. It is not uncommon for such stories to refer to events which were hardly humorous and even dramatic, but are, however, recounted jovially to elicit a humorous response in the addressee.[47]

In the archive we are left with the narrative text but not the narrative event. In consequence, the selections made here represent the submissions where the humour remains evident in the text alone and which emerged from the subject matter more than from in-the-moment banter.

The sheer volume of narratives gathered in digital form on the site allows researchers to note and explore patterns otherwise nigh invisible or buried in hundreds of lengthier published autobiographical materials and oral history archives. The first publication based on the site was by Housden and Zmroczeck who drew on their experiences to explore the role of war memories in helping older people to 'maintain a sense of identity, sometimes in the face of multiple losses'.[48] Historians have focused on the themes found within the submissions: in previous publications I have explored the potential of the site in two different research areas: the flouting of the combat taboo by female auxiliaries, and the ubiquity of the banana in wartime reminiscences.[49] Lucy Noakes drew on the BBCPW for her engagement with wartime loss, not least because it includes memories marginal to representations of the war at the time and since. Noakes also explored the latter in a paper on the site as a mode of remembrance and commemoration.[50] As she argued,

> The BBC's 'People's War' website exists as a space where the dominant cultural memory of the war, which positions it as a pivotal event in British history and a defining moment in the articulation and mobilization of the shared mores and

---

[47] Dynel, 'Beyond a Joke', 1295. See also Alessandro Portelli on the significance of volume, velocity, tone, and rhythm, not 'reproducible in writing'. Alessandro Portelli, 'What Makes Oral History Different', in R. Perks and A. Thomson (eds.), *The Oral History Reader* (London: Routledge, 2006), 61–74, here 63.

[48] Housden, and Zmroczek, 'Exploring Identity in Later Life'.

[49] Peniston-Bird, 'Of Hockey Sticks and Sten guns', 13–22 and '"Yes, we had no Bananas": Sharing Memories of the Second World War', in Mary Addyman, Laura Wood and Christopher Yiannitsaros (eds.), *Food, Drink, and the Written Word in Britain, 1820-1945* (London: Routledge, 2017).

[50] Lucy Noakes, '"War on the Web": The BBC's 'People's War' Website and Memories of Fear in Wartime in 21st-Century Britain', in Lucy Noakes and Juliette Pattinson (eds.), *British Cultural Memory and the Second World War* (London: Bloomsbury Publishing Plc, 2013); Lucy Noakes 'The BBC "People's War" Website', in Michael Keren and Holger H. Jefferson (eds.), *War, Memory, and Popular Culture: Essays on Modes of Remembrance and Commemoration* (North Carolina: McFarland & Company, 2009).

values which are still understood as being central to a shared national history and identity, interacts with more personal individual or family memories of the war, which may not always accord with the dominant narrative.[51]

Humour aligns with this observation in that it can clearly speak to and draw upon dominant narratives but is also often rooted in the particular and familiar. For example in her discussion of rationing, Margaret Hartrey, a teen in Cardiff, narrated how 'I remember my mother going for our share [of offal] and being told that there wasn't any left, so she answered back with "Well, I suppose you're going to tell me that the animals are being born without innards, for the duration!"' a story which captures both her mother's wit and wartime frustrations.[52]

The timing of the BBC project thus needs to be considered in relation to the dominant cultural memory of the Second World War at the beginning of the twenty-first century. It followed the fiftieth anniversary of the end of the war in 1995, in which the inclusion of the Home Front experience had been particularly marked. Janet Watson has observed how between the anniversaries of the 1980s and 1990s the emphasis shifted from the veteran to the Home Front: 'What made "total war" total was its breadth: no longer about just armed forces, total was everyone's war, perhaps especially the civilians' war, and that's what "total anniversary" was about, too.'[53] This is evident in the BBCPW also, and the project thus drew upon and fed existing tropes in the recollections of the Second World War. Mark Connelly has explored British cultural memory of the Second World War up to the period of the story-gathering, and the key tropes that he identifies (Churchill and Monty, Dunkirk and the Battle of Britain, Standing Alone, the People's War and ultimately victory and the welfare state) are clearly in evidence in both the narratives and their categorizations on the site.[54] As intimated with many of the examples in this chapter, tales of aerial bombardment and the Blitz, for example, are ubiquitous, repeating the same components and themes: blacking out windows, managing shattered glass, dust and rubble, the different shelters available, damage and death, resilience,

---

[51] Her paper considered 'the extent to which the participatory nature of the internet provides a challenge to the hegemonic nature of cultural memory, opening up public space to a variety of conflicting and oppositional voices that have previously been marginalized'. Noakes, 'War on the Web', 63. A perfect example of this can be found in the contribution by John Nicholls, A4049462 BBCPW, 11 May 2005.
[52] Margaret Hartrey, A2704727, BBCPW, 5 June 2004.
[53] Janet Watson, 'Total War and Total Anniversary: The Material Culture of Second World War Commemoration in Britain', in *British Cultural Memory and the Second World War*.
[54] Mark Connelly, *We Can Take It!: Britain and the Memory of the Second World War* (Harlow: Pearson, Longman, 2004).

defiance and resolution, but capturing also the individual experience of such common themes, including fear and boredom.

Don Howell offers another surreal anecdote in this vein. Don, who had served in the RAF, had been intending to dictate his story of how he had come to crash in his Hudson in Portugal, but was distracted when he overheard the staff commenting that no stories that day had been 'funny'.[55] Musing first 'can there be humour in war? Emphatically no! How can conflagration which gives place to such carnage be humorous?', Don overcame his scruples to list a series of comic anecdotes and jokes, beginning with a story of a parachute mine exploding when he was home on leave in Tottenham, London. Mobilizing his ARP training, Don hoped he might be of some help and

> went down the road towards the High St and heard a voice calling out quite plaintively, drawing nearer one could see against the lightening sky that the whole of one wall was missing and there sitting on the toilet was an elderly man saying over and over again, "but I only pulled the chain!"

Such a punchline merited repetition, and Don continued, 'Picking my way through the debris I entered the parlour then the hall way and up the stairs to assist him down all the while he was repeating "but I only … …"'[56] This story suggests the spoken performance that underpins its humour and overtly states the impetus behind the recollection. Curiously, a variation on this story is repeated on the site. It remains located in London, but is this time narrated by Joan Windsor, a young married woman on outbreak of war. In contrast to Don's story, told in the first person and building in a crescendo, Joan tells it as a story that was funny at the time rather than for comic effect, capturing a moment in time rather than delivering a performance. Having joined civil defence, she remembered how one night,

> one man, a real character, a trader in Petticoat Lane came back laughing. We asked him what was so funny and he relayed how a house had fallen down and they'd dug a bloke out. Apparently, once rescued he said, "I thought it was a bit strange, I was only sitting on the toilet, I pulled the chain and the house fell down"! That is a story that has stuck in my mind. We did laugh about that.[57]

It proved impossible to ascertain how widely this story was in circulation in the war or whether both narrators experienced the same night in London and beat

---

[55] Don Howell's Hudson story can be found under Article ID: A4445291 BBCPW, 13 July 2005.
[56] Contributed by BBC Southern Counties Radio featuring Don Howell, A4516625 BBCPW, 22 July 2005. You can see an image of a pull chain flush here: 'The Bathroom and Lavatory of a British 1940s Suburban House', https://www.1900s.org.uk/1940s-house-bathrooom, accessed 12 April 2021.
[57] Contributed by stjohnscentre featuring Joan Windsor, A4369007, BBCPW, 5 July 2005.

the odds to repeat it for the same archive. The different tones adopted reflect the different personalities of the speakers, and are dependent also on perceptions of the audience, with Don's a direct response to the staff whose observations he overheard. But the contrast between the two also suggests the different temporal relationships at stake: the first is told as a story set in the past which remains amusing in the present; the second places the amusement in the past too. The audience can get the joke, but are not invited into it.

There is thus a contrast between humour positioned firmly in the past, and that dependent on the passage of time. As examples of the former, both direct speech and indirect speech on the site celebrate wartime banter and witticisms: Esther Bruce, 'a black Londoner at war', related how 'Things were so bad they started selling whale meat, but I wouldn't eat it. I didn't like the look of it. We made a joke about it, singing Vera Lynn's song *We'll Meet Again* with new words, "Whale meat again!"'[58] One story appears at least three times (set in Belfast, and Newcastle-under-Lyme), perhaps because dentures remain a material object both funny-ha ha and funny-peculiar across time. The set up involves a female family member or neighbour taking too long to seek shelter in an air raid because of hunting for her false teeth. Notice the switch to the historic present to add colour and authenticity: 'My cousin Bobby was shouting at her "Mother, for goodness sake would you hurry up!" She was so big she couldn't really rush. She says "For God's sake Bobby would you hold on, I'm looking for my false teeth". "Mother," he says, "It's not bread they're dropping, its bombs!"'[59] The variations change the cast and the retort, reversing the punchline: 'The neighbour said to Maggy, "you are going, come on without your teeth, Hitler's dropping bombs not blooming sandwiches!"'[60] and 'Never mind your teeth Elsie – They're dropping bloody bombs – Not pork pies!'[61] Such repetition may suggest the appropriation and adaptation of wartime jokes, but may equally likely reflect wartime individuals coining original but not unique witticisms in response to common experiences.

Retrospective humour often positions a memory of a specific point in the past in relation to other time periods, however. A common trope for example is the buying power of money; the ridiculousness, in current terms, of being able to buy a week's worth of sweets for 25p, for example, or taking home a salary of £2 a

---

[58] Stephen Bourne, A Black Londoner at War, regarding his aunt Esther Bruce, A2045828, BBCPW, 15 November 2003.
[59] Hazel Collins, A4509092, BBCPW, 21 July 2005.
[60] 'V.E. Day, Sirens, and Maggie's Teeth', Silver Threads Club, A3484802, BBCPW, 8 January 2005.
[61] 'Elsie forgets her Teeth!' Contributed by Newcastle-staffs-lib featuring Mr Morris and Family and Mr and Mrs Jones; A3307862, BBCPW, 21 November 2004. See also 'Toothless!' contributed by brssouthglosproject featuring Margaret Hillman and Family, A5212171 BBCPW, 19 August 2005.

week, neither of which were funny at the time.[62] Such humour depends upon the narrator and the addressee sharing knowledge granted by experience or context denied the subject. The reader is prepared by crescendo and a question for the niece's reveal in this story:

> My Uncle Alan was a young boy during the war. He grew up with rationing and food shortages – fruit was a luxury that hardly ever came his way. At the age of 4 he was given his first banana. He was thrilled by the sight of this exciting and new piece of food. He took his first bite and spat it out in disgust. He never looked at a banana for the next 20 years. The reason for this violent reaction? He ate the banana with the skin on!![63]

Uncle Alan was not alone in this experience according to the archive, and its inherent humour depends on the interplays: the child and the adult s/he became, the disjuncture between the present and past availability of bananas, the shared expertise of the narrator and the recipient audience at the expense of the butt of the joke. Not all such narratives seek to provoke mirth in the here and now, however. Edith Taylor's story of a suspected gas attack would require a more deliberate reveal of the difference between the feared and the actual to be funny. Instead, the audience is asked to sympathize with the initial experience rather than its subsequent interpretation:

> When off duty one evening my husband shouted that gas had been dropped and we all hurriedly donned our gasmasks. We later found that the smell came from smoke generators which were designed to cover the towns with a sheet of thick black smoke. Although it seemed funny later it was very traumatic at the time.[64]

Memories which narrate laughter but do not seek to reproduce it are an interesting trope on the site. Humour that thrives on the disjunctures between then and now relies on incongruity. One of the most striking examples of this genre was submitted by Alice Burman who spoke of her sister Doris's experiences in the London Ambulance Service in the East End and drew on the cultural constructions of the resilience of that area:

---

[62] 'To give you some idea of just how much £ were in those days: in 1951 Dad landed his first job, in which he earned £2 a week. This was 6 years later! Today we are very lucky.' 'The Black Banana', contributed by sparklingjosephine, on Robin Campbell Burgess, A1956323, BBCPW, 3 November 2003.

[63] Contributed by Stoke_on_trentlibs on behalf of Dawn, A2430352, BBCPW, 16 March 2004. A similar story was intended to amuse during the war in 'Bananas in Moscow', *The Times*, 5 September 1944. Another example from the BBCPW: 'I don't ever remember being without food, but I do remember trying to eat a banana with the skin on – this must have been at the end of the war – and also I remember sharing an orange with a friend and my part was the skin!' Contributed by salisburysouthwilts featuring Mrs Steve Weathurburn A5858643. BBCPW, 22 September 2005.

[64] Edith Taylor, A2499519, BBCPW, 7 April 2004.

.... the old East End spirit survived, although living in such difficult circumstances, they remained at their posts and also managed to get a few laughs out of certain droll situations. One such situation was related by Doris after it had occurred, on one awful night of continuous raids and many casualties she and her driver were picking up pieces of dead bodies, the ambulance was soon filled – they had the unpleasant task of attempting to sort and put together the respective arms, legs and torsos, into body bags, cart them to a hospital (any hospital!) where an overworked doctor was to certify them dead ... [then] off went the ambulance straight to the local morgue, where the vehicle was quickly emptied. They returned to the fray assisting and caring for further casualties, only to find out that the mortuary received a direct hit later that night, and all the bodies, so carefully sorted, had been blown to smithereens, and mixed up once more! Looking back I suppose it was a shock reaction but they laughed helplessly, at the wasted effort. It was good that everyone could laugh, after all there was no counselling then, you were alive, so you carried on.[65]

This manner of narration serves to distance the modern-day audience and contemporary approaches to trauma from those who experienced the raids rather than bridging the gulf between past and present. Awareness of such a gulf was reflected on the site with observations such as 'We had more out of life than any other generation. Maybe because of we all went through in the war we have an appreciation that those who haven't experienced it wouldn't understand.'[66] Here the gulf of experience traditionally positioned between civilian and service personnel in wartime is positioned between temporal periods instead, and erodes the former distinction. Such narratives stand in contrast with the comparisons which note qualitative change – usually the abundance of the present in comparison to the deprivation or frugality of the past – but not rupture: 'in those days we didn't have as many clothes as youngsters seem to have nowadays.'[67]

The contemporary context of reminiscence can add layers of disjuncture, poignance, outrage, nostalgia and resentment, embedded in, masked or illuminated by humour. Whether an audience is present or imagined to be, the use of humour speaks to relationship and draws upon narrative structures shared by speaker and audience; it underpins the identity formation of the individual and the relationship and impact sought on the intended audience. In the interplay of temporalities within reminiscences, humour can function

---

[65] Contributed by London Borough of Newham Public featuring Alice Burman, A1904771, BBCPW, 21 October 2003.
[66] Contributed by ActionBristol featuring Valerie Strickland, A4021101, BBCPW, 7 May 2005.
[67] Sylvia Radford, A3484398, BBCPW, 6 January 2005.

to bridge the gulf between the past and the present and provoke recognition, sympathy and congruence, but it can also be mobilized in order to deepen the gulf, to underline distinction and to distance experience from appropriation.[68] Much of the humour here that conveys more than the wit of the speaker reveals how the experience of war is brought home by the juxtaposition of the usual and the unusual, innocence and experience, comedy and tragedy. The humour that is shared on the BBC People's War seldom reflects the critical, counter-narrative edge for which humour can be the ideal vehicle, but it does convey the surreality of the experience of war. Thus the value of the archive lies not only in its expansive collection of the exceptional and the mundane, but in the juxtaposition of the two. As the philosopher Simon Critchley observed, 'Humour views the world awry, bringing us back to the everyday by estranging us from it.'[69] As the Second World War fades from living memory it becomes all the more important to be conscious of the paradox inherent in our familiarity with, and estrangement from, the war.

Bibliography

Lynn Abrams, *Oral History Theory* (London: Routledge, 2010).
BBC WW2 People's War, bbc.co.uk/ww2peopleswar.
Martha Rose Beard, 'Re-thinking Oral History – a Study of Narrative Performance', *Rethinking History*, 21, no. 4 (2017), 529–48.
Mark Connelly, *We Can Take It! Britain and the Memory of the Second World War* (Harlow, England: Pearson, Longman, 2004).
Simon Critchley, *On Humour* (London and New York: Routledge, 2002).
Graham Dawson, *Soldier Heroes: British Adventure, Empire and the Imagining of Masculinities* (London: Routledge, 1994).
Mary Douglas, 'Do Dogs Laugh? A Cross-Cultural Approach to Body Symbolism', *Journal of Psychosomatic Research*, 15, no. 4 (1971), 387–90.
Henk Driessen, 'Humour, Laughter and the Field: Reflections from Anthropology', in Jan Bremner and Herman Roodenburg (eds.), *A Cultural History of Humour* (Cambridge: Polity Press, 1997), 222–41.
Marta Dynel, 'Beyond a Joke: Types of Conversational Humour', *Language and Linguistics Compass*, 3, no. 5 (2009), 1284–99.

---

[68] For a similar triad, see Nancy Walker, 'Humor and Gender Roles: The "Funny" Feminism of the Post-World War II Suburbs', *American Quarterly*, Special Issue: American Humor, 37, no. 1 (1985), 98–113.
[69] Simon Critchley, *On Humour* (London; New York: Routledge, 2002), 65.

Sigmund Freud, *Der Witz Und Seine Beziehung Zum Unbewußten* [*Jokes and Their Relation to the Unconscious*] (Leipzig and Vienna: Franz Deuticke, 1905).
Paul Fussell, *Wartime: Understanding and Behavior in the Second World War* (New York: Oxford University Press, 1989).
Richard Godfrey, 'Soldiering on: Exploring the Role of Humour as a Disciplinary Technology in the Military', *Organization*, 23, no. 2 (2016), 164–83.
Virginia Graham, *Consider the Years, 1938–1946* (First ed. Jonathan Cape, 1946; London: Persephone Books, 2000).
Lynn Hilditch, *Wonder and Horror: An Interpretation of Lee Miller's Second World War Photographs as 'Surreal Documentary'* (PhD dissertation, University of Liverpool, 2010).
Sarah Housden and Jenny Zmroczek, 'Exploring Identity in Later Life through BBC People's War Interviews', *Oral History*, 35, no. 2 (2007), 100–8.
David Low, *British Cartoonist's Caricaturists and Comic Artists* (London: William Collins of London, 1942).
Edward Madigan, '"Sticking to a Hateful Task": Resilience, Humour, and British Understandings of Combatant Courage, 1914–1918', *War in History* (Special Issue on Courage and Cowardice in Wartime), 20, no. 1 (2013), 76–98.
Francois Maon, Adam Lindgreen, Joelle Vanhamme, Robert J. Angell and Juliet Memery, *Not All Claps and Cheers* (Milton: Routledge, 2018).
Andy Medhurst, *A National Joke: Popular Comedy and English Cultural Identities* (Abingdon: Routledge, 2007).
Michele A. Court, 'Are Women Funny (and other stupid questions)', http://micheleacourt.com/are-women-funny-and-other-stupid-questions/.
Daniel Miller and Jolynna Sinanan, *Visualising Facebook: A Comparative Perspective* (London: UCL Press, 2017).
Gabriel Moshenska, *Material Cultures of Childhood in Second World War Britain* (Abingdon: Routledge 2019).
Siân Nicholas, 'The People's Radio: The BBC and Its Audience, 1939–1945', in Nick Hayes and Jeff Hill (eds.), *Millions Like Us?: British Culture in the Second World War* (Liverpool: Liverpool University Press, 1999), 62–92.
Lucy Noakes, 'The BBC "People's War" Website', in Michael Keren and Holger H. Jefferson (eds.), *War, Memory, and Popular Culture: Essays on Modes of Remembrance and Commemoration* (North Carolina: McFarland & Company, 2009), 135–149.
Lucy Noakes, '"War on the Web": The BBC's 'People's War' Website and Memories of Fear in Wartime in 21st-Century Britain', in Lucy Noakes and Juliette Pattinson (eds.), *British Cultural Memory and the Second World War* (London: Bloomsbury Publishing Plc, 2013), 47–65.
Lucy Noakes and Juliette Pattinson (eds.), *British Cultural Memory and the Second World War* (London: Bloomsbury Publishing Plc, 2013).
Neal R. Norrick, 'Retelling Stories in Spontaneous Conversation', *Discourse Processes*, 25, no. 1 (1998), 75–97.

Neal R. Norrick, 'Humour in Oral History Interviews', *Oral History*, 34, no. 2 (Autumn 2006), 85–94.

C.M. Peniston-Bird and Penny Summerfield, '"Hey, you're dead!": The Multiple Uses of Humour in Representations of British National Defence in the Second World War', *Journal of European Studies*, xxxi (2001), 413–35.

Corinna M. Peniston-Bird, '"All in It Together" and "Backs to the Wall": Relating Patriotism and the People's War in the 21st Century', *Oral History*, 40, no. 2 (2012), 69–80.

Corinna M. Peniston-Bird, 'Of Hockey Sticks and Sten Guns: British Auxiliaries and Their Weapons in the Second World War', *Women's History Magazine*, Autumn, no. 76 (2014), 13–22.

Corinna M. Peniston-Bird, '"Yes, we had no bananas": Sharing Memories of the Second World War', in Addyman Mary, Laura Wood and Christopher Yiannitsaros (eds.), *Food, Drink, and the Written Word in Britain, 1820–1945* (London: Routledge, 2017), 165–86.

Alessandro Portelli, 'What Makes Oral History Different', in R. Perks and A. Thomson (eds.), *The Oral History Reader* (London: Routledge, 2006), 61–74.

J.B. Priestley, *English Humour* (London: Heinemann, 1976).

Sillince, *We're All in It* (London: Collins, 1941).

Nancy Walker, 'Humor and Gender Roles: The "Funny" Feminism of the Post-World War II Suburbs', *American Quarterly*, Special Issue: American Humor, 37, no. 1 (1985), 98–113.

Janet Watson, 'Total War and Total Anniversary: The Material Culture of Second World War Commemoration in Britain', in Lucy Noakes and Juliette Pattinson (eds.), *British Cultural Memory and the Second World War* (London: Bloomsbury Publishing Plc, 2013), 175–94.

Alan Weeks, *Cheer Up Mate: Second World Humour* (Stroud: The History Press, 2011).

9

Exploring *The Real Dad's Army* in the Imperial War Museum, London

Kasia Tomasiewicz

There is a spectre haunting any critical analysis of humour and the Second World War – *Dad's Army*. A continually popular sitcom produced and broadcast by the BBC, *Dad's Army* remains a cultural phenomenon with its success spanning many decades, and like a rolling juggernaut, film and television remakes. This chapter analyses a lesser known part of its far-reaching cultural heritage: *The Real Dad's Army*, a small but significant exhibition in the Imperial War Museum, London (IWM), during the mid-1970s. Emerging as part of a new approach to attract larger audience numbers during a time of economic turbulence, the exhibition brought the theme of comedy into the war museum in an unprecedented way by very directly drawing on the imaginative possibilities afforded by the already popular BBC television programme *Dad's Army*. Given the Museum's role as a powerful historical site for the dissemination of war narratives, such an approach was not without risk, mainly because war and comedy can prove an unstable mix. Highlighting that the context of the 1970s – especially a sense of economic decline – ensured a continued popular cultural appetite for the war years, this chapter argues that exhibitions on popular war-themed programmes legitimize the narratives offered within them as accurate portrayals of war.

Dad's Army focused on the trials and tribulations of a group of Local Defence Volunteers (LDV), later known as the 'Home Guard', in the fictional town of Walmington-on-Sea during the Second World War. It was the first British comedy about the war years but proved, against initial critique, to be a success. It ran for nine series between 31 July 1968 and 13 November 1977, attracting an average of 12 million viewers a week, and reaching a peak of 18 million in 1972.[1]

---

[1] Penny Summerfield and Corinna Peniston-Bird, *Contesting Home Defence: Men, Women and the Home Guard in the Second World War* (Manchester: Manchester University Press, 2007), 170.

It was so popular that it was adapted into a film (1971), a radio series (1974), stage show (1975) and, as this chapter will explore, an exhibition.

The Real Dad's Army exhibition at the IWM opened to the public on 17 October 1974 and it endeavoured to show the 'weapons, equipment, documents, photographs, paintings and cartoons relating to the Home Guard' from its inception in 1940 to its disbandment in 1944.[2] Part of the exhibition was also dedicated to the sitcom itself, making it an exhibition on both the 'real' Home Guard and the 'real' *Dad's Army*. It proved popular and attracted 29,007 visitors in the first three months of opening, a fair number for a special exhibition at the time, and before its closure on 29 June 1975 it raised via an entrance fee a considerable £3,789.31 (the equivalent today of £40,500).[3]

While these visitor numbers pale in comparison to the millions of television viewers *Dad's Army* attracted, it is important to remember the symbolic potential of the narratives displayed in museums, which can have a profound effect on the memory of war. At their core, museums show glimpses of historical pasts through material culture that act as 'witnesses' to the past. While this gives them much of their cultural authority, museums are generally trusted as purveyors of 'factual' narratives that give objects meaning. As Lucy Noakes suggests, museums are 'powerful sites of cultural transmission and public education; they are an embodiment of knowledge and power, important hegemonic instruments'.[4] Indeed, writing about the memory of Vichy France, Henry Rousso highlights that museums among other cultural spaces and signifiers are important 'vectors of memory' through which narratives of the past are constructed.[5] This makes exhibitions significant cultural interventions, but also markers of the accepted social and cultural boundaries of war narratives.

Importantly, although museums appear from the outside as static monoliths, they do not just shape, but are in turn shaped by wider contexts. The popularity of *Dad's Army* would be one such wider context that invariably shaped the Museum's public programming. *Dad's Army's* success was due to its two defining features: it is a comedy, a particularly popular genre of programming, and it is based on the Second World War, a cultural touchstone that permeated into cultural and social life long after 1945. Initially, these aspects appear incompatible. On the

---

[2] Imperial War Museum press notice, IWM Central Files in EN4/15/d/s.
[3] Internal memorandum dated 13 January 1975, IWM Central Files in EN4/15/d/s.
[4] Lucy Noakes, 'Making Histories: Experiencing the Blitz in London's Museums in the 1990s', in M. Evans and K. Lunn (eds.), *War and Memory in the Twentieth Century* (Oxford: Berg, 1997), 89–104; 90.
[5] Henry Rousso, *The Vichy Syndrome: History and Memory in France since 1944* (Cambridge, MA: Harvard University Press, 1991).

one hand, comedy is a powerful narrative framing device, and although comedy is subjective, *Dad's Army* could be classed as a 'good' and 'funny' comedy in the sense that it made people laugh, and as a result they continued to watch it. On the other hand, the Second World War was the most devastating global war of the twentieth century.

Combining comedy and the Second World War then proves an unstable mix, with a high potential to offend, perhaps why prior to *The Real Dad's Army* the IWM avoided comedic representations of the war.[6] This was partially due to what Andrea Witcomb calls the 'politics of respect' to the war living and dead that frame representations in war museums.[7] As Jay Winter notes, the function of war museums is to convey historical narratives as the 'sacred' or the commemorative, and as the 'profane' or educational.[8] Traditionally, comedy does not appear to fall into either realm. And yet, in being created in the same tradition as a long line of experiential imperial exhibitions, the IWM was also a site for entertainment.[9] It amazed audiences with machinery, material culture and the politics and poetics of exhibition design.[10] While entertainment is an aspect that is often overlooked in critical war museum analysis, this chapter will highlight how comedy was incorporated into these spaces.[11]

Frustratingly, museums themselves have been slow to recognize and archive their own contributions to historical memory. No document exists, for example, that fully maps the exhibition narrative of *The Real Dad's Army*, and instead this analysis relies on archival correspondences and a chance discovery of a number of photographs in an institutional 'yearbook' album. Despite this archival scarcity, however, examining the traces of museum exhibitions and the circumstances

---

[6] See also controversy over *Blackadder Goes Forth* (1989) in Emma Hanna, *The Great War on the Small Screen: Representing the First World War in Contemporary Britain* (Edinburgh: Edinburgh University Press, 2009), 133.

[7] Andrea Witcomb 'Remembering the Dead by Affecting the Living: The Case of a Miniature Model of Treblinka', in Sandra Dudley (ed.), *Museum Materialities* (Routledge: London, 2009), 39–52.

[8] Jay Winter, 'Museums and the Representation of War', *Museum and Society*, 10, no. 3 (November 2012), 150–63.

[9] Steven Cooke and Lloyd Jenkins, 'Discourses of Regeneration in Early Twentieth-century Britain: From Bedlam to the Imperial War Museum', *Area*, 33, no. 4 (December 2001), 382–90.

[10] See Sarah Byrne, Rodney Harrison and Anne Clarke (eds.), *Unpacking the Collection: Networks of Material and Social Agency in the Museum* (New York: Springer, 2011); Henrietta Lidchi, 'The Poetics and the Politics of Exhibiting Other Cultures', in Stuart Hall, et al., (eds.), *Representation: Cultural Representations and Signifying Practices*, 2nd ed. (London: Sage, 2013), 120–57; Paul Cornish, 'Sacred Relics: Objects in the Imperial War Museum 1917–1939', in Nicholas J. Saunders (ed.), *Matters of Conflict: Material Culture, Memory and the First World War* (London: Routledge, 2004), 35–50; 37.

[11] For further analysis of war museums spaces see Kasia Tomasiewicz, '"We are a Social History, not a Military History Museum": Large Objects and the "Peopling" of Galleries In the Imperial War Museum, London', in Kate Hill (ed.), *Museums, Modernity and Conflict: Museums and Collections in and of War Since the Nineteenth Century* (London: Routledge, 2020), 213–34.

by which they come to be staged, enjoyed or critiqued offers us an invaluable window into the creation and legitimization of historical narratives in the past.

Exploring the tensions and negotiations around the staging and inclusion of comedy in the IWM, this chapter focuses on the launch and content of *The Real Dad's Army* exhibition. First, it argues that the popularity of *Dad's Army* meant that despite being an exhibition on predominantly the 'real' Home Guard, the inclusion of *Dad's Army* related material meant that the exhibition might have been read as reflective of the historical narratives shown in the fictional *Dad's Army*. The argument here is not that visitors couldn't differentiate between the 'real' history of the Home Guard in authentic material culture and the 'inaccurate' portrayal of historical events in *Dad's Army*, but that *Dad's Army* powerfully inflected readings of historically contemporaneous material culture, and vice versa. Having established the influence of the programme, this chapter then interrogates why, given the clear potential challenges in displaying comedy, the IWM held such an exhibition in the mid-1970s. It argues that economic turbulence framed a wider appetite for war-themed cultural products, a culture that the IWM shrewdly capitalized on.

The Real Dad's Army

On 16 October 1974, journalists gathered in the forecourt of the IWM to snap photographs of the cast members of *Dad's Army* in full uniform. They posed for photographs and enacted various scenes with 'Jones' meat van', a key prop in the show. As a comedy heavily dependent on character-based gags and storylines, these photographs appear to show the characters of *Dad's Army* 'in real life'. In one photograph even when smiling Arthur Lowe appears officious as the leader of the unit Captain George Mainwaring, John Le Mesurier looks bored as his long-suffering deputy Sergeant Arthur Wilson, Clive Dunn's limbs appear as a blur, true to the character of Lance Corporal Jack Jones the local butcher who could never salute on time, John Laurie looks thoughtful as the 'doomed' Private James Frazer, Arnold Ridley is hunched and looks sleepy like the calm conscientious objector Private Charles Godfrey, and Bill Pertwee stands tall as one might expect from the officious Chief Air Raid Warden Hodges. The only central characters of the unit absent at the exhibition launch were Ian Lavender as the 'mummy's boy' Private Frank Pike, and James Beck the crafty cockney 'spiv' Private Joe Walker, who had died suddenly the year before.

My reading of the scene shown in the photograph is of course subjective, but I would suggest that it is a reading familiar to anyone who has seen *Dad's Army*, including contemporaries, partially because the writers of the sitcom Jimmy Perry and David Croft developed comprehensive character histories. These were then developed by the actors who added personal anecdotes, or as in the case of John Le Mesurier, based their acted character on themselves.[12] There is a warmth and joy – a familiarity – felt at seeing the characters in 'real life', which is best summarized by Jeffery Richards's comment that 'from the first they were characters, never caricatures … [T]hese were three-dimensional characters who became old friends'.[13] In the television programme, one of the ways in which the characters appeared fully formed was through the wearing of both military and civilian clothing while 'on' and 'off' duty. Similarly, a photograph from the exhibition launch of a tired Arnold Ridley sat down sipping sherry allows us to imagine that while not in uniform he is still Godfrey, the sweet octogenarian.

And yet, crucially, these photographs are simultaneously a reminder that the cast aren't *really* yours or Jeffrey Richards's wartime friends. There are cars in the background that don't seem typical of the war years, visitors mill around the front of the Museum and John Le Mesurier's contemporary shoes appear to jar a little with his 'uniform'. Equally, in another, a mannequin of a nurse can be spotted through the window just above Ridley. The cast may look familiar, but they are out of place and out of their time; they are no longer in the early 1940s in the Walmington-on-Sea church hall, but at the IWM in 1974. It is worth reminding ourselves of this because these 'three dimensional characters' are, and were, so culturally resonant that they can powerfully shape how we understand aspects of the past. They can also significantly shape museum spaces that attempt to show some sense of 'what really happened' in the past.

So strongly are the acted characters associated with the Home Guard, that authentic Home Guard-related material culture appears uncannily similar to members of the cast. A photograph of Clive Dunn in full uniform, posing next to a portrait of a real member of the Home Guard painted by S. Morris Brown to whom he looks eerily similar shows this most clearly. Visitors to the exhibition may not have seen this photograph of Dunn next to the painting, but those who watched the programme would have been struck by the physical similarities of the man in the painting and Dunn. Even when showing authentic material, therefore, visitors would be engaging with the exhibition and its representation of the past through the imagery of, and representations in *Dad's Army*. In a fairly

---

[12] Graham McCann, *Dad's Army: The Story of a Classic Television Show* (London: Fourth Estate, 2002), 69–75.

[13] Jeffrey Richards 'Dad's Army and the Politics of Nostalgia', in *Films and British National Identity: From Dickens to Dad's Army* (Manchester: Manchester University Press, 1997), 351–66; 366.

profound way, this allows for a drawing of connections between the narrativized fictional experience of the sitcom and the authentic objects on display.

Here, it should also be noted that in naming the exhibition *The 'Real' Dad's Army*, the Museum from the start made particular claims as to authenticity and historical accuracy of the exhibition. This is not to say it did not display authentic objects. Indeed, key material culture including improvised weapons, wartime cartoons by Giles and Stube, the original 'Sea Lion' invasion directive signed by Hitler and King George VI's Sten gun.[14] These authentic objects sat alongside objects related to the television programme, including a recreation of Captain Mainwaring's office, and a map of the fictional Walmington-on-Sea. And yet, the name appears an anachronism in showing the 'real' Home Guard given that *Dad's Army* as a descriptive term was only made popular following the launch of the television programme.[15] Of course, this name is clearly a cultural shorthand, and one that was so common that veterans themselves referred to their own experiences in those terms.[16] And yet, it is precisely this cultural shorthand that is of interest, because it allows for the imaginative possibilities of *Dad's Army* to dominate and, therefore, to blur the boundaries between real and fictional. In such a title the 'real' Home Guard is described *as Dad's Army*, and as such the representations in the sitcom gain a historical significance.

Historical significance was something that was frequently visible in the sitcom itself. Episodes were 'anchored' to historical events, often through the inclusion of 'real life' Churchill speeches. So frequent were such references, that as Bernd Lenz notes Churchill 'is omnipresent: either visible or, if invisible, as an encouraging leader in the background'.[17] Additionally, as Penny Summerfield notes, the greatest care was taken during the filming of the sitcom to make settings authentic including the use of genuine wartime ephemera, products, clothes, weapons and vehicles, and although the theme tune by Bud Flanagan was a pastiche of those he would sing in the war, authentic wartime songs featured in many scenes.[18] The creators of the programme also consistently stressed the sitcom's factual accuracy, given that characters have been largely

---

[14] Imperial War Museum press notice, IWM Central Files in EN4/15/d/s.
[15] C. Peniston-Bird notes how a reference to *Dad's Army* appeared 'in a Giles cartoon in the Sunday Express of 23 March 1969 commenting on the British invasion of the Caribbean Island of Anguilla' in 'I wondered who'd be the first to spot that', 183–202, 188.
[16] This phenomenon is well documented in Summerfield and Peniston-Bird, *Contesting Home Defence*.
[17] Bernd Lenz '"Your Little Game": Myth and War in Dad's Army', in Jürgen Kamm and Birgit Neumann (eds.), *British TV Comedies* (London: Palgrave, 2016), 36–50; 42.
[18] Penny Summerfield, 'Dad's Army, the Home Guard and the Memory of the British War Effort', in M. Riera and G. Schaffer (eds.), *The Lasting War: Society and Identity in Britain, France and Germany after 1945* (London: Palgrave Macmillan, 2008), 86–99; 90–1.

based on Perry's own experiences in the LDV as a teenager. Private Pike was based on Perry himself, and Lance Corporal Jack Jones's catchphrase 'they don't like it up 'em' was frequently said by someone in Perry's battalion who had, like Jones, fought at Omdurman in 1898.[19]

And yet, such assertions by the creators of the programme blur the boundaries between a constructed television in the 1970s and 'what really happened' in the 1940s. As previously mentioned, however, veterans of the Home Guard too blurred their own war experiences with those narrativized in *Dad's Army*. The popularity of *Dad's Army* clearly made it an accessible reference point for a force 'which did not fit neatly either into recollections of civilian service (given the military roles of the force), nor into discussions of military service (its members had civilian status)'.[20] As such, *Dad's Army* provided a narrative framework around which veterans could organize and understand their own experiences and memories.

By the early 1970s, the war had been over for almost thirty years. As a result, it was still a history within graspable living memory. While Churchill had died in 1965, it feels pertinent that key figures in the creation of the Home Guard were able to attend the exhibition launch, including former Prime Minister Sir Anthony Eden. Eden, who opened the exhibition, was a fitting choice as he had announced on the radio the creation of the Local Defence Volunteers (LDV), later to be called the Home Guard, on 14 May 1940 in a speech that had featured in the first episode of *Dad's Army* 'The Man and the Hour'. In the letter of invitation to Eden, Head Trustee Sir Deric Holland-Martin outlined the exhibition aim as 'fairly light-hearted in character but at the same time we are anxious to pay due tribute to the courage and patriotism of the men who joined the Home Guard'.[21] Interestingly, the careful reassurances by Holland-Martin to pay 'tribute' highlight the tensions over representing comedic narratives of the Second World War at the time.

These tensions can be seen in the inclusion of a fairly large memorial wall in the exhibition of flags, newspaper articles and a memorial plaque. This was an important addition, in that exhibitions in IWM as a rule didn't always include memorial spaces or markers. The comedic nature of *Dad's Army* meant that the Museum needed to show that – despite the widespread public acceptance of

---

[19] Jimmy Perry, *A Stupid Boy: The Autobiography of the Creator of Dad's Army* (London: Century, 2002).
[20] C Peniston-Bird 'I wondered Who'd Be the First to Spot That', 183–202.
[21] Letter from Sir Deric Holland-Martin to Sir Anthony Eden, IWM Central Files in EN4/15/d/s.

Dad's Army at this point – it wasn't making a mockery of the memory of the Home Guard and so was appropriately observing Witcomb's 'politics of respect'.[22]

Attempts to reconcile these differences are also clearly seen in *Dad's Army* itself. As a form of public damage control, the first episode is framed as a memory-based retrospective account by situating the sitcom in 1968, thus deflecting critique of any scenes deemed inappropriate as being fictionalized constructions of memory. In a clearer nod to commemoration, in the sitcom's final episode 'Never Too Old' the cast turn to the camera and, breaking the fourth wall, raise a toast 'To Britain's Home Guard!' This is not a scene that would have necessarily featured in other fictional war-themed television programmes. Perhaps unusually then, in navigating the acceptable boundaries of war representation, comedy quite directly incorporates commemoration into its framing of the war, meaning that as we laugh, we are also reminded to remember those who fought and died. This emphasis on commemoration as a means to prove respectfulness makes comedy a powerful vector for shaping the memory of the war.

And yet, what was being 'remembered' in the exhibition was prescriptive. In repurposing the name of the programme, instead of the more neutral Home Guard, the exhibition can be seen to be reproducing the implicit values the programme represented. One clear example of this is its gendered construction of the Home Guard. In the sitcom, women predominantly performed the roles of love interests, wives and mothers, or as in one episode 'Mum's Army', a female recruit; such roles were always either supporting or fleeting. The very name of the programme, relating specifically to the male father, meant that '*Dad's Army*', as Summerfield and Peniston-Bird note, powerfully limited the visibility of some 40,000 women who joined the Home Guard from 1943.[23] As there is no cohesive exhibition list or narrative, it is unclear if women were wholly excluded from the exhibition. Nevertheless, the urge to pay tribute to, as Holland-Martin suggested, the 'men who joined' (although this could have been meant in the gender-neutral plural) goes some way in highlighting how little room was afforded explicitly to the memory of the women who joined the Home Guard.[24]

This leads us to question more broadly why, given its cultural authority, the IWM did not simply produce an exhibition on the Home Guard. Indeed, as we have seen comedy can be both an unstable and powerful framing device of war narratives. It is to the circumstances that led to the exhibition that we now turn.

---

[22] Witcomb, 'Remembering the Dead', 39–52.
[23] Summerfield and Peniston-Bird, *Contesting Home Defence*.
[24] The gendered nature of home defence has been explored by Lucy Noakes, '"Serve to Save": Gender, Citizenship and Civil Defence in Britain 1937—41', *Journal of Contemporary History*, 47, no. 4 (2012), 734–53.

Nostalgia and crisis

Responses to the initial preview of the pilot of *Dad's Army* were poor, with some audience members wondering if 'the authors know the war's over?'[25] *Dad's Army* was the first British comedy to air about the war since the immediate postwar years, although the Home Guard had featured in some comic representations of the war, notably during the conflict in films such as *Get Cracking* (1943), and afterwards in *Whiskey Galore* (1949).[26] Some audiences read the sitcom as a satire that showed the unpreparedness of civil defence and the failure of leadership during the Second World War. Many more, however, read it as a celebration, with some seeing the Walmington-on-Sea Home Guard as 'nothing short of a symbol of British heroism'.[27] As Summerfield argues, much of this was due to a wider sense of postwar economic decline. It was aired just months after a number of sterling crises, a context found in the first episode during which Mainwaring stated he was 'Backing Britain' in reference to the contemporaneous 1968 campaign to boost the British economy.[28]

This economic turbulence continued through much of the early 1970s, partially due to the Oil Crisis of the autumn of 1973, the subsequent miners' strike and the three-day working week.[29] The beginning of 1974, the year *The Real Dad's Army* was held, was marked by the 1973 Christmas number one soundtrack in which glam rock band Slade's utopian optimism encouraged Britain to 'look to the future now', while power rationing meant shops closed early and shoppers had to conduct their business by candlelight. And yet, Britain seemed culturally to only want to 'look back'. As commentators such as critic Leonard Buckley noted in *The Times* in January 1974, 'Television is obsessed with the Second World War'. It was precisely because of these economic conditions that *Dad's Army* flourished, and yet as Summerfield notes '*Dad's Army* fed this wave of Second World War nostalgia.'[30]

Nostalgia is often understood as a passive yearning for and rose-tinted representation of an idealized past. For Svetlana Boym, however, nostalgia is a complex historical phenomenon, made up of nostos (home) and algia (longing)

---

[25] David Croft quoted in McCann, *Dad's Army*, 81.
[26] *Get Cracking* Dir. Marcel Varnel (1943); *Whiskey Galore* Dir. Alexadner Mackendrick (1949).
[27] Summerfield, 'Dad's Army, the Home Guard and the Memory of the British War Effort', 93–5.
[28] For more on this see S. Newton, 'The Sterling Devaluation of 1967, the International Economy and Post-War Social Democracy', *The English Historical Review*, CXXV, no. 515 (2010), 912–45.
[29] R. Lowe, 'Life Begins in the Seventies? Writing and Rewriting the History of Postwar Britain', *Journal of Contemporary History*, 42, no. 1 (2007), 161–9. For a popular account see Andy Beckett, *When the Lights Went Out: What Really Happened in Britain in the Seventies* (London: Faber and Faber, 2010).
[30] Ibid.

and it '... is a rebellion against the modern idea of time, the time of history and progress'.[31] This implies that rather than nostalgia embodying a simple, passive 'return to the past' it can also have future-orientated and transformative potentialities, that rather than maintaining 'progress' reclaim aspects of a more definable past. As Richards points out, nostalgia is also a love, motivated by rage and frustration at the present, and as such can be a powerful force for societal transformation. The 1970s, for example, gave rise to blossoming campaigns for green spaces, better food, real ale and lead-fee petrol.[32] For Robin Nelson, Richards's optimistic view of a return to past practice for future mobilization 'betrays an uneasy slippage between traditionalism and his [Richards] conception of nostalgia as a vital force for good'.[33] And yet, what matters here is how nostalgia can be understood in terms of both a longing for the times of the past that becomes visible in the 1970s during a time of decline, but could also be a form of mobilizing utopianism (whatever the values of that utopianism may be) as a response to perceived crisis.

Indeed, as historical debate on the early 1970s has shown, the *perception* of crisis was as important a factor as the actual material impact of decline in real terms, given that generally at the beginning of the decade standards of living improved.[34] As a case in point, television ownership grew significantly. In 1951 fewer than 10 per cent of Britons owned a television set, a figure that rose to 91 per cent by 1975.[35] In their important research re-contextualizing the 1970s, Emily Robinson et al. show how along with perceptions of crisis there was a chance of flourishing – of new technologies, new ideas, new ways of living and new cultural moods.[36]

Certainly, the IWM had been changing and adapting during this time. Reflecting in his autobiography, Noble Frankland highlighted how during this time he aimed to soften the image of the Museum in that 'I aimed to convert the Museum into a centre of historical study but I also wanted to soften its

---

[31] Svetlana Boym, 'Nostalgia and Its Discontents', *The Hedgehog Review*, 9, no. 2 (2007), 7. Essay adapted from her monograph *The Future of Nostalgia* (New York: Basic, 2001).
[32] Jeffrey Richards, *Films and British National Identity*, 365.
[33] Robin Nelson initially sent out 120 questionnaires and conducted interviews on the continuing importance of *Dad's Army* in 'They do "like it up 'em": "Dad's Army" and myths of old England', in Jonathan Bignell and Stephen Lacey (eds.), *Popular Television Drama: Critical Perspectives* (Manchester: Manchester University Press, 2005), 64.
[34] See Lawrence Black, Hugh Pemberton and Pat Thane (eds.), *Reassessing 1970s Britain* (Manchester: Manchester University Press, 2013) who have queried the usefulness of deconstructing 'crisis', given that many perceived there to be a crisis despite material wealth. Also see Colin Hay's 'Narrating Crisis: The Discursive Construction of the "Winter of Discontent"', *Sociology*, 30, no. 2 (1996), 253–77, Alyn Turner, *Crisis? What Crisis?: Britain in the 1970s* (London: Aurum, 2008).
[35] Gavin Schaffer, *The Vision of a Nation* (London: Palgrave Macmillan, 2014), 3.
[36] See the excellent Emily Robinson, et al., 'Telling Stories about Postwar Britain: Popular Individualism and the "Crisis" of the 1970s', *Twentieth Century British History*, 28, no. 2 (June 2017), 268–304.

forbidding impression by the introduction of a measure of socializing and, by this means, to enlist the support of people of influence and of learning.'[37] One way of visibly doing this was to stage exhibitions on popular pre-existing cultural interventions in the memory of the war, and to invite to exhibition launches high-profile actors, well-known members of state, war veterans, as well as cultural people of interest such as novelist Jilly Cooper whose husband Leo was a military book publisher. The Coopers, and later the actress Joanna Lumley, were exactly the kinds of 'socializing', 'people of influence and learning' that IWM wanted to refashion its image towards.[38] This approach sought to foster networks of museum influence, but as the press invitation to take photographs of the opening of *The Real Dad's Army* shows, it was also a shrewd move to court press interest in order to generate publicity.

From the early 1970s, publicity had increasingly become a concern of museums as their financial viability was increasingly debated. On 21 June 1971, for example, Margaret Thatcher, then Minister of Education, gave a speech to parliament defending a motion formed by Lord Eccles on the introduction of museum entrance fees. The speech, beginning with the 'several things upon which we can all agree', raised concerns about the adequate housing of collections, the agreement of partial funding by the Exchequer, and the cost of museum visiting on the taxpayer.[39] Although the government was prepared to partially finance museums, alternative means of raising additional funds were urged.

In 1972, the British Museum's *Tutankhamun* exhibition proved that a timely exhibition with lots of publicity could generate significant capital. This quickly became a model for how museums aspired to generate revenue, and it became particularly important when fees were eventually introduced from 1 January 1974.[40] For IWM, an opportunity was luckily provided in the autumn of 1973 by

---

[37] Noble Frankland, *History at War: The Campaigns of an Historian* (London: Giles de la Mare, 1998), 168.

[38] The Director and Jilly Cooper appear in their correspondence in IWM Central Files as good friends. This point is less about their relationship, however, and more so about a changing sense of cultural prestige. Ben Highmore's research on the shop Habitat in the 1970s has helped to guide this thinking, in 'Feeling It: Habitat, Taste and the New Middle Class in 1970s Britain', *New Formations*, 88, no. 88 (2016), 105–22.

[39] Margaret Thatcher, speech on 'Museums and Galleries (Admissions Charges) in the House of Commons', *Hansard* HC Deb (21 June 1971), https://api.parliament.uk/historic-hansard/commons/1971/jun/21/museums-and-galleries-admission-charges#S5CV0819P0_19710621_HOC_230, accessed 19 February 2022.

[40] In main editorial in the 'Editorial', *Museums Journal*, 72, no. 1 (January 1972), 1–2, remarked that the slow pace of the government in implementing museum entrance fees was the one aspect that visitors would rejoice. A similar remark was made in the editorial of the 'Editorial', *Museums Journal*, 73, no. 4 (March 1973), 1–2 edition, which suggested that as it has taken so long, perhaps it will not be fully implemented until the end of the decade.

the *Radio Times* to launch a collaborative exhibition on the new series of Prisoner-of-War-themed drama *Colditz* (1972–4). In emulating the Tutankhamun model of being a timely exhibition supported by a press outlet, it proved exceptionally popular, attracting 300,000 visitors over nine months at a time the Director-General noted as being 'a period when we are normally slack'.[41]

To answer why the IWM staged an exhibition called *The Real Dad's Army* as opposed to one that just referred to Home Guard, we can see a picture emerging of a desire to court publicity and facilitate growth by utilizing the imaginative possibilities of popular television programmes during a period of economic uncertainty. Importantly, the IWM has not been the only cultural producer to do this. As Stephen Cullen notes the publishing industry has used *Dad's Army* as a cultural touchstone in order to sell books on the Home Guard. He even notes how 'the marketing department of Pen and Sword Books was insistent that it be used again in the title of this [his own] book'.[42] Interestingly, however, the impetus for claiming something was 'real' in the context of *Dad's Army* appears to have originated from Norman Longmate's book *The Real Dad's Army* that was launched in conjunction with the IWM exhibition, which Longmate also gathered much of the material and wrote the captions for. Such an association was mutually beneficial, but for the Museum it boosted the image of it as a 'centre of historical study' as per Frankland's aims. It was also, however, crucial for maintaining the image that IWM had not fallen foul of a much-feared museum sector-wide Faustian bargain, in which museums trade their integrity as sites of robust scholarship in favour of popular exhibitions with high visitor turnovers but low intellectual credibility.

What is crucial here is that *Dad's Amy* captured public imagination, and in order to increase publicity, existing cultural producers increasingly framed their outputs as extensions of the sitcom. There were clear financial incentives to this. As the long queues for *Colditz* showed, visitors were prepared to pay 10p (£1.07 today) for adults and 5p (£0.53 today) for children to visit, at a time the Director-General noted as 'especially useful in the first month of admission charges'.[43] This fee rose to 20p (£2.14) for adults and 10p for children for *The Real Dad's Army*. It is perhaps because of this new approach towards other cultural producers that by mid-1974, as Hugh Jenkins Labour Minister for the Arts made clear, IWM

---

[41] IWM Central Files, EN4/15/q.
[42] Stephen Cullen, *In Search of the Real Dad's Army: The Home Guard and the Defence of the United Kingdom, 1940–1944* (Barnsley: Pen & Sword Military, 2011), 201.
[43] IWM Central Files, EN4/15/q.

was one of the few national museums that supported entrance fees.[44] From the potential revenue-generating capabilities of their new approach towards existing popular television programmes, it is clear why.

And yet, working with external partners does not just create challenges with regard to the implicit values of exhibitions but can also be challenging to form and sustain. Attempting to repeat the model of *Colditz*, in the proposal of *The Real Dad's Army*, the Museum actively sought a working relationship with the *Radio Times*. Frankland suggested, for example, that alongside working collaboratively on the exhibition the *Radio Times* and the BBC might also advertise in both Norman Longmate's book and the exhibition space. Despite the 'thoughtful suggestion', however, his proposition was rejected by K. J. Bristow, Publications and Promotional Services Manager at the *Radio Times*.

While this must have come as a blow, later correspondence show that the Museum believed it had reached a 'gentleman's agreement' with the BBC to advertise the exhibition after the airing of weekly episodes of *Dad's Army*. In a letter to Huw Weldon, Managing Director at the BBC, however, Christopher Dowling of the Museum noted how the reassurances he had received had not materialized, and the exhibition was not being advertised. He urged the BBC to rectify this urgently as 'an exhibition of this character depends heavily for success upon publicity. Time now is of the essence'.[45] Nevertheless, he was rebuffed by the BBC who said no such reassurances could have been given as they breached the broadcaster's charter.

Given the rejection of *The Real Dad's Army* as a cooperative venture by the *Radio Times* and BBC, the motivations for the *Dad's Army* actors and the sitcom's writers to appear at the exhibition launch are difficult to determine. Little exists in the IWM's archives as to why the cast decided to join, but there is no mention in the scant archival trace of them being paid. Their attendance then might well be understood perhaps partially to raise awareness of the new series of *Dad's Army*, or exclusively as a philanthropic gesture to raise publicity for the Museum's exhibition. And yet, photographs of them playing around in the exhibition are interspersed with photographs of them thoughtfully looking at historical materials. This gives some indication that they were interested and invested in the lives of those they tried to portray.

---

[44] Robert Hewison notes that 'All of the Museums, with the Exception of the Imperial War Museum, were Opposed to Charging', in *Culture and Consensus: England, Art and Politics Since 1940* (London: Routledge, 2015), 171. Also see correspondence between IWM and Jenkins in IWM central files, EN4/15/q.

[45] Letter from Christopher Dowling to Huw Wheldon 6 December 1974, IWM central files in EN4/15/q.

Perhaps this is an over sentimental reading, but the photographs explored in this chapter do appear to show a genuine attempt by the actors and the Museum to both celebrate and pay appropriate respect to those who served in the Home Guard. While they would not have had to do this, the acceptable boundaries of representation of the Second World War within a comedy meant that both celebration and commemoration were carefully engaged with side-by-side. The photographs of the exhibition launch, of which this chapter has only been able to show a very select number, allow us to see the range of individuals who were invested in this dual purpose as well as the success of the launch and exhibition. As a letter on the exhibition launch from Sir Peter Masefield, a key stakeholder and Trustee shows, 'I thought that it all went very well indeed and that it was the best of such events yet … I am sure the exhibition will be a great success – even in these rather gloomy days'.[46] And yet, it was precisely because of these rather 'gloomy days' that *Dad's Army* proved popular, and the exhibition was held at all.

Conclusion

The Real Dad's Army proved a continued departure in representing a historical past in the IWM. Rather than appealing to audiences solely through the allure of authentic material culture, the exhibition's main cultural authority did not singularly stem from the authentic objects or didactic narrative histories it showcased, but equally to a sense of proximity to a popular television comedy programme. Comedy, a hitherto seldom represented aspect of war, proved attractive to visitors. It also powerfully framed narratives of the war precisely because during a moment of perceived 'crisis' there was a cultural need for humour and nostalgia that provided some relief from present conditions.

Crucially, in being so closely associated with the TV programme, the Museum framed the experiences of the historical Home Guard directly with the representations of *Dad's Army* that occupied a substantial position within the cultural memory of civil defence during the war. Although stressing the historical accuracy of the exhibition, the Museum had less control over the narratives and claims to being historically representative, precisely because the crowds that were drawn to the Museum would understand the Home Guard through the multitude of emotional resonances of *Dad's Army* that acted as a powerful

---

[46] Letter to the Director, 18 October 1974 as found in IWM central files in EN4/15/q.

shaping framework for the exhibition. The exhibition was, therefore, defined by and in turn played its own role in restricting, perpetuating and legitimizing particular imaginative possibilities of wartime experience, even as it used innovative approaches to attract new visitors to the IWM.

As this chapter has shown, it was the potency of the convergence of (real or perceived) crisis and the success of a nostalgic comedy that combined the imagined and authentic, that has shaped a powerful British memory of the Home Front during the Second World War. Crucially, however, as we have moved temporally further from the war years, the blurring of the authentic and facsimile that may have been distinguishable some thirty years after the war ended to contemporaries visiting *The Real Dad's Army*, has become increasingly harder to differentiate. This is in no small part due to *Dad's Army* being a continually popular comedy; it can be easily watched long after it was first aired while its narrative offerings about who 'we are' during wartime remain potent. The continuing importance of the 1970s in shaping a continued memory of the war years, therefore, cannot be underestimated, and the exhibition and its launch offer us a glimpse into the tensions, negotiations and feelings of the decade.

Filmography

Dad's Army (1968–78).
Colditz (1972–4).
Blackadder Goes Forth (1989).

Bibliography

Primary sources
Archives

Colditz exhibition. IWM Central Files, EN4/15/q.
The Real Dad's Army exhibition. IWM Central Files, EN4/15/d/s.
Margaret Thatcher, speech 'Museums and Galleries (Admissions Charges)' in the House of Commons, *Hansard* HC Deb (21 June 1971), https://api.parliament.uk/historic-hansard/commons/1971/jun/21/museums-and-galleries-admission-charges#S5CV0819P0_19710621_HOC_230, accessed:19 February 2022.

Newspaper articles

Longmate, Norman, 'Dad's Army Was a Strikingly Accurate Portrayal of the Home Guard', *The* Guardian, 2 February 2016.
Masters, Tim, 'Dad's Army: A Box Office Battle?' *BBC News website*, 29th April 2014.

Books

Jimmy Perry, *A Stupid Boy: The Autobiography of the Creator of Dad's Army* (London: Century, 2002).

Journals

'Editorial', *Museums Journal*, 72, no. 1 (January 1972), 1–2.
'Editorial', *Museums Journal*, 73, no. 4 (March 1973), 1–2.

Secondary sources

Andy Beckett, *When the Lights Went out: What Really Happened in Britain in the Seventies* (London: Faber and Faber, 2010).
Lawrence Black, Hugh Pemberton and Pat Thane (eds.), *Reassessing 1970s Britain* (Manchester: Manchester University Press, 2013).
Svetlana Boym, 'Nostalgia and Its Discontents', *The Hedgehog Review*, 9, no. 2 (2007), 7. Essay adapted from her monograph *The Future of Nostalgia* (New York: Basic, 2001).
Sarah Byrne, Rodney Harrison and Anne Clarke (eds.), *Unpacking the Collection: Networks of Material and Social Agency in the Museum* (New York: Springer New York, 2011).
Steven Cooke and Lloyd Jenkins, 'Discourses of Regeneration in Early Twentieth-century Britain: From Bedlam to the Imperial War Museum', *Area*, 33, no. 4 (December 2001), 382–90.
Paul Cornish, 'Sacred Relics: Objects in the Imperial War Museum 1917–1939', in Nicholas J. Saunders (eds.), *Matters of Conflict: Material Culture, Memory and the First World War* (London: Routledge, 2004), 35–50; 37.
Stephen Cullen, *In Search of the Real Dad's Army: The Home Guard and the Defence of the United Kingdom, 1940–1944* (Barnsley: Pen & Sword Military, 2011).
Noble Frankland, *History at War: The Campaigns of an Historian* (London: Giles de la Mare, 1998).
Emma Hanna, *The Great War on the Small Screen: Representing the First World War in Contemporary Britain* (Edinburgh: Edinburgh University Press, 2009).
Colin Hay, 'Narrating Crisis: The Discursive Construction of the Winter of Discontent', *Sociology*, 30, no. 2 (1996), 253–77.

Robert Hewison, *Culture and Consensus: England, Art and Politics Since 1940* (London: Routledge, 2015).

Ben Highmore, 'Feeling It: Habitat, Taste and the New Middle Class in 1970s Britain' *New Formations*, vol. 88, no. 88 (2016), 105–22.

Bernd Lenz, '"Your Little Game": Myth and War in Dad's Army', in Jürgen Kamm and Birgit Neumann (eds.), *British TV Comedies* (London: Palgrave, 2016), 36–50.

Henrietta Lidchi, 'The Poetics and the Politics of Exhibiting Other Cultures', in Stuart Hall, et al. (eds.), *Representation: Cultural Representations and Signifying Practices*, 2nd ed. (London: Sage, 2013), 120–57.

R. Lowe, 'Life Begins in the Seventies? Writing and Rewriting the History of Postwar Britain', *Journal of Contemporary History*, 42, no. 1 (2007), 161–9.

Graham McCann, *Dad's Army: The Story of a Classic Television Show* (London: Fourth Estate, 2002).

Robin Nelson, 'They Do "like it up 'em": "Dad's Army" and Myths of Old England', in Jonathan Bignell and Stephen Lacey (eds.), *Popular Television Drama: Critical Perspectives* (Manchester: Manchester University Press, 2005), 64.

S. Newton, 'The Sterling Devaluation of 1967, the International Economy and Post-War Social Democracy', *The English Historical Review*, CXXV, no. 515 (2010), 912–45.

Lucy Noakes, 'Making Histories: Experiencing the Blitz in London's Museums in the 1990s', in M. Evans and K. Lunn (eds.), *War and Memory in the Twentieth Century* (Oxford: Berg, 1997), 89–104; 90.

Lucy Noakes, '"Serve to Save": Gender, Citizenship and Civil Defence in Britain 1937–41', *Journal of Contemporary History*, 47, no. 4 (2012), 734–53.

Corinna Peniston-Bird, '"I Wondered who'd be the First to Spot that": Dad's Army at War, in the Media and in Memory', *Media History*, 13, no. 2–3 (2007), 183–202.

Jeffrey Richards, *Films and British National Identity: From Dickens to Dad's Army* (Manchester: Manchester University Press, 1997), 351–66.

Emily Robinson, et al., 'Telling Stories about Postwar Britain: Popular Individualism and the "Crisis" of the 1970s', *Twentieth Century British History*, 28, no. 2 (June 2017), 268–304.

Henry Rousso, *The Vichy Syndrome: History and Memory in France since 1944* (Cambridge, MA: Harvard University Press, 1991).

Gavin Schaffer, *The Vision of a Nation* (London: Palgrave Macmillan, 2014).

Penny Summerfield, 'Dad's Army, the Home Guard and the Memory of the British War Effort', in M. Riera and G. Schaffer (eds.), *The Lasting War: Society and Identity in Britain, France and Germany* after 1945 (London: Palgrave Macmillan, 2008), 86–99.

Penny Summerfield and Corinna Peniston-Bird, *Contesting Home Defence: Men, Women and the Home Guard in the Second World War* (Manchester: Manchester University Press, 2007).

Kasia Tomasiewicz, '"We Are a Social History, not a Military History Museum": Large Objects and the "Peopling" of Galleries in the Imperial War Museum, London', in Kate Hill (ed.), *Museums, Modernity and Conflict: Museums and Collections in and of War since the Nineteenth Century* (London: Routledge, 2020), 213–34.

Alwyn Turner, *Crisis? What Crisis?: Britain in the 1970s* (London: Aurum, 2008).

Andrea Witcomb, 'Remembering the Dead by Affecting the Living: The Case of a Miniature Model of Treblinka', in Sandra Dudley (ed.), *Museum Materialities* (Routledge: London, 2009), 39–52.

10

Listening very carefully to *'Allo 'Allo*: British comedy and the path to Brexit

Gavin Schaffer

Amid the deep and diverse roots of Brexit, the extent to which British feelings remain rooted in memories of the Second World War is notable. For decades preceding the 2016 referendum, historians and social scientists of Britain and Europe had highlighted the prevalence of British Euroscepticism and Europhobia, evident time and again for all to see in the rhetoric of politicians and the editorials of British newspapers.[1] Similarly, the ambivalence of the British public towards Europe and the desire to stand apart from the Continent were laid bare in numerous cultural outputs on television and film since the 1960s. Antoinette Burton has recently asserted, 'as half a century of British television alone makes clear, there have been regular, even ordinary, intimations of embryonic Brexit experiences and protean Brexit subjects across many fields of vision'.[2]

This chapter highlights the extent to which such British 'embryonic' estrangement from the Continent was rooted in nationalist renderings of memory of the Second World War. As Pänke has recently observed, the 'historical parallel' drawn in British thinking between the War and contemporary Europe is 'obvious'.[3] Indeed, in the rhetoric of British debates about Europe, past and

---

[1] See Stephen George, *An Awkward Partner: Britain in the European Community* (Oxford: Oxford University Press, 1994); Andrew Gamble, 'The Reluctant Europeans', in *Between Europe and America: The Future of British Politics* (Basingstoke and New York: Palgrave, 2003), 108–31; Wolfram Kaiser, 'Using Europe and Abusing the Europeans: The Conservatives and the European Community, 1957–94', *Contemporary Record*, 8, no. 2 (1994), 381–99; and Philip Stevens, *Britain Alone: The Path from Suez to Brexit* (London: Faber and Faber, 2020).

[2] Antoinette Burton, 'When Was Brexit? Reading Backward to the Present', *Historical Reflections*, 47, no. 2 (2021), 1–8.

[3] Julian Pänke, '"The Fourth Reich Is Here": An Exploration of Populist Depictions of the European Union as a German Plot to Take over Europe', *German Politics and Society*, Issue 134, 38, no. 3 (2020), 54–76.

present, the War has never been far away. As Reynolds has noted, amid the Brexit vote, 'the Churchillian moment – 1940 as the country's "finest hour" – continues to exert magnetic appeal'.⁴ Understanding British readings of European relations and the War, in this context, offers one starting point for understanding British-European relations more broadly as they have evolved in the postwar period. And there is nowhere better to see the showcasing of British attitudes, this chapter argues, than British situation comedy (specifically the hugely popular BBC series 'Allo 'Allo that ran from 1982 to 1992).

At one level, targeting sitcom in this way is a response to Burton's demand for scholars 'to develop a new set of narratives large and small that enable us to see more clearly that Brexit and its histories have been hiding in plain sight'.⁵ This call to arms reflects something of my own long-held irritation that comedy, as a genre, has been neglected as an access point to historical analysis, an approach I share with other authors in this volume who have similarly sought to illuminate the significance of the lampooning and mockery of wartime enemies within British culture. Shining a light on what was the BBC's most successful comedy series of a decade, a war comedy beloved by tens of millions of people, is, to my mind, a historically obvious thing to do, yet 'Allo 'Allo (and television comedy writ large) has mostly not been approached by scholars: hiding in plain sight indeed.⁶

Situation comedy has been given such little scholarly attention, it seems, amid a snobbery and dismissiveness about the lack of substance of the genre. Sitcom, it is easy to argue, is not written or performed to be held under a microscope and interrogated. It is inherently ephemeral, throwaway television. Such attitudes have been, to a certain extent at least, reinforced by the way that British television itself has valued its entertainment output. Many programmes from the early days of British sitcom (from the 1950s and 1960s) were 'wiped' after their broadcast, so that records are either lost forever or very hard to access, though there are usually workarounds for historians who seek them.⁷

---

⁴ David Reynolds, 'Britain, the Two World Wars, and the Problem of Narrative', *Historical Journal*, 60, no. 1 (2017), 197–231, 231.

⁵ Ibid., 2.

⁶ Academic discussions of 'Allo 'Allo have been limited to say the least. One exception is Valerie Deacon, "'A Jolly Romp We Were Always Destined to Win'": The BBC's 'Allo 'Allo and British Memories of Downed Aircrew in Occupied France during the Second World War', *Contemporary European History*, 26, no. 1 (2017), 139–59.

⁷ The BBC has attempted to recover missing programmes, launching a campaign for public support, https://www.bbc.co.uk/cult/treasurehunt/missing/. Where broadcasts are missing, it is sometimes possible to at least read scripts of programmes, retained in the BBC Written Archive Centre.

Some scholars, however, have argued that the very nature of sitcoms should make us sit up and take notice. Whereas academics are often drawn towards serious, substantial and inherently less popular cultural forms of expression, there is much to be said for engaging the material that drew the interest of the greatest number of people. Frequently, comedy programmes have been, and continue to be, shows that garner huge audiences and shape the cultural fabric of the nation, the way we speak, behave and identify. As Mills points out, sitcoms create 'a valuable public space which, significantly, the mass is likely to feel belongs to them'.[8] The feeling of sharing a joke or a set of jokes, of belonging within a family of humour, has been explained by Bailey as an access point for social inclusion, drawing audiences into a shared 'knowingness', an elective temporary incorporation into a 'conspiracy of meaning' whereby a fleeting moment of perceived unity gathers everyone together (around the joke that they understand and enjoy).[9] Bailey was writing about music hall audiences when he made this argument but the same, I would argue, is true of sitcom in the age of television. While it is important to understand that audiences don't all laugh for the same reason, sitcoms can garner feelings of togetherness around a set of shared (at least to a certain extent) meanings.[10] These feelings may well, as Medhurst has put it, be 'a fiction', but they are a fiction 'from which solidarity and sustenance can be drawn'.[11]

Analysis of jokes, Davies has argued, may enable us to 'measure, record and indicate what is going on' (or at least what many people think is going on) in a social moment, to take, as he put it, a reading of a 'social thermometer'.[12] In this way, the silliness of sitcom, precisely its lack of seriousness, is a key ingredient because it frees both creators and audiences from restrictions and standards that need to be observed in more serious settings, a 'carnivalesque' licence, as Bakhtin might have seen it.[13] In this way, comedy, according to Zupančič, enables us to

---

[8] Brett Mills, *Television Sitcom* (London: BFI, 2005), 154. Also see David Sutton, *A Chorus of Raspberries: British Film Comedy 1929–39* (Exeter: University of Exeter Press, 2000), 24.
[9] P. Bailey, *Popular Culture and Performance in the Victorian City* (Cambridge: CUP, 1998), 137.
[10] In the wake of Stuart Hall's famous analysis of the way that meanings come through to television production to audiences, there has been substantial debate across fields on the ways the audience interpret programmes. See Stuart Hall, *Encoding and Decoding in the Television Discourse*, (Centre for Contemporary Cultural Studies, Birmingham, 1973). Also see John Fiske and John Hartley, *Reading Television* (London: Methuen, 1978); David Morley, *Television, Audiences and Cultural Studies* (London: Routledge, 1992); and Phil Wickham, *Understanding Television Texts* (London: BFI, 2007).
[11] Andy Medhurst, *A National Joke: Popular Comedies and English Cultural Identities* (London and New York: Routledge, 2007), 19.
[12] Christie Davies, *Ethnic Humor around the World: A Comparative Analysis* (Bloomington: Indiana University Press, 1990), 9.
[13] See Mikhail Bakhtin, *Rabelais and His World*, trans. Hélène Iswolsky (Bloomington: Indiana University Press, 1984).

engage 'things that really concern us, things that concern the very kernel of our being', themes that otherwise would not be permissible for discussion.[14] Or put another way, it is perhaps possible to say more of what you really feel if you can immediately justify your outburst with the idea that you were only joking.[15]

Nowhere was the idea of 'only joking', saying things that were only permissible amid an absence of the serious right mind, more prominent than in perhaps the most famous scene of postwar British sitcom, John Cleese and Connie Booth's engagement with 'the Germans' in Fawlty Towers in 1975. Here, Britain's relationship with Europe, in the context of the lasting trauma of the Second World War, was employed as the elephant in the room, through the rantings of a concussed and confused character, hotelier Basil Fawlty, who was liberated by his head injury to say things that he would otherwise have considered taboo. In one of the most famous comedy lines of all time, now a well-used British expression to describe any situation where cordial relations depend on something sensitive yet important being left unsaid, Fawlty repeatedly cautioned his staff: 'don't mention the war' when two German couples visited his hotel.[16]

Unfortunately for all involved, Fawlty's advised discretion fell by the wayside after he concussed himself, was hospitalized and returned to the hotel, head bandaged and confused. The context of his ranting about British-German relations was Britain's first referendum on joining more closely with its neighbours, the United Kingdom European Communities membership referendum of June 1975 (in which the British public were asked to confirm support for the previous government's decision to enter the European Communities in January 1973).[17] Broadcast only months after a resounding 'yes' vote in this referendum, Basil Fawlty picked up the mantle of the discussion as he told his German guests his views on the ballot and its outcome: 'I didn't vote for it myself quite honestly but now that we're in I'm determined to make it work so I would like to welcome you all to Britain'.

The War lingered millimetres beneath the surface of Fawlty's European politics. His failure *not* to mention it poked fun at, and pointed to, the proximity of the conflict in the way that Britons thought about Europe. Tending to his German guests it all poured out, a seeping wound, which clearly (for Fawlty at

---

[14] A. Zupančič, *The Odd One in: On Comedy* (Cambridge, MA and London: MIT Press, 2008), 182.
[15] Michael Billig, 'Humour and Hatred: The Racist Jokes of the Ku Klux Klan', *Discourse and Society*, 12, no. 3 (2001), 267–89. Also see Michael Billig, *Laughter and Ridicule: Towards a Social Critique of Laughter* (London: Sage, 2005).
[16] Fawlty Towers, 'The Germans', *BBC*, tx. 24 October 1975.
[17] For analysis of this campaign see Rob Saunders, *Yes to Europe! The 1975 Referendum and Seventies Britain* (Cambridge: Cambridge University Press, 2018).

least) was not healing quickly. The encounter ended with the hotelier reminding the Germans that they (not the Nazis but really all Germans) had started the conflict. While he assured his guests in the least convincing way that the War was 'all forgotten now and let's hear no more about it', the famous scene, as Fawlty uncontrollably spewed out war reference after reference, serves to characterize a broader tendency in British thinking, where the War remained incredibly prominent to British worldviews, especially when it came to the subject of Europe.

The point being made by Cleese and Booth was clear. Under the thin veneer of growing postwar cooperation and unity, British approaches to Europe were still underwritten by a raw and powerful war memory. While of course Europe was not simply Germany, Fawlty's conflation of British-German relations and British-European relations was telling. Scratch the surface of British attitudes towards Europe and you were never far from old enmities and anxieties in British thinking. A bang to the head, like the one that fuelled Fawlty's concussion (perhaps exemplifying the power of comedic licence more broadly) could bring it all to the surface. Piloting seven years after the first broadcast of *Fawlty Towers*, the BBC's *'Allo 'Allo* gave extended treatment to British attitudes towards Europe. Once again, the theme (and in this case the setting) was the Second World War, and a war-inspired rendering of the conflict and the nature of its protagonists sat at the centre of the comedy.

David Croft, co-creator of *'Allo 'Allo*, was no stranger to comedy writing about the Second World War. Before coming to *'Allo 'Allo* he had co-written two other iconic and successful sitcoms based on the British War experience, *Dad's Army* and *It Ain't Half Hot, Mum*. Beginning in 1968, *Dad's Army* was a successful BBC sitcom that found a pitch to deal with the sensitive subject of the Home Front, including bombing and evacuation in a gentle, nostalgic, manner. Written by Croft with Jimmy Perry, the series initially sparked concerns at the BBC about the appropriateness of lampooning the British war effort from any angle. Aside from the fact that Croft and Perry were both ex-Home Guards themselves, reassurance came in the form of a comedy formula which made light of personal idiosyncrasies and competences but seldom questioned the essential goodness and bravery of the British war effort and its soldiers.[18] This was, as Summerfield has observed, a 'humour of the victors rather than the

---

[18] Corinna M. Peniston-Bird, 'I Wondered Who'd Be the First to Spot That: Dad's Army at War in the Media and in Memory', *Media History*, 13, no. 2–3 (2007), 183–202. Croft recalls the extent to which the material for not only *Dad's Army* but also *It Ain't Half Hot, Mum* and *'Allo 'Allo* stemmed from his personal service in *You Have Been Watching: The Autobiography of David Croft* (London: BBC Books, 2004), 101.

vanquished'.[19] While British suffering and loss during the War remained prominent in the public consciousness, Allied victory (along with the absence of the introspection triggered in other countries by the consequences of Nazi invasion or collaboration) rendered the War, on a certain set of terms, possible for television comedy. Comedic construction, moreover, facilitated a particular War in British memory, a finest hour, albeit a funny and fortunate one, where the greatness of the nation was ultimately realized.

In *Dad's Army*, the War was painted as a period of national cooperation and human interaction ... [providing] evidence that Britain once truly was "Great Britain".[20] That the aged, flawed and incompetent characters of the Home Guard (as they were portrayed in *Dad's Army*) were prepared to stand and fight despite their own personal inadequacies became an exemplar of British character, reinforced by the fact that they always found a way (by hook or by crook) to be victorious. The "Germans" observation at the end of *Fawlty Towers*, 'How ever did they win?', is important here. Only in Britain could such incompetence not compromise victory. And you needed to be British to understand that! Amid this wallowing in national triumph, tones and subjects that might have told a different story, or brought the trauma of the War too close into vision, were avoided. For example, Croft's original ending credits of *Dad's Army*, which included in the background 'the explosion of a tank and also a stream of refugees' was replaced by a less disturbing (and fictional) backdrop.[21]

Alongside renewing and recreating a national war identity, *Dad's Army* drew its laughs from a set of character stereotypes which came together as a vision of Britishness across nations and classes. The show drew humour from the Scottish miser and pessimist, the 'spiv', the entitled public-school boy, the brave but ignorant shop owner. And, at the centre of it all, the pompous, ludicrous but ultimately triumphant middle-class British bank manager. These regional and class stereotypes that together pointed towards Britishness were similarly evident in Croft and Perry's subsequent foray into war sitcom, *It Ain't Half Hot, Mum*, which focused its attention on the British army in India. Running from 1974 to 1981, *It Ain't Half Hot, Mum* set the idiosyncrasies of British servicemen in the context of an imperial concert party, injecting a significant set of queer characters, juxtaposed against a screaming, disapproving Sergeant Major.

---

[19] See Penny Summerfield, 'Dad's Army, the Home Guard and the Memory of the British War Effort', in Monica Riera and Gavin Schaffer (eds.), *The Lasting War: Society and Identity in Britain, France and Germany after 1945* (Palgrave: Basingstoke and New York, 2008), 86–99; 96.
[20] Peniston-Bird, 'I Wondered Who'd Be the First to Spot That', 186.
[21] Croft, *You Have Been Watching*, 178.

The Indian setting allowed for the teasing out of British relations with local Indian people, who entered the show in subaltern roles serving and supporting the troops. Here crystalized an approach to jokes about ethnicity and race which would go on to be important in *'Allo 'Allo*. At one level, *It Ain't Half Hot, Mum*'s approach focused on popping the bubble of British perceived superiority. The Indian characters in the show, especially the Bearer (Rangi Ram), outwitted the feckless British time and again, making it possible to argue that no sort of cultural or racial superiority was being asserted in the story.[22] Nonetheless, the gulf between the Indians and their British masters was ever present, especially in the Indian characters' failure to master British culture, in a way which left little doubt about the essential difference between the British troops and local populations.[23] Rangi Ram was played by a white actor (Michael Bates), an indication of the many ways in which *It Ain't Half Hot, Mum* painted ethnic types through a white British gaze. For Croft, challenges that held that the programme was racist, or problematic, indicated a lack of humour on the part of critics and a failure to see the verisimilitude of the comedic performances. He argued: 'It was founded in truth and deserves a place among our classic comedies'.[24]

The idea that the War could be rendered comedic through national, ethnic and sexual stereotypes came through clearly in *'Allo 'Allo*, which drew its laughter from little else. For Croft, now writing with Jeremy Lloyd, *'Allo 'Allo* revisited the subject of ethnic and national war interactions, albeit without a colonial dimension. The sitcom was set in the northern French town of Nouvion during the Nazi occupation, telling the story of a sexually incontinent, cowardly café owner, Rene Artois, (played by Gorden Kaye), trying to navigate his way unscathed through the Second World War, troubled at every turn by the occupying German forces who frequented his business, the French Resistance who constantly attempted to co-opt him to the cause, and his overbearing wife (played by Carmen Silvera). Often described as a conscious parody of resistance drama such as the BBC's *Secret Army* (which ran until 1979), *'Allo 'Allo* was the BBC's comedy success of the decade. It ran through eighty-five episodes and nine series, drawing an audience at peak of 17 million viewers. By 1989 the show had been sold to twenty-eight countries, earning the BBC an estimated two million pounds – and this was only the beginning of the story.[25]

---

[22] Gavin Schaffer, *The Vision of a Nation* (Basingstoke: Palgrave, 2014), 199–206.
[23] Ibid.
[24] Croft, *You Have Been Watching*, 200–1.
[25] ''Allo 'Allo – They're Laughing all the Way to the Bank', *Daily Mail*, 5 July 1989. Also see Richard Webber, *30 Years of 'Allo 'Allo! The Inside Story of the Hit Show* (London: Carlton, 2012), 6.

The series spawned an official stage version which ran over 1,000 times including 'sell-out nationwide and international tours and several London runs'.[26] *'Allo 'Allo*, moreover, inspired a myriad of local amateur productions, and is performed as a play around Britain right up to the present day. 'According to those who publish the amateur rights', Lloyd claimed in 2012, 'it is one of the most successful of their shows both in the UK and internationally'.[27]

A sitcom that was easy to imitate because of the prevalence of distinct uniforms, costumes, and personal idiosyncrasies, loved for its bawdy farcical humour, steeped in sexual *double entendre*, *'Allo 'Allo* became a show to watch and imitate. As one journalist explained in 1986:

> All over the country groups are forming 'Allo 'Allo clubs and costume hirers report a phenomenal demand for German uniforms and French maid outfits. Even teachers of French complain that classes are messing them about with catch phrases from the show like: "Leesten vairy cairfully ... I will say theese only wunce.[28]

Like *Dad's Army*, *'Allo 'Allo* visited the war through a wide array of national characteristics, incorporating many European nations. Britons in the series were foppish and stupid, the French were sexually promiscuous and cowardly, (ditto the Italians but even more so) and the Germans ludicrous, camp, sexually deviant and occasionally fastidious and sinister. This gorging on national stereotypes grated on some critics who felt that such comedy brought out the worst in people and was increasingly stale. David Sinclair wrote in the *Sunday Times*:

> I find 'Allo 'Allo (BBC1, Saturday) one of the most offensive programmes on television. It is not so much the off-colour humour – that can be funny when sensitively handled – but the proposition undermining the entire series; that foreigners are intrinsically funny, and more so when they try to speak English. I should have thought xenophobia was widespread enough in this country (viz the man who said on radio recently that he was opposed to the Channel Tunnel because he didn't want English culture to be "diluted") without playing to its prejudices in the names of entertainment.[29]

But it wasn't the national stereotyping but its treatment of the War that fuelled most criticism of *'Allo 'Allo*. The programme's making light of the French Resistance and the Nazi occupation of France, and its humanizing of Nazi

---

[26] Webber, *30 Years of 'Allo 'Allo*, 226.
[27] Ibid., 4.
[28] Barry Wigmore, "Allo 'Allo Fever', *The People*, 7 September 1986.
[29] David Sinclair, 'A Pretty Hopeless Situation', *Sunday Times*, 6 December 1987.

soldiers, drew a furious response in some quarters. Following the pilot, one letter written to the authors reminded them that there were 'thousands of people in this country who suffered, directly, at the hands of the Germans, and thousands more whose early years were turned into nightmares'. Furious that Croft and Lloyd would see the matter as ripe for comedy, the writer told them: 'You make a mockery of bravery and loyalty and you make me sick'.[30]

This kind of criticism was levelled too in parts of the press. Writing in the *Daily Mail*, Herbert Kretzmer complained:

> Millions died in Europe because of the Nazi terror. Millions more who survived them are still alive today, tending their wounds and mourning their dead. To them, no doubt, the very sight of a Nazi uniform on TV is a memory of a dark and bloody age.[31]

It was not only the potential re-triggering of trauma that concerned critics, but the idea that a programme like *'Allo 'Allo* might inadvertently mislead younger people about the historical truths of the War and the Holocaust, skewing its moral parameters. Patrick Stoddart wrote in *Broadcast*: 'I couldn't help wondering whether children watching all that good-natured claptrap won't grow up convinced that Hitler, the gas chambers and the Holocaust are simply the overblown figments of their ga-ga grandparents' imaginations'.[32]

Beyond the War, *'Allo 'Allo*'s approach to non-British people was also a cause for concern to some. At the show's outset, Lucy Hughes-Hallett, writing in the *London Evening Standard*, shared a worry that *'Allo 'Allo* 'reinforces all the prejudices of the British'.[33] With its neat designation of European nationalities into behavioural boxes it was certainly arguable that *'Allo 'Allo* was feeding from a deep reservoir of long-held xenophobia, constructing European relations according to the pre-existing prejudices of many British people. Whether or not such a programme could serve to reinforce public prejudices is matter of considerable scholarly doubt.[34] It does seem reasonable, however, to question whether the way that *'Allo 'Allo* constructed Britain's European neighbours might have reflected something of the way that Britons felt about British/European relations, tapping into a vein of thinking that was rooted in war memory, and still potent in the 1980s, even if it didn't serve to add to it.

---

[30] BBC Written Archive Centre, Caversham (WAC), T70/41/1, 'Allo 'Allo, Letter to Lloyd and Croft, 30 December 1982.
[31] 'Herbert Kretzmer's View: It's No Joke Being Witty about the War', *Daily Mail*, 23 October 1985.
[32] Patrick Stoddart, 'Oh Not Such a Lovely War', *Broadcast*, 2 November 1984.
[33] Lucy Hughes Hallett, 'Allo 'Allo, *Standard*, 31 December 1982.
[34] See footnote 10 above for debates on the impact of television on its audiences.

On these terms, *'Allo 'Allo*, it may be argued, might tell us something about British attitudes to Europe, how they were changing and not changing in this period. The 1980s saw Britain edging into closer bonds with her European neighbours, culminating in the Maastricht Treaty of 1992, yet these closer bonds were achieved amid widespread underlying Euroscepticism embodied (until her ousting by keener European conservatives) by the political leadership of Margaret Thatcher. British voices of Euroscepticism never deviated too far from suspicions rooted in the War, amid perceptions of threat and difference which still, for many Britons, merited attention when considering the forming of tighter bonds. After all, as one letter writer told the *Radio Times* about *'Allo 'Allo's* construction of Nazi officers: 'It may suit our new Common Market image to portray the Germans as harmless loons, the reality was so different'.[35]

Mirroring something of British peoples' ambivalence about Europe, *'Allo 'Allo* can be read both as a deliberate attempt to put to bed the Germanophobia of the War (and work through European war trauma), and at the same time as an example of just how different the British felt that Europeans were from themselves. For the writers of *'Allo 'Allo*, the programme's handling of the European past was presented as a means to catharsis and healing, offering lessons about the essential similarities of all people, and holding up to ridicule the considerable space given over in British drama (and in British popular culture more broadly) to the Second World War stories which perpetuated difference and trauma. In asserting such a role for their sitcom, Croft and Lloyd were tapping into an argument that had repeatedly been made in defence of the British sitcoms which had dealt with racial difference through the use of bigoted characters.[36] Most famously perhaps, the writer Johnny Speight, defending the airing of racist views through his character Alf Garnett in the BBC's *Till Death Us Do Part* (1965–75), had spent years arguing that joking about prejudices, and making prejudiced people the butt of jokes, was a valuable way to draw public attention to the absurdity of racism. As Speight famously put it, 'Why not bring racial prejudice into the open, show people how ignorant they are about it, and make them laugh at themselves?'[37]

In *'Allo 'Allo*, the writers made the case that the story disarmed xenophobic stereotyping as the main characters of all nationalities revealed themselves to be very similar in their wartime conduct; specifically, they all shared a desire to

---

[35] DJ Wears to the *Radio Times*, 31 December 1982.
[36] See Schaffer, *The Vision of a Nation*, 178–230.
[37] Speight was defending his approach in an interview with *The Sun*, 12 September 1966.

get through the War and go home to their families, as well as an absence of zeal, fundamentalism and heroism. As Gorden Kaye told one journalist, this reality was designed to serve as an antidote to well-meaning war films that were riddled with unrealistic heroism. In 'Allo 'Allo, he explained, there were no 'stiff upper lips – only very wobbly ones'.[38] On these terms, the Nazi occupiers were given characters that were much like everyone else in the story, a portrayal of moral equivalence that drew considerable criticism from some viewers. Jeremy Lloyd explained to the *Daily Mirror*, 'All human failings are there: the airmen from the RAF are just as big a pair of idiots as the Germans. No one is spared – they are all as good or bad as everyone else'.[39] In one 1985 episode, Rene, driving a stolen Nazi tank, hit the Nazi colonel's car but doesn't worry about it. It was ok, he explained, because the Colonel would simply blame the Resistance and 'shoot a couple of peasants'. Then, in a line delivered straight to camera he quipped, 'How easy it is to slip into the ways of being a Nazi'.[40] Recalling the pedagogic intentions of this particular scene, Croft told the *Radio Times*, 'Most of our audience did not laugh when he said it. A few gave a philosophical twitter. I think this is a good sign'.[41]

The presenting of characters as fundamentally similar even went as far as the characterization of the Gestapo, represented in the show by Richard Gibson playing Herr Otto Flick, a limping, ostensibly sadistic Nazi ideologue, who became an icon in his own right. Otto Flick, in his relationship with the German soldier (and his screen lover) Helga (Kim Hartman), played tough, was certainly kinky, but was no kind of monster. Indeed, the humour of the character was repeatedly drawn from his soft centre, which undermined any performative desire to be a Nazi hardman. In one episode, for example, Flick instructed Helga to stand in the corner for ten minutes as a punishment for burning his toast and, as if this admonition was too mean, for good measure he kept her boiled egg warm under a tea-cosy. She told him, 'Herr Flick, you have a very kind streak in your nature' and he replied, 'I nearly failed my Gestapo exams because of it'.[42]

Among British audiences, Gibson's Flick became an icon in his own right. A 1986 article in the *News of the World* claimed: 'Every week, he has to plough through hundreds of kinky letters, poems and songs … There are a hell of a lot of ladies in our land wanting to enjoy the dubious delights of flagellation,

---

[38] David Lewin, 'Can You Resist Them?', *News of the World*, 10 October 1985.
[39] David Lewin, 'Good Moaning We Vill Say Zees Onlee Once: Bye Bye 'Allo! 'Allo!', *Sunday Mirror*, 15 November 1992.
[40] 'Allo 'Allo, 'The Policeman Cometh', tx. 4 November 1985.
[41] Croft replies to a critical letter in the *Radio Times*, 7 December 1985.
[42] 'Allo 'Allo, 'The Policeman Cometh', tx. 4 November 1985.

being dominated, forced to stand in corners and be chastised like naughty schoolgirls'.[43] Yet while the innocence and allure of Helga and Flick's kinky love were a significant draw to many, some people in Britain had grave misgivings about the humanization of the Gestapo, and Nazis in general, in this lighthearted way.

'Allo 'Allo's concession to such concerns was (generally) to stay away from Jewish characters and storylines, avoiding the Holocaust and Nazi anti-Semitism as a step too far for humour. Nonetheless, as Andy Medhurst pointed out in a piece of contemporary criticism in *The Listener*, this 'sensitivity' did not extend to homosexuality, which was ever present through the character of Lieutenant Gruber (Guy Siner). Perhaps, Medhurst mused, Croft and Lloyd didn't 'know that many thousands of homosexuals were victims of the concentration camps, but even so Gruber's presence is difficult to accept'.[44]

And despite the general absence of Jewish storylines in the narrative, where it suited the 'Allo 'Allo team, even Jews were not off-limits. In one early episode the German officers found themselves working alongside the French against the Gestapo, and needed to secure some counterfeit uniforms. These were parachuted in from England in the form of two Jewish tailors, 'Solomon' and 'Klein'. The irony of bringing in Jews to help the Nazis played through in the objections of the German Colonel Von Strohm, who complained about the tailors, 'It's the principle of the thing. If I'd have known they were employing Jewish tailors things would have been different'.[45] In typical 'Allo 'Allo style, Strohm's adjunct, Captain Gerring, confirmed that things would indeed have been different had he known in advance that Jewish (read as high quality) tailors were being flown in: 'We could have ordered some extra shirts', he replied to the Colonel.

In 'Allo 'Allo, where characters were driven by their essential human needs and desires and rarely by ideology or zeal, the horror of racial genocide receded from the war story. Nazi officers were not extremist anti-Semites. They were just ordinary men, to borrow Christopher Browning's famous formulation, trying to get by, much like anyone else.[46] One letter to the BBC about Colonel Von Strohm joined in with this joke play by pointing out that, in his experience, Von Strohm was actually a Jewish name. Croft replied to him personally, 'I was

---

[43] Mervyn Edgecombe, *News of the World*, 7 December 1986.
[44] Andy Medhurst, 'Race Riot', *The Listener*, 27 October 1988.
[45] 'Allo 'Allo, 'Pigeon Post', 21 September 84.
[46] See Christopher Browning, *Ordinary Men: Reserve Police Battalion 101 and the Final Solution in Poland* (New York: HarperCollins, 1992).

slightly shocked to hear that Von Strohm was a Jewish name. I am sure it will give the cast a good laugh when I tell them.'[47]

For many observers and participants in the phenomenon of 'Allo 'Allo, the brand of humour that underpinned the show, bawdy *double entrendre* and playful stereotyping with a heavy dose of self-deprecation, signposted the very core of Britishness. Richard Webber, explaining the success of 'Allo 'Allo in his book to celebrate its thirtieth year, argued that it was 'quintessentially British'.[48] For Sam Kelly (who played Captain Gerring), what made this the case was the willingness of the British to draw themselves into the ridicule. He told the *News of the World*, 'We are sending ourselves up rotten because we English have the facility for laughing at ourselves.'[49]

This argument, that there was something specifically British about being able to laugh at yourself (along with the attending assumption that this quality differentiated the British from others not so far away), was key to much of the public affection for 'Allo 'Allo and, I would argue, helps to explain British-European relations in this period by illustrating the extent to which British people considered their outlook, and principles, different and exceptional. For Kelly's claim to mean anything at all, it requires the existence of an opposite type, creating boundaries of humour and character that differentiate the British from other people who simply do not have *our* sense of humour and humility. As Hilary Kingsley put it, writing in the *Daily Mirror*, 'I bet the Germans and the French have nothing as funny on their TV as 'Allo 'Allo. How could they?'[50] If people don't like 'Allo 'Allo, another journalist explained in the *Daily Telegraph*, 'they simply don't understand the way we go about things.'[51]

In 'Allo 'Allo, as in all comedy, the jokes drew boundaries between those who laughed and those who didn't, between those who were in on the joke and those who weren't, and could never be.[52] Here was Bailey's 'knowingness' and 'conspiracy of meaning', a privileged status 'earned by the audience's own well-tested cultural and social competence'.[53] Getting the joke indicated a special status, it was in Medhurst's words 'a shortcut to community'.[54] And in 'Allo 'Allo, the humour stemmed *not* from the common frailties of human character, or from

---

[47] WAC, T70/44/1, 'Allo 'Allo, Letter to David Croft, 3 December 1984.
[48] Webber, *30 Years of 'Allo 'Allo!*, 6.
[49] David Lewin, 'Can You Resist Them?', *News of the World*, 10 October 1985.
[50] Hilary Kingsley, 'Super French Sauce', *Daily Mirror*, 22 October 1985.
[51] *Daily Telegraph*, 6 December 1986.
[52] See Billig, *Laughter and Ridicule*.
[53] Bailey, *Popular Culture*, 137.
[54] Medhurst, *A National Joke*, 19.

a common European-ness, but from a specific and exceptional British approach to the Second World War, which was created and performed to stand apart from all other European war narratives. Indeed, the joke was only so funny amid the realization that others would not get it at all. On these terms, a BBC spokesman gleefully reported in 1984 that the show was 'bound to provoke European TV chiefs'.[55] Reporting on the deal to take 'Allo 'Allo to the United States in 1987, a journalist in the *Independent* delighted in its inaccessibility to Britain's nearer neighbours.

> The American success of 'Allo 'Allo contrasts with the hostility it arouses in France because it treats the Resistance as a joke. It was also viewed last month by West German programme buyers who told Mr Gwenlan [Gareth Gwenlan: head of BBC comedy]: '"We are probably the only five Germans who will ever see it."[56]

Gorden Kaye showed a little more humility, but echoed the same understanding of what made 'Allo 'Allo work, as he explained the show's failure in Germany in 1991, 'They don't find the SS uniform very funny over there and I can understand that'.[57]

In the end, 'Allo 'Allo entrenched British difference and delighted in it. It painted a picture of the Second World War that could not be equally appreciated in Germany, France or Italy, countries working through histories of victimhood, collaboration and guilt in a way that Britain was not. 'Allo 'Allo's writers seem to have sincerely thought that the show had the potential to unify, and aspired to take their creation to the widest possible international audience. And yet, at the same time, all involved knew that for 'Allo 'Allo to be appreciated abroad, non-British audiences had to see things from the British vantage point. There was a desire for this to happen, but at the same time a revelling in the distance between us and them.

Watching the impact and sprawl of 'Allo 'Allo over decades, thousands of British people donning Nazi uniforms and French maids outfits, complete with funny walks and accents, sent a message about the ways in which British people remembered the War, and the contrasting ways that they thought their European neighbours did so. While much of Europe strove towards an eradication of difference and ever closer ties, Britain remained a country that very much saw itself as exceptional and superior, and retained a rather idiosyncratic view of the

---

[55] Patrick Hill, *The London Evening Standard*, 8 June 1984.
[56] *The Independent*, 24 March 1987. The series was belatedly sold to German television channel ProSieben Sat 1 for broadcast in 2008. See "Allo 'Allo to Invade German Screens', *The Independent*, 11 March 2008.
[57] 'Rene's Allo to Germany', *Sunday Mirror*, 22 December 1991.

values and behaviours of the people who lived on the other side of the English Channel, and did not have the same sense of humour.

In the end, funny as it sounds, the wartime humour of *'Allo 'Allo*, its enduring success in Britain and resonance with broader British war memory, amplifies some of the thinking that underpinned the decision of the British electorate to walk away from the European Union in 2016. The show, taken to the hearts of so many Britons, presented a Britishness that required Europeans to see things as we did, and told the story of a people that just weren't ready to slip into a European melting point, attached as they were to a non-negotiable vision of how things came to be the way they are. This tendency cannot easily be explained in political discourse so that to understand British thinking, there are very good reasons to listen very carefully to the laughter of the British sitcom.

In 2018, *'Allo 'Allo* nostalgia was still going strong. In error, columnist and author Yasmin Alibhai Brown, re-tweeted a photograph from the 'Gloucester Goes Retro' festival, in which Vicky Michelle, Richard Gibson, Gun Siner and Kim Hartman, had posed as their *'Allo 'Allo* characters in full regalia (which saw all but 'French maid' Michelle in various Nazi outfits). Missing the point of the original tweet (which was set up as a joke about the resurgence of British racism) and not knowing, or remembering, who these people were, Alibhai Brown asserted that the characters on display were 'the real scary threat posed by the hard right'.[58] Of course, these actors were and are nothing of the sort; this was a simple matter of mistaken identity, of the boundaries of 'knowingness', as Bailey might put it. But in the fraught and fragile atmosphere after Brexit (and given that it was over twenty-five years since the final episode of *'Allo 'Allo* had been broadcast) it was perhaps not surprising that Nazi uniforms on the streets of Brexit Britain caused alarm and distress.[59]

While many who loved and remembered *'Allo 'Allo* would have been delighted to see their old favourites out and about, the continuing presence of this kind of humour inadvertently points to something of a British blind spot about the legacy of the War and the barriers which stand firm between Britain and the rest of Europe. In the end, what lurks in the shadows of this treasured sitcom is a nation deeply ill at ease with its European neighbours and itself, still working through its own history of the War and its aftermath. Listening very carefully to *'Allo 'Allo* reveals a story of a nation that remains unready for further European integration.

---

[58] 'UK Journalist Mistakes 'Allo 'Allo! Cast Reunion for a Hard Right Threat', *The New Statesman*, 30 August 2018.

[59] 'Allo 'Allo's final episode aired in 1992, although a one-off special episode was broadcast in 2007.

Bibliography

Peter Bailey, *Popular Culture and Performance in the Victorian City* (Cambridge: Cambridge University Press, 1998).

Mikhail Bakhtin, *Rabelais and His World,* trans. Hélène Iswolsky (Bloomington: Indiana University Press, 1984).

Michael Billig, 'Humour and Hatred: The Racist Jokes of the Ku Klux Klan', *Discourse and Society*, 12, no. 3 (2001): 267–89.

Michael Billig, *Laughter and Ridicule: Towards a Social Critique of Laughter* (London: Sage, 2005).

Christopher Browning, *Ordinary Men: Reserve Police Battalion 101 and the Final Solution in Poland* (New York: HarperCollins, 1992).

Antoinette Burton, 'When Was Brexit? Reading Backward to the Present', *Historical Reflections*, 47, no. 2 (2021): 1–8.

David Croft, *You Have Been Watching: The Autobiography of David Croft* (London: BBC Books, 2004).

Christie Davies, *Ethnic Humor around the World: A Comparative Analysis* (Bloomington: Indiana University Press, 1990).

Valerie Deacon, 'A Jolly Romp We Were Always Destined to Win': The BBC's 'Allo 'Allo and British Memories of Downed Aircrew in Occupied France during the Second World War', *Contemporary European History*, 26, no. 1 (2017): 139–59.

John Fiske and John Hartley, *Reading Television* (London: Methuen, 1978).

Andrew Gamble, 'The Reluctant Europeans', in *Between Europe and America: The Future of British Politics* (Basingstoke and New York: Palgrave, 2003), 108–31.

Stephen George, *An Awkward Partner: Britain in the European Community* (Oxford: Oxford University Press, 1994).

Stuart Hall, *Encoding and Decoding in the Television Discourse*, (Centre for Contemporary Cultural Studies, Birmingham, 1973).

Wolfram Kaiser, 'Using Europe and Abusing the Europeans: The Conservatives and the European Community, 1957–94', *Contemporary Record*, 8, no. 2 (1994), 381–99.

Andy Medhurst, *A National Joke: Popular Comedies and English Cultural Identities* (London and New York: Routledge, 2007).

Brett Mills, *Television Sitcom* (London: BFI, 2005).

David Morley, *Television, Audiences and Cultural Studies* (London: Routledge, 1992).

Julian Pänke, '"The Fourth Reich Is Here": An Exploration of Populist Depictions of the European Union as a German Plot to Take Over Europe', *German Politics and Society*, Issue 134, 38, no. 3 (2020), 54–76.

Corinna Peniston-Bird, 'I Wondered who'd be the First to Spot that: Dad's Army at War in the Media and in Memory', *Media History*, 13, no. 2-3 (2007), 183–202.

David Reynolds, 'Britain, the Two World Wars, and the Problem of Narrative', *Historical Journal*, 60, no. 1 (2017), 197–231.

Rob Saunders, *Yes to Europe! The 1975 Referendum and Seventies Britain* (Cambridge: Cambridge University Press, 2018).

Gavin Schaffer, *The Vision of a Nation* (Basingstoke: Palgrave, 2014).

Philip Stevens, *Britain Alone: The Path from Suez to Brexit* (London: Faber and Faber, 2020).

Penny Summerfield, 'Dad's Army, the Home Guard and the Memory of the British War Effort', in Monica Riera and Gavin Schaffer (eds.), *The Lasting War: Society and Identity in Britain, France and Germany after 1945* (Palgrave: Basingstoke and New York, 2008), 86–99.

David Sutton, *A Chorus of Raspberries: British Film Comedy 1929–39* (Exeter: University of Exeter Press, 2000).

Richard Webber, *30 Years of 'Allo 'Allo! The Inside Story of the Hit* Show (London: Carlton, 2012).

Phil Wickham, *Understanding Television Texts* (London: BFI, 2007).

Alenka Zupančič, *The Odd One in: On Comedy* (Cambridge, MA, and London: MIT Press, 2008).

Index

absurdity 2, 13, 27, 28, 46, 65, 75, 76, 81, 96, 138, 139, 147, 149, 151, 156, 157
Air Raid Precaution (ARP) 4, 36, 80, 95, 103
air warfare 127, 152, 161–2, 167, 173
'Allo 'Allo 7, 161, 200–15
Americans 20, 22, 36, 37, 42, 56, 65, 67, 68, 70, 71, 72–3, 76, 117, 165, 212
artist 87, 89, 111, 112, 114, 116, 119, 121, 131, 132, 149
Atlantic Convoy 143–57

Battle of Britain 28, 173
Blitz 2, 5, 23, 28, 30
Brexit 199–200, 213
British Army *See* men's services
British Association of Plastic, Reconstructive, and Aesthetic Surgeons (BAPRAS) 112, 119
British Broadcasting Corporation (BBC) 7, 11, 12, 13, 22, 23, 24, 32, 33, 37, 55, 57, 63–85, 169, 181, 193, 200, 203, 205, 206, 208, 210, 212
British Broadcasting Corporation World War II People's War (BBCPW) 11, 12, 13, 37, 163
British Cartoon Archive 85–110, 161
Britishness 2, 55, 57, 204, 211

caricature 90–1, 128–30, 145, 146, 148
cartoonists
    Carl Giles 85, 89, 94, 907, 102, 186
    David Low 23, 86, 88, 89, 97, 163
    Fougasse (Bird, Cyril Kenneth) 17, 22, 90, 91
    KEM 91–3
    Sidney Stube 186
cartoons 10, 11, 12, 13, 18, 21, 21, 85–110, 111–35, 138–51, 156–7, 161, 162, 163, 186

Chaplin, Charlie 25, 33, 66
Churchill, Winston 32, 68, 73, 77, 93, 173, 186, 187, 200
civilian men 80, 102–6
class 12, 17, 19, 20, 22, 34, 37, 45, 54–5, 70, 80, 142, 155, 204
comedians 18, 19, 21–4, 32, 36–7, 48, 53, 64, 65, 67, 71, 72, 73, 78, 162n
Connelly, Mark 28, 173
conscription 30, 97, 103, 162
Croft, David 7, 185, 203–5, 207, 208, 209, 210
Crown Film Unit 44, 49, 51, 123
Czechoslovakia 3, 50, 55–6, 86n

Dad's Army 7, 9, 161, 181–98, 203–4, 206
Dunkirk 30, 173

empire 1, 56–7, 71, 82
Englishness 2, 72
European Union 213

film 5–6, 7, 8, 11, 24, 25, 33, 37, 41–62, 68, 72, 77, 78, 88, 91, 103, 105, 115, 123, 132, 137 162, 181, 182, 189, 199, 209
food 2, 5, 35, 48, 52, 74, 76, 77, 95–6, 143, 163, 168, 176, 190
Formby, George 5, 21, 25, 33–4, 55
France 28, 29, 31, 68, 69, 143, 182, 206, 212
    Battle of 29, 31
    Fall/invasion of 28, 143

gender 13, 17, 34, 37, 45, 51, 63, 85, 97–107, 113, 121–3, 141, 149, 157, 162, 165, 168, 169, 180
Germany 28, 37, 67, 68, 93, 203, 212
Greece 29, 86
Guinea Pig Club 115–17, 127

Index

Harrisson, Tom 18, 78
Hitler, Adolf 5, 13, 28, 29, 31, 47, 52, 65–8, 71, 75, 89, 90, 91, 93, 148–9, 175, 186, 207
Holocaust 207, 210
Hollywood 20, 25, 132
Home Front 7, 11, 13, 20, 32, 43, 47, 63, 72, 73, 93–7, 102–3, 105–6, 112, 113, 161, 162, 163, 164, 168, 173, 195, 203
Home Guard 7, 8–9, 31, 71, 181–98, 203, 204
hospitals 111–36, 177
    Hill End Hospital 111, 113, 114–15, 124, 126
    Park Prewett Hospital 114–15, 131–2
    Queen Victoria Hospital 114–15, 116, 118, 127, 131–2

Imperial War Museum 43, 181–98
incongruity 51, 95, 103, 138, 140–5, 149–56, 176
It's That Man Again (*ITMA*) 5, 13, 63, 74–80, 161
It Ain't Half Hot, Mum 7, 203, 203n, 204–5
Italy 29, 34, 212

Japan 27, 34
Jennings, Humphrey 18, 50

Lloyd, Jeremy 7, 205, 207, 208, 209, 210
Local Defence Volunteers (LDV) *See* Home Guard

Mass-Observation 2, 11, 12, 17–40, 45, 46–7, 49, 50, 53, 54–5, 70, 78
memory 7, 9, 12, 14, 21, 63, 153, 161–80, 182, 183, 187–8, 191, 194, 195, 199, 203, 204, 207, 213
men's services
    Army 30–1, 46, 69, 71, 88
    Royal Air Force 7, 17n, 28, 53–54, 55, 71–2, 78, 92, 126, 163, 174, 209
    Royal Navy 29, 71, 98, 137–60
Ministry of Information (MOI) 17, 42–8, 53, 55, 56, 58
mockery 5, 28, 31, 52, 55–6, 72, 89, 93, 157, 162, 188, 200, 207
morale 1, 3, 4, 6, 7, 18, 70, 78, 106, 114, 115, 117, 118, 161, 162

mundane 4, 13, 27, 48, 95, 162, 163, 164, 178
museums 169, 181–98

national identity 8, 11, 51–7
national stereotypes 53, 80, 204, 206, 208, 211, 216
    French 216
    German 52–3, 216
nostalgia 72, 177, 189–94, 213

performance 121, 123, 164–5, 165, 171, 174
photographs / photography 62, 166n, 182, 183, 184–5, 191, 193–4, 213
Priestley, J.B. 41, 55, 163
promiscuity 36, 37, 101
propaganda 7, 17, 37, 41–60, 73–80, 86, 90–1, 157
Punch (Magazine) 17, 22, 23, 26, 64, 87, 89, 94, 95, 101, 103, 104

race/ethnicity 56, 91, 205
    Jewishness 3, 33, 86, 210
radio 1, 3, 4, 5, 7, 11, 12–13, 23, 63–84, 91, 93, 146, 161, 166, 169, 171, 182, 187, 206
rationing 5, 12, 19, 27, 28, 47, 77, 79, 85, 95, 96, 162, 168, 169, 173, 176, 189
regional and national humour 2, 5, 23, 33, 55, 112, 204
    Clydeside 2
    Cockney 3, 17, 65, 68–9, 74, 76, 184
    Dorset 2
    Englishness 2
    Irish 3, 124
    Jewish 3, 210
    Scottish 2, 32, 204
    Yorkshire 55
Reith, John 33, 63
remembered humour 14, 153–6, 161–80

sitcom 9, 12, 181–215
Stalin 31, 93
surreal 46, 48, 78, 82, 166, 166n, 168, 174, 178

Trinder, Tommy 5, 48

U-boats 127, 143, 145–7, 149
United States of America 20, 22, 24, 29, 32, 36, 37, 42, 56, 65, 67–8, 70–3, 76, 117, 165, 212

Western Approaches Command 143–51, 157
women 2, 8, 35–7, 51, 93, 94, 97–106, 142, 162n, 188

women's services
    Auxiliary Territorial Service (ATS) 35–6, 71, 99, 105
    Women's Auxiliary Air Force (WAAF) 35–6, 100, 170
    Women's Royal Naval Service (WRNS) 35–6, 101, 143, 149–50, 155

xenophobia 206, 207

www.ingramcontent.com/pod-product-compliance
Lightning Source LLC
Chambersburg PA
CBHW052108300426
44116CB00010B/1577